# Bloomsbury Studies in Continental Philosophy

## Derrida, Badiou and the Formal Imperative

Bloomsbury Studies in Continental Philosophy

*Bloomsbury Studies in Continental Philosophy* is a major monograph series from Bloomsbury. The series features first-class scholarly research monographs across the field of Continental philosophy. Each work makes a major contribution to the field of philosophical research.

# Derrida, Badiou and the Formal Imperative

Christopher Norris

**B L O O M S B U R Y**
LONDON • NEW DELHI • NEW YORK • SYDNEY

*For Douglas and Lynne*

**Bloomsbury Academic**
An imprint of Bloomsbury Publishing Plc

50 Bedford Square        1385 Broadway
London        New York
WC1B 3DP        NY 10018
UK        USA

**www.bloomsbury.com**

**Bloomsbury is a registered trade mark of Bloomsbury Publishing Plc**

First published in 2012 by the Continuum International Publishing Group Ltd
Paperback Edition first published 2014 by Bloomsbury Academic

**British Library Cataloguing-in-Publication Data**
A catalogue record for this book is available from the British Library.

ISBN: HB: 978-1-4411-2832-4
PB: 978-1-4725-2592-5

**Library of Congress Cataloging-in-Publication Data**
A catalog record for this book is available from the Library of Congress.
Norris, Christopher, 1947-
Derrida, Badiou, and the formal imperative/Christopher Norris.
p. cm. – (Continuum studies in Continental philosophy)
Includes bibliographical references and index.
ISBN 978-1-4411-2832-4 – ISBN 978-1-4411-3992-4 (ebook (pdf)) 1. Derrida, Jacques. 2. Badiou, Alain. 3. Continental philosophy. 4. Analysis (Philosophy) I. Title.
B2430.D484N67 2012
194–dc23
2012004675

Typeset by Deanta Global Publishing Services, Chennai, India

# Contents

# Acknowledgements

Many thanks (once again) to my colleagues and post-graduate students in the Cardiff Philosophy Section for providing a lively and congenial environment in which to think through some of the knottier issues raised in this book. I have prefaced a good many other books with similar expressions of gratitude over the past 20 years or so but I am happy to say it once again, with some new colleagues and a great many new students presently in mind.

Beyond that, thanks also to the various people who have helped with comments, queries or suggestions along the way, or who have made some other contribution – perhaps unknowingly – in the course of conversation or by way of correspondence. In one way or another this mostly had to do with my growing interest in Badiou and their willingness to invite me as a visiting speaker, or to comment on various items of work-in-progress, or to take me on as their PhD supervisor (this being just the right way to phrase it since I have learnt a great deal from our exchanges over the past couple of years). Although the list is very far from complete, let me mention especially Alison Assiter, Burhan Baki, Manuel Barbeito, Jason Barker, Tom Constant, Paul Ennis, Fabio Gironi, Peter Hallward, Kathy Kerr, Christian Kerslake, Rafe McGregor, Dmitris Vardulakis and Patricia Waugh. Then of course there were those nearer home who helped me, if not to get the work/life balance right, then at least to get it a bit less drastically out of kilter. Anyway I have many reasons to thank Robin Attfield, Clive Cazeaux, Ray Davies, Andrew and Grace Edgar, David Edwards, Terry Hawkes, Wendy Lewis, Laurence and Helen Peddle, Meic Petersen, Rhian Rattray, Rob and Helen Stradling, Chris and Sue Thorkelson, Alison Venables, Barry Wilkins and Robin Wood. Shelley Campbell saw me through all manner of crises, major and minor, as the work went along and managed to strike just the right balance between sympathetic concern and sanity-restoring amusement.

Among the three very helpful, generous and expert anonymous readers whom Continuum asked to review this project at an embryonic stage was (I surmise) Antonio Calcagno whose own book *Badiou and Derrida: Politics, Events and Their Time* had appeared some three years previously, also from Continuum. I must confess that I came to his study belatedly – after the present work had gone to press – but of course made a point of chasing it up when I learnt of its existence. As it happens, or as luck would have it, he and I go very different ways around in constructing our respective cases for the deep affinity that we both perceive between Derrida's and Badiou's projects. Where the emphasis of my book falls mainly on Derrida's earlier, more 'analytical' texts – those that give maximum purchase for an approach *through* philosophy of language, logic and the formal sciences – Calcagno looks chiefly to the later Derrida and to writings that explicitly address or *thematize* the kinds of issue flagged in his book's subtitle. Where my own focus is very much on Badiou's mathematical thinking as a formal point of entry and key to his thinking about philosophy, politics and art, Calcagno is more directly concerned with Badiou's idea of the life- or world-transformative 'event' as that which institutes a radically changed relationship between subjectivity and its various defining, that is, truth-oriented projects and conditions. In consequence, Calcagno has a lot more to say about Derrida's expressly political texts, most of them dating from his last two decades and treating what he takes to be the deeply paradoxical or aporetic nature of ethically charged *topoi* such as hospitality, forgiveness, democracy, justice, decision and responsibility. While making occasional reference to those texts – and seeking to point up their continuities with what went before – I put the case that any adequately theorized 'politics of deconstruction' will need to go by way of a formal analysis that starts by engaging the logical complexities of the early work and only then, on the strength of that, proceeds to an assessment of the later Derrida's more overt social and ethico-political concerns. As a result, we present two sharply contrasting accounts of Derrida and Badiou, not only as regards their individual aims, methods and priorities but also with respect to those points of convergence between their two projects that Calcagno and I both seek to bring out but which we interpret in very different ways. At any rate, I am grateful to him for airing some pertinent queries at a timely stage and for not letting these differences get in the way of a constructive and thoughtful review.

Some chapters of this book include revised versions of material that has previously appeared in the journals *Filolog, Modern and Contemporary France, Revista Portuguesa de Filosofia* and *Speculations*. I am very grateful to the editors and publishers concerned for their permission to incorporate that material here.

**Cardiff**
*December 2011*

# Introduction

## I

There have been clear signs over the past decade or so that some kind of rapprochement was at last shaping up between so-called analytic and so-called continental philosophy, although in just what form and on just whose terms it is less easy to say. Of course there are still those – whether diehard analytics or all-embracing continental revisionists – who take it that the opposing ranks have run out of intellectual steam and will soon collapse exhausted into the arms of their old opponents. However, theirs is not the predominant view at present, as it was 20 years ago when hostilities were running high and when the issue was (or was considered to be) pretty much epitomized in mutually baffled and hostile exchanges like that between Derrida and Searle. Or again, it worked out as the quarrel between a 'post-analytic' and continentally oriented thinker like Richard Rorty and the community to which he had once very squarely belonged but which he now wished to transform out of all recognition. However, such outright antagonisms, if hardly a thing of the past, have since then been overtaken by a range of conciliatory or at any rate tentatively bridge-building efforts which presume the obsolescence of that bad old dichotomy.

Some of these initiatives have come from analytic philosophers, especially those with an interest in cognitive science or artificial intelligence, who argue that any adequate grasp of the scope and (more pointedly) the limits of a purely physicalist approach must look beyond the science-led concepts and categories of analytic thought and take stock of the alternatives offered by various continental (e.g. phenomenological or hermeneutic) thinkers. Others have come from those with a background or early main interest in continental philosophy who have decided – perhaps as a result of certain well-publicized postmodernist excesses – that some components of the 'other', analytic tradition might provide a needful corrective. Nothing in what follows should be taken as in any way attacking, decrying or calling into question the desirability and indeed necessity of such a rapprochement if Anglophone philosophy is to find some way beyond its currently far from vibrant condition. Still the reader may well have reflected that when people use phrases like 'Nothing I say should be taken . . .' so as to deny that they are denying this or that item of belief, then the chances are that they are doing just that – raising some large question marks over the claim – despite their pious protestations. I suppose that my arguments here might arouse that suspicion since they do enter a range of caveats concerning what I take to be the more facile, premature or ill-thought-out proposals for a *ménage à deux* or marriage of convenience between the two schools. However, I also want to say – and submit my claim to that reader's best judgement – that this is a book written very much in the interests of establishing a better, more open-minded and communicative intellectual culture where typecast oppositions like that between 'analytic' and 'continental' are no longer able (as with the ill-starred Derrida/Searle exchange) to conjure animosity or downright incomprehension. My concern is that productive debate on substantive issues might be pushed even further out of reach by a range of misconceived or under-argued gambits – like those often canvassed under the name of 'post-analytic' philosophy – which tend to conjure up a false sense of problems solved or issues now shown to be non- or pseudo-issues.

Thus, for instance, I question the idea currently doing the rounds that Derrida's thinking about speech-act 'iterability' and the problems with Austinian speech-act theory can be assimilated pretty much without remainder to post-analytical proposals for a 'minimalist semantics' that would simply have done with all that tedious old business of conceptual analysis. Such approaches run the two-fold risk of underestimating Derrida's work as regards its own, in many ways heterodox yet nonetheless rigorous modes of analysis while at the same time overstating the extent to which analytic philosophy – in the more commonplace, localized or parochial sense of that term – has indeed run out of intellectual steam. Of course, there are those like Richard Rorty who would view them not so much as risks or damaging errors but, on the contrary, as consummations devoutly to be wished. On their account Derrida is best read as an inventor of novel language-games, styles of self-description, or fresh-minted 'metaphors we can live by', while analytic philosophy has surrendered all claim to the allegiance or interest of anyone beyond a tiny academic coterie by reason of its narrowly technical concerns, inability to solve its own self-induced problems and utter lack of such inventiveness or creativity. My argument here is that the analytic/continental 'dialogue' – if that is the right term, with its somewhat too placid or emollient character – had best keep a sense of those unresolved issues that still have the power to strike sparks in any mooted convergence of the twain. It stands to benefit less through an outlook of benign ecumenism or a flattening-out of troublesome differences than by focusing on just those points where a meeting of the two philosophical cultures can be seen to generate conflicts or at any rate symptomatic tensions of precept and practice. No doubt it will be said that this is already to skew the issue in favour of a *modus operandi*, like Derrida's, which thrives on precisely the idea of philosophy as always and everywhere marked by such moments of strictly irreducible aporia between and within the texts of its formative tradition. I shall have more to say in this respect as concerns, among other instances, Derrida's meticulous teasing-out of those aporias that emerge through the encounter of Husserlian phenomenology with the structuralist 'revolution' in thought that challenged some of its most basic premises. However, I shall also put the case that such deconstructive modes of thought can likewise be found in philosophers deemed to stand squarely in the analytic mainstream. This still leaves room for the acknowledgement of certain salient differences rather than seeking to suppress, sublate or transcend them in what is apt to strike partisans on either side as more like a hostile takeover-bid than a friendly overture.

Another focal issue throughout this book is the debate between realism and anti-realism, along with that between relativism and various (mostly truth-based and realist) arguments against it. Here I seek to disentangle the various, often conflicting and confusing senses that present-day philosophers – mainly philosophers of language and science – have attached to each of these terms. More specifically, I illustrate the ways in which anti-realism trades on its claim to deliver a knockdown riposte to objectivist or realist claims. Such claims are supposed to involve the appeal to a realm of absolute, mind-independent or recognition-transcendent truth that by very definition exceeds the limits of humanly attainable knowledge and hence leaves the door wide open to scepticism and sundry forms of relativist or 'strong'-constructivist thinking. I contest that supposition by rehearsing the various alternatives to anti-realism in the logico-semantic-metaphysical guise set forth most influentially by Michael Dummett. In particular, I instance those strains of robust (ontological) realism that reject many central doctrines of mainstream philosophic thought as it has developed in the wake of both Kant's epistemological 'revolution' and the latter-day linguistic turn. As it happens, the single most ambitious recent attempt to pass the 'two traditions' of post-Kantian thought in synoptic review and lessen the perceived distance between them – Lee Braver's impressive book *A Thing of This World* – comes at the topic from an avowed anti-realist standpoint and takes that approach to hold out the best (indeed only) hope for more productive dialogue. The title seems to me rather oddly chosen given his view of Kant's inaugural role in making anti-realism the default position or ensuring that it set the main agenda for subsequent debate in both philosophical lines of descent. The implication, in brief, is that only by bringing truth safely back within human cognitive or epistemic reach – only by excluding all thought of truth as objective or potentially recognition-transcendent – can philosophy indeed become a 'thing of this world', presumably in the sense 'this world as we human beings inhabit, experience, and know it'. My own view is that this gets things exactly back-to-front, since anti-realism in its different analytic and continental forms has, if anything, tended to deepen the rift between those totemic camps as well as the problems and misunderstandings within them. At any rate, my book will take a contrary position and argue for realism, rightly (i.e. non-prejudicially) construed, as the best source of unifying insights and the firmest ground on which to build a case for this promising convergence of interests.

That Derrida and Badiou happen to be two of the most inventive, intelligent, profound and at times highly problematical thinkers in the history of post-war French philosophy is a decent (but surely not the best) rationale for a twin-focus study such as this. That they have each exerted a powerful influence on developments within and beyond academic philosophy – and conjured up what seems an equal and opposite force of resistance – is a bit nearer the mark since it means that there is useful work to be done in sorting those responses *pro* and *contra* that can claim adequate warrant from those that fall short on that score. However, the strongest justification is that Derrida and Badiou have enough in common for this not to be a merely procrustean exercise while also having differences enough – differences ranging over many areas of ontology, epistemology, metaphysics, politics, ethics and aesthetics – for the exercise to have real point as a comparative study. In addition they are both highly original thinkers whose work never strains for novelty but always acknowledges its manifold debts to a diverse range of formative encounters with texts which nevertheless they read with a critical eye to various conceptual, argumentative and ideological blind-spots. Neither displays the least sign of that 'anxiety of influence' famously expounded by Harold Bloom as the ground-bass of literary history and the motivating force behind all major intellectual and creative achievements.

## II

This emerges to particularly striking effect in Badiou's posthumous tribute to Derrida, published in the volume *Pocket Pantheon*. The essay is a miniature *tour de force* which achieves, in its 20-page span, three extraordinary feats. First, it succeeds in shifting the emphasis from Derrida as textual close-reader of incomparable subtlety and power to Derrida as a political thinker, a shift seen not only in his later (post-1980) writings where politics very often came to the fore but also throughout his entire, massively imposing *oeuvre*. Second, and yet more notably, it manages to present Derrida's thinking about politics in terms that derive – quite openly so – from Badiou's own treatise *Logics of Worlds*, the sequel to *Being and Event*. In brief, he takes it that deconstruction has to do with multiplicities, worlds, appearances in worlds, degrees of existence or inexistence and the forcible inscription of presence or absence. Moreover – alluding directly to Derrida's *Spectres of Marx* – it points the way towards a differential ontology which allows us to explain how that which undeniably has *being* in a given world (as does the proletariat in the world of twenty-first century global capitalism) can all the same be lacking in *existence*, here defined as the capacity to assert its interests or make its material presence felt. My own first response was to count this a singular display of strong-revisionist reading or creative 'misprision' in precisely Bloom's sense, although one that did capture something of the political valence that Derrida's 'left' readers were quick to detect in his earlier work without being able to define it more specifically. Now I would make the point rather differently and say that Badiou is here producing (discovering? educing? positing? eliciting? maybe 'inventing' in the classical rhetoricians' sense: 'hitting upon through some happily apt though nonetheless exacting procedure') certain truths about Derrida's thought that came into focus – that passed from latent to fully articulate and operative status – only through their exposure to a reading of just that kind. After all, this is precisely how Badiou conceives the 'event' of truth, that is to say, as marking the decisive break with a given, pre-existent state of knowledge and the passage to a new order of thought along with a radically transformed or expanded ontology which brings the resources to articulate problems and envisage solutions unknown to the earlier paradigm.

Not that he is at all prone to underestimate the differences of intellectual temperament as well as political outlook that led Derrida, in this respect very unlike Badiou, to distance himself from the more militant leftist groupings during the late 1960s high-point of French activism. He attributes that stance chiefly to Derrida's 'diagonal obstinacy', his 'dislike of abrupt metaphysically derived divisions' and a long-cultivated habit of mind 'clearly not suited to stormy times when everything comes under the law of decisiveness, here and now' (*Pocket Pantheon*, p. 138). More specifically:

This is what kept Derrida apart from the truth of the Red Years between 1968 and 1976. Because the truth of those years spoke its name with the words: 'One divides into Two'. What we desired, in poetic terms, was the metaphysics of radical conflict, and not the patient deconstruction of oppositions. And Derrida could not agree about that. He went into exile, so to speak. (Ibid., pp. 138–9)

It is an eloquent passage, not without some overlay of irony, even perhaps a certain good-humoured mockery along with the tolerant acceptance of Derrida's (imputed) 'anything-for-a-quiet-life' attitude. Nor is one left in much doubt that Badiou's patience is in shorter supply than Derrida's and that it is liable to run out rather swiftly if confronted with too many examples of the painstaking textual analysis that might have kept some disciples of Derrida away from the barricades. All the same, it is a passage that impresses for its rare combination of a steadfast refusal to yield ground on issues of principle with a readiness to acknowledge the variety of human motives – political motives included – and the distinct possibility that good-willed others might go a very different way around. What some mistake for arrogance or dogmatism in Badiou's writing is much more a matter of his carrying across from mathematics into other disciplines that axiomatic-deductive mode of thought which he shows to have achieved such signal results in its primary (or its hitherto most successful since rigorously formalized) context of deployment. That it can perfectly well go along with openness to criticism, challenge and possible refutation is a lesson borne out by many developments in the history of mathematics, among them – paradigmatically – those set-theoretical advances that for Badiou typify the truth-event and its break with some pre-existing state of knowledge.

In Derrida's case also, I suggest, there is the same appeal open from past or present best knowledge to recognition-transcendent truth, an appeal pre-emptively closed off by anti-realist or verificationist doctrines that deny the possibility of any such thing. Here the process of discovery involves a meticulous close-reading of texts which reveal hitherto ignored complications – moments of aporia or unresolved conflict – and thereby signal the limits and the stress-points of some given interpretative schema. Hence my choice of that phrase 'the formal imperative' as a part of this book's title and as an indication of the single most important connecting thread that weaves through and across or between these two thinkers' work. This is why I devote a good deal of space in subsequent chapters to the task of defining more exactly the relationship between, on the one hand, deconstruction and classical (bivalent or true/ false) logic and, on the other, deconstruction and those various deviant, non-bivalent, or paraconsistent logics that have lately been proposed in order to address problems with the classical conception. I hope that one beneficial result of reading Derrida in conjunction with Badiou will be to point up those formal elements in his work – for instance, its concern with undecidability in the strict (Gödelian) logico-mathematical sense – which are apt to escape notice among his more 'literary' followers or else be treated, by analytic philosophers, as merely gesturing towards that kind of hard-won formal rigour and precision. At the same time, and to likewise beneficial effect, one result of reading Badiou in conjunction with Derrida will be to bring out the depth and acuity of Badiou's critical engagement with a great range of past thinkers from the ancient Greeks to Derrida himself. Thus, it may help to offset the commonplace idea – by no means wholly wide of the mark – that the strength of Badiou's mathematical orientation, or the 'formal imperative' embodied in his work, must render him in principle averse to the practice of textual close-reading which Derrida brought to such a high point of refinement. Despite his emphatic rejection of the 'linguistic turn' in its diverse forms, from post-structuralism to various schools of analytic philosophy, there is every sign that Badiou's readings of Plato, Aristotle, Descartes, Spinoza, Leibniz, Hegel, Heidegger and others are themselves the upshot of a textual engagement that is equally probing and acute although not conducted 'on the page' in Derrida's meticulously detailed way.

These are some of my reasons for offering a study of two thinkers whom I regard not only as preeminent figures in the history of post-1960 French thought but also as counting among the most significant philosophers of this or any time. Another is the fact that both have an ethical dimension to their thought which is often overlooked or misunderstood. In Badiou's case this is mainly on account of his oft-stated hostility to ethics in just about every present-day philosophical, socio-political or more broadly cultural form. That hostility is grounded in his vehement rejection of the various, nowadays dominant, discourses – especially those of a purported liberal or social-democratic character – that in his view have worked to legitimize an order based on the exclusion or enforced disenfranchisement of anyone not matching certain criteria for communal inclusion. Hence what is surely the most distinctive and, for many readers, most difficult and challenging aspect of his work: its constant recourse to mathematics and specifically to post-Cantorian set theory as the basis for a critical ontology which aims to define the precise points of rupture marking the transition from being to event. Only thus, according to Badiou, can we hope to provide an adequate account of how social structures perpetuate particular forms of injustice such as the enforced civic and political invisibility of certain groups who occupy the outermost margins of society. Yet it also provides the best means to understand how those structures on occasion come up against some stubbornly anomalous or discrepant instance that cannot be contained within the 'count-as-one' or the currently prevailing (ideologically determined) conception of *bona fide* membership within some given socio-political or communal mode of existence. Hence the standing possibility – however rare the occurrence – that there will suddenly appear an 'evental site' where the multiple in question asserts its existence against the officially maintained pretence that the count is a representative tally which includes all its parts as members.

To this extent Badiou is indeed concerned to elaborate an ethics of principled resistance to social injustice in its diverse forms, especially as concerns the plight of undocumented (*sans-papiers*) immigrants to France mainly from North African countries. At the same time he sees ethics, or the discourse that conventionally bears that name, as a constant temptation to seek refuge from these harsh realities in the reassuring sense – one with a major philosophical source in Kant – of belonging to a *sensus communis* that transcends and reconciles such merely quotidian disparities of status, power and citizenly membership. On the negative side, I show how he traces the genealogy of that way of thinking to a certain avowedly detached or contemplative attitude towards politics that again points back to Kant and which finds its latter-day representatives in figures such as Hannah Arendt and a host of lesser apologists for the currently prevailing liberal consensus. This *modus vivendi* has again been encouraged by the 'linguistic turn' – in whichever of its protean contemporary forms – through the reduction of concepts such as truth, justice and progress to so many culture-relative products of sundry 'language-games', 'discourses', 'conceptual schemes', 'frameworks', 'paradigms', cultural 'life-forms' and so forth. On the positive side, I seek to elucidate the complex order of relationship, as Badiou sees it, between ontology (set theory) as that which affords us maximum purchase on whatever legitimately 'counts' according to existent, more or less partial modes of inclusion and the different kinds of evental occurrence that might always emerge to resist, subvert and potentially transform that dominant order.

Along the way I offer various comparisons in order to specify the distinctive or indeed – in a sense of that grossly over-used adjective which he has been at pains to define with great precision – the revolutionary bearing of Badiou's thought on a range of ethical and socio-political issues. Above all I stress the unique combination in his work of an *engagé* conscience keenly attuned to such matters of real-world practical commitment with an intelligence sharply focused on substantive and challenging questions as regards the formal practice and historical development as well as the philosophy of mathematics. To this extent it stands in marked contrast to the humdrum and conceptually undemanding character of so much discussion in the analytic mainstream, as typified by the Wittgenstein-inspired debate about rule-following or continuing a numerical sequence. Then there is the constantly reiterated (pseudo-)dilemma with regard to how truth in mathematics could be both objective (or potentially recognition-transcendent) and, despite that, at least sometimes brought within the compass of human cognition. If Badiou offers a striking antidote to philosophy conceived in this strictly subaltern, mathematically uninteresting role, it is on account of his readiness to *work through* the various problems that have marked the history of mathematics to date – especially those thrown up by reflection on the infinite by thinkers from Plato to Cantor and beyond – and thus gain access to the most advanced and revealing modes of investigative thought, namely the formal procedures by which 'paradox turns into concept'.

To describe Badiou's project in these terms is to bring it very much within the ambit of recent analytic philosophy, and – in particular – to point up its bearing on the current debate between realists and anti-realists with regard to issues of truth and knowledge in the formal, physical and (albeit with salient differences of emphasis) the social and human sciences. I have done so mainly because I see his work as having much to contribute in that 'other' philosophical context by way of an approach whose speculative scope extends far beyond the often rather narrow confines of the mainstream analytic tradition yet which also manifests the kind of conceptual precision and logical rigour that are usually taken as its trademark virtues. Thus, there might well be benefits for analytically trained philosophers of mathematics – so often hung up on what Badiou would consider artificial and trivial pseudo-problems with their source in a widespread failure of intellectual nerve – if they followed his example of actively engaging with those real (as opposed to philosophically hyper-cultivated) problems that have often surfaced in the course of set-theoretical research. Moreover, they might also have something to learn with regard to the limits imposed upon thought by that received analytical division of philosophic labour which decrees that there exist certain specialist areas of discourse and corresponding areas of special expertise such as to render any breach of their boundaries an offence against standards of professional, intellectual and ethical propriety alike. This would make it strictly inconceivable that (for instance) the approach to certain foundational issues in philosophy of mathematics should be thought to have a bearing on issues in political theory, or that the discovery of set-theoretical paradoxes and the techniques used to resolve them might have decisive implications for our thinking about questions in spheres far beyond mathematics, logic and the formal sciences.

All the same – lest this give the wrong impression – Badiou shows clearly by precept and practice that he is far from endorsing that strain of postmodernist thought which holds that received ideas of what properly counts as a distinct or autonomous discipline of thought are in truth nothing more than conventional products of a certain, quite recent and wholly academic (i.e. university-based) mindset. On this view the best way forward is one that bids a long overdue farewell to those orthodox ideas and a welcome to any kind of interdisciplinary venture offering a sense of the creative prospects afforded by an attitude of breezy indifference to the ruling generic proprieties. For Badiou, conversely, there is no prospect of advancement or constructive thinking in any domain – whether mathematics, physical science, politics or art – except on condition that it strive to achieve the utmost clarity with regard to its own conceptual and justificatory grounds. This in turn requires that such thinking maintain a respect for intra-disciplinary standards or those laid down by its development to date as a progressively unfolding sequence of discoveries guided (as appears to most striking effect in the case of mathematics) by a likewise deepening and sharpened sense of what constitutes genuine progress. Hence Badiou's insistence on carefully leading his reader through those various signal stages of advance in the history of set-theoretical research – along with equally decisive episodes in other disciplinary quarters – which would otherwise amount to no more than a series of loosely analogical events. Only thus could Badiou be justified in attempting so massively ambitious a project, one that cuts across so many well-established academic and intellectual boundaries while nonetheless refusing to have any truck with the sorts of all-purpose anti-disciplinary thinking promoted by sundry postmodernists, neo-pragmatists and other subscribers to what he impugns as the latter day revival of age-old sophistical doctrines.

# III

One aim of my book is, therefore, to lay out the conceptual foundations of Badiou's work for the benefit of those (analytic philosophers for the most part) with a primary interest in philosophy of mathematics and the formal sciences. Since they are likely to start as resisting readers – suspicious of anything 'continental', even (or especially) where it strays onto territory colonized by thinkers in the analytic line of descent – I return at many points to various aspects of Badiou's work on mathematics and his distinctive (though far from eccentric) deployment of conceptual resources drawn from post-Cantorian set theory. Most important here is his emphasis on Cantor's discovery of a means to reckon with the existence of real, as distinct from merely virtual, orders of the infinite and moreover on the need to recognize that these occupy a scale of progressively larger 'sizes' or cardinalities. My second aim – again with a view to convincing sceptical readers – is to offer a justificatory account of Badiou's claim that such breakthrough advances in the realm of mathematics have a crucial bearing on issues of political justice and social concern. What I seek to bring out is the tight relationship that exists between certain highly specific aspects of Badiou's mathematical thinking, among them his axiomatic commitment to some (and not other) set-theoretical precepts and certain likewise specific aspects of his thinking about politics and ethics. My proposal is that we should take these claims at full philosophical strength, rather than treating them as loose or fanciful cross-disciplinary ventures. By so doing, we might achieve both a transformative conception of political justice and an incentive to move beyond some of the more cramping (and philosophically rather than mathematically driven) fixations of recent philosophy of mathematics.

There is, I should acknowledge, no such tight connection that can plausibly be claimed – or no such formally elaborated range of precise structural analogies – when one turns to those passages in Derrida's writing where he invokes certain kindred *topoi* such as Gödel's undecidability-theorem or the limits of classical (bivalent) logic as revealed by its encounter with textual complications beyond its power to resolve or accommodate. Nor should one expect this to be the case, given the fact of his primarily textual focus and the further consideration that Derrida's work had its formative moment in the conflict – more aptly, the shuttling exchange of priorities – between structuralism and phenomenology as they competed for the high theoretical ground in France during the late 1950s and early 1960s. That debate was conducted in large part by way of its perceived implications for philosophy of language, theoretical linguistics and the various other disciplines – literary criticism among them – where the issue played out (as it did for Derrida) through the distinctly chicken-egg issue concerning whether structure or expression should be thought to take priority in methodological or conceptual-explanatory terms. I shall have more to say about this later on, chiefly with a view to showing how Derrida's work relates to the fitful interest in Husserlian phenomenology displayed by some analytic philosophers at different times during the past five decades, from Gilbert Ryle to Michael Dummett. I shall also put the case that their failure to pursue that interest more doggedly through the various challenges it posed – as Derrida most emphatically does in those early books and essays – left them with a number of unresolved (and on their own terms strictly unresolvable) problems that can nowadays be seen to have defined the very nature and ultimate limits of their enterprise. For introductory purposes I shall simply make the point that while Derrida's project started out very much under the aegis of language as a principal ground of dispute between phenomenology and structuralism, it very soon and *for just that reason* took on a distinctively formal aspect and a concern with conflicting structures of logical implication that very clearly mark its distance from any version of 'linguistic philosophy' properly so called.

Derrida is at one with Badiou to this extent at least: that his thinking finds its most adequate articulation in a mode of analysis whose point of departure may be textual or linguistic but whose province is finally philosophy of logic rather than philosophy of language. This is why I spend a good deal of time in the following chapters seeking to locate Derrida's thought with reference to certain specific developments in analytic philosophy over the past half century or so. I stress the specificity of focus here because there is already a good amount of work, including some earlier work of my own, that adopts a more generalized approach to the contrasts and comparisons involved. Chief among the issues I examine are (1) the relationship between deviant, non-classical or non-bivalent logics as they operate in Derrida's texts and in the thinking of various analytic (or 'post-analytic') philosophers and (2), following directly from this, the issue of realism *versus* anti-realism in the logico-semantic form which that issue has taken since Michael Dummett's decisive intervention. These in turn raise (3) the question of priority between conceptual and linguistic modes of analysis, a question posed both *within* the analytic tradition and *between* it and various movements in recent 'continental' thought. Lastly, (4): there is the topic of creativity in philosophy, one that has to do both with Derrida's practice as a highly inventive close-reader of texts and also, more broadly, with deconstruction when viewed in light of its reception-history among philosophers on the one hand and literary critics/theorists on the other.

In each case, Derrida's work has been drastically misunderstood not only by its mainstream-analytic detractors but also by disciples – whether literary theorists or 'post-analytic', continentally inclined philosophers – insufficiently attentive to aspects of it that don't fit in with their preconceptions. For they would otherwise have seen that Derrida is very far from endorsing a version of anti-realism based on the rejection of bivalent (classical) logic along with a commitment to some ill-defined postmodernist theses concerning the supposed non-existence of objective truth-values, the linguistic (or textual) construction of reality, and hence the irrelevance of Question (4) above, since philosophy *just is* another literary 'kind of writing'. On the contrary, deconstruction could not possibly exert such critical leverage on classical conceptions of truth, reference, logic and language in its various (e.g. constative and performative or philosophical and literary) modes except on condition – a condition he defines with great clarity – that it respect those classical requirements *right up to the point* where they encounter resistance from the text or particular topic in hand. Only thus can it marshal the kind of distinctly philosophical, as opposed to merely persuasive or rhetorical warrant that enables Derrida to call into question certain received or institutionally accredited modes of thought. Moreover, this approach has the signal merit of explaining the deep though elusive continuity between Derrida's early texts on the deviant logics of supplementarity, *différance*, parergonality, etc. and his later writing on topics such as death, forgiveness, the gift, hospitality, the auto-immune and non-human animality. To that extent, it bears out my claim – and the basic rationale for this book – that with Derrida, as with Badiou, there is a close and reciprocal dependence between aspects of their work amenable to treatment in formal or logical terms and aspects of it that engage directly with issues of real-world practical, ethical and socio-political concern.

Chapter 1 discusses both thinkers in more or less equal measure and is basically a further drawing out of the claims advanced by way of summary introduction here. Other chapters focus primarily either on Derrida or Badiou although with various points of cross-reference, overt or implied, which I hope make this a properly comparative study rather than a twin-pronged exercise conducted in a vaguely analogical or bridge-building spirit. My approach in Chapter 1 is partly through Badiou's brief though remarkably subtle and suggestive tribute to Derrida in the volume *Pocket Pantheon*. However, I also take a wider view of the various points of intersection between their two projects. In particular, I show how the under-recognized formal dimension of Derrida's work is thrown into sharp relief by Badiou's set-theoretically based conception of ontology, along with his theory of the event as that which arrives to perturb and transform an existing order of knowledge, politics or artistic practice. This chapter seeks to rectify the bias of much of Derrida commentary, friendly and hostile alike, by stressing the qualities of logical rigour, conceptual precision and analytic acuity that characterize his best work; hence the very marked intellectual kinship that finds voice in Badiou's tribute to Derrida and can be seen to have its ultimate source in their shared devotion to certain distinctive formal procedures. These include (for Badiou) the set-theoretical technique of 'forcing', as developed by the mathematician Paul Cohen, and (in Derrida) the various modes of deconstructive close-reading whose aporetic outcome can best be understood by analogy with Gödel's incompleteness or undecidability theorem. In both cases – though more explicitly in Badiou – the aim is to show how truth must be thought of as always potentially exceeding the compass of present best knowledge, proof or ascertainment yet also as signalled by the contradictions or anomalies that exist (and will at length be shown to have existed) within that current paradigm.

It is in keeping with this formal imperative that Derrida formulates his various deviant or non-classical logics of supplementarity, *différance*, parergonality and so forth. With Badiou, it leads to a highly developed and refined application of set-theoretical concepts which extends beyond the realm of mathematics, logic and the formal sciences to encompass issues in philosophy of art and – absolutely central to his project – a radically transformed conception of politics. This requires the commitment to a resolute thinking-through of certain hitherto progress-blocking problems such as that which Bertrand Russell famously confronted in his attempt to place set theory on a purely logical basis. Or again, as with Derrida, it may involve pressing hard on some textual crux and then pursuing its longer-range implications to the point where there emerge certain hitherto unnoticed complications of logic, sense and reference. Such 'symptomatic' readings – which also take a cue from Louis Althusser's approach to the writings of Marx and Jacques Lacan's structuralist-inflected account of Freudian psychoanalysis – very often go strongly against the grain as regards the express (author-warranted) meaning of the text or its commonly accepted import as handed down through a canonical tradition of authorized scholars and exegetes. Nevertheless, Derrida's deconstructive commentaries can be seen to argue their case with the utmost fidelity to matters of detail and logical implication. Although Badiou doesn't go in for close reading in anything like so minutely attentive a way, he does make a regular point, especially in *Being and Event*, of defining his own position *vis-à-vis* the arguments of earlier thinkers, some of whom he subjects to a forceful critique of their basic presuppositions while others (the majority) he treats in a mode of partial and carefully qualified endorsement. Indeed his practice of textual exegesis can best be seen as a further working-out of his case with respect to developments in set theory, that is to say, as showing how advances come about through a close engagement with problems or anomalies which thereby offer the critical purchase for a leap beyond received or doxastic habits of thought.

This brings him close to the deconstructive standpoint adopted by those, like Derrida, who examine texts for the moments of unresolved tension between opposed orders of logic and sense which often betoken some deeper philosophic or ideological conflict of interests. Indeed, it is fair to say that Badiou must have learnt a good deal from Derrida's many, themselves now canonical, essays on the great thinkers of the Western philosophical canon. However, Badiou is distinctly wary of what he sees as the nexus between deconstruction and other variants of the linguistic turn – from Frege-type logico-semantic analysis to Wittgensteinian–Austinian 'ordinary language' philosophy – that, in his view, very often deploy their concern with theories of signification or minutiae of everyday usage as a means to avoid any deeper engagement with genuine philosophical, let alone political issues. Here he is at one with those seventeenth-century rationalists who regarded natural language as at best a relatively clear and efficient means of communication and at worst a grossly distorting medium which philosophy should either seek to reform or (ideally) replace with a logical symbolism or conceptual language of its own devising. Moreover, he is thereby placed – to this extent at least – in the company of mainstream analytic philosophers, from Frege and Russell down, who have likewise very often tended to suppose that one of philosophy's primary tasks is to reform (i.e. clarify or disambiguate) the vagaries of 'ordinary', natural language.

All the same, Badiou's rationalism and consequent hostility towards most versions of the linguistic turn never goes so far as to pitch him against the basic claim – in his case chiefly of structuralist provenance – that language enters into all our dealings with the world and also into much (though not everything) that rationalists might think of as strictly *a priori* and hence in no way subject to linguistic mediation or structuring. Otherwise he could scarcely find so much room – and at so deep a level of his own thinking in matters of foremost concern – for the claims of a psychoanalyst such as Lacan or a political theorist such as Althusser, both of whom made a programmatic point of reading their source-texts (Freud and Marx) through a conceptual lens informed by the insights of structural linguistics. Although Derrida doesn't loom so large among Badiou's intellectual sources, his influence does emerge clearly in the latter's critical yet nonetheless constructive manner of engagement with philosophers from Plato to Heidegger. More specifically, it forms the basis of Badiou's frequent claim to have discovered certain crucial fault lines in the structure of their thought – localized symptoms of a larger non-coincidence between what the author explicitly says and what the logic of the text constrains them to imply – which open the way to such a jointly diagnostic and (in Badiou's as in Derrida's case) appreciative account. This is not to deny that Badiou is very deeply at odds with some of those thinkers whose work he passes in critical review from stage to stage in the unfolding sequence of historically, thematically and dialectically structured argument that constitutes *Being and Event*. All the same, these differences are brought out by means of a reading that is also (in the true sense) a critical encounter, that is, a coming-up against problems unlooked-for on other, more orthodox accounts. What Derrida has to say about the various deviant or paraconsistent logics of the *pharmakon* (Plato), 'supplementarity' (Rousseau), the *parergon* (Kant), *différance* (Husserl) or 'iterability' (Austin) finds a close analogue in Badiou's reading of those philosophers from Plato down whom he regards as having somehow proleptically grasped – albeit in a faltering, intermittent or largely unconscious way – truths that would arrive at the point of formal expression only with the advent of Cantorian set theory. Despite being so far in advance of orthodox thinking at their time as obliquely to prefigure certain temporally distant conceptual advances, they were still in the grip of other powerful preconceptions that stood in the way of any conscious or deliberative means of ascertaining those truths.

# IV

So there is a strong case that Badiou's mode of critical engagement with his major precursors has much in common with Derrida's deconstructive exegeses of texts in the mainstream Western philosophical tradition. Self-evidently any such engagement will need to argue its case through a close attentiveness to crucial and (very often) problematical passages in the works that represent those thinkers' various truth-claims, doctrinal commitments, conceptual priorities and so forth. However, to repeat, what Badiou does very forcefully disown is the extreme version of this claim proposed by some post-structuralists not to mention Wittgensteinians and adepts of the present-day 'linguistic turn' in its more extreme versions. On this view, there is simply no way that thinking can get some critical, diagnostic or corrective purchase on language, since language is the very element of thought or the absolute horizon of intelligibility beyond which it cannot purport to go without falling into manifest nonsense. Such is the cultural–linguistic–relativist notion that Badiou denounces with admirable force in his reflections on the prevalence of sophistry as a substitute for genuine thought in much that nowadays passes for philosophy on both sides of the English Channel. It is one reason why he evinces an attraction to Spinoza's philosophy – despite contesting some of its most basic ontological theses – insofar as Spinoza likewise regarded thought as intrinsically prior to language and language as a more or less adequate means of communicating thoughts rather than a matrix or shaper of them. It is also why Badiou can justifiably claim to read Plato, Aristotle, Leibniz, Rousseau, Hegel and others in a way that respects the conceptual integrity of their work while nevertheless finding that work to signify something other and more than could plausibly be held to have figured in the authors' conscious or deliberate design. Although not a sedulously close reader or prober of textual doubts and complications in Derrida's way, Badiou can be seen to raise similar questions about the sometimes divergent, even contradictory relationship between overt (avowed or intended) meaning and what the text actually implies, presupposes or logically entails.

Indeed Badiou's distinctive line of approach to these issues through mathematics is one that may help to correct those prevalent misunderstandings of Derrida which fail to recognize the formal (logico-semantic) rigour of his work and consequently treat it – whether in praise or blame – as an exercise in the 'textualist' or strong-descriptivist vein designed to show that philosophy is just one 'kind of writing' among others. To understand why Badiou is so squarely opposed to this idea on political and social as well as on 'purely' philosophical grounds is at the same time to grasp why Derrida's thought has been so travestied by analytically minded detractors, on the one hand,

and, on the other, by an appreciative company of literary-cultural theorists along with some 'post-analytic' or continentally oriented philosophers. Here again it needs stating – *contra* both parties – that Derrida's work is centrally concerned with issues in philosophy of logic and language that have also been a main focus of interest for philosophers in the 'other', that is, analytic or mainstream Anglophone tradition. Moreover, it engages them in such a way as inescapably to raise further issues of an epistemological and ontological character that are also very active topics of debate on the analytic side. They include, as I have said, the ongoing dispute between realists and anti-realists with respect to the question whether truth can properly or intelligibly be conceived as transcending the limits of available evidence, present best knowledge or attainable proof. I maintain that Derrida can be seen to espouse a realist position not only in logico-semantic terms – the terms on which this discussion is most often conducted nowadays – but also as a matter of strong metaphysical and ontological commitment. Indeed, if this were not the case, then there could be no justification for the claim – implicit throughout his work – that a deconstructive reading can discover (rather than project or invent) hitherto unrecognized complexities of sense and logic. These in turn serve to indicate hitherto unrecognized problems or shortfalls in the current state of knowledge concerning one or other of those numerous topic areas that Derrida addresses by way of such a reading.

Hence his insistence, as against the routine charge, that he is not for one moment rejecting or ignoring the referential component of language but rather pointing out the kinds of complication – the uncertainties of scope or instances of contextual under- or over-determination – which tend to escape notice on other, more simplified or doctrinaire accounts. If paradox is the great engine of change for Badiou, especially the kinds of paradox that arise through reflection on the infinite and issues of set-theoretical membership/inclusion, then for Derrida that role is most notably played by the emergence of aporias or logical–semantic–referential aberrations whose discovery marks the break with some existing state of knowledge and the moment of advance into unexplored regions of thought. What links these two, in other ways dissimilar thinkers is a critical impulse that takes the form of a rigorously argued undoing of certain hegemonic yet questionable truth-claims by means of a discourse that stakes its credit on the power – the logical and conceptual power – to reveal just where those claims run up against unexpected obstacles, dilemmas or aporias. That Badiou sets about this project *more mathematico* and Derrida seemingly *more linguistico* should not be allowed to disguise their kinship as thinkers who explore the capacity of reason to transcend the kinds of limit imposed by any in-place currency of knowledge or belief.

So this book goes various ways around in making its case against those equally various kinds of preconception or downright prejudice that have typified the long-running spat between 'analytic' and 'continental' philosophy. First, it argues that the rift cannot be characterized in terms of the typecast oppositions (realist *versus* anti-realist, logic-based *versus* logically promiscuous, science-led *versus* science-hostile, rigorous *versus* impressionistic or muddle-headed, etc.) that have often – though not quite so often of late – been peddled by those in the analytic camp. Second, it sets out to show through engagement with the work of Derrida and Badiou that the analytic virtues (in a proper or generic rather than partisan, sectarian or parochial sense of the term) are virtues fully shared – even, in some respects, surpassed – by some work in that 'other' tradition. Third, it takes certain of Derrida's texts as striking confirmation of the fact that a discourse on and of philosophy can exhibit the highest, most exacting standards of conceptual analysis while also exhibiting the power to invent or create new concepts whereby to challenge received habits of thought. Gilles Deleuze has been most explicit in stressing this contrast between philosophic approaches that seek only a somewhat more perspicuous (logically accountable) rendition of existing ideas or idioms and on the other hand approaches – nonetheless philosophical for that – which bring about a transformation in the scope of what's thinkable at any given time. The former conception is one that takes shape in various kinds of analytically approved methodology such as purebred logico-semantic analysis in the Frege–Russell line of descent, or a Wittgenstein-sanctioned deference to the problem-solving wisdom enshrined in 'ordinary language', or the appeal to certain kinds of thought-experiment as affording access to truth or knowledge through the witness of 'straightforward' (rational or common sense) intuition. What all such procedures have in common is the tendency – indeed, the fixed determination – to prop up the existing conceptual and institutional status quo against any too drastic departure from its own governing norms.

In other words, they are subject to a generalized version of the 'paradox of analysis' that first struck G.E. Moore. This was the puzzling fact that if analytic philosophy, true to form, aspired to the order of logical self-evidence possessed by the analytic proposition then by achieving that goal it would become altogether redundant or devoid of substantive content. Any strict continuation of the project set in train by thinkers such as Frege, Russell, Carnap and Tarski – the basically logicist project carried on with great vigour and confidence until the hammer-blow of Quine's 'Two Dogmas' and in somewhat more restricted specialist quarters thereafter – would end up by having nothing of substance to say since all its statements would be self-evident truths in virtue of their logical form and hence strictly tautologous. This point has mostly been treated as a 'paradox' by commentators within the broad analytic tradition or regarded as a curious, maybe worrisome but in no way disabling objection. Thus it has not, on the whole, been accorded anything like the same destructive force as those arguments that pretty conclusively discredited the logical-positivist verification principle by remarking that it failed to satisfy either of its own criteria (empirical warrant or logical self-evidence) and was thus plainly self-refuting. Still the two cases are sufficiently similar – both of them turning on the problems with a certain conception of logic *vis-à-vis* other, that is, empirical or evidence-based modes of enquiry – for the travails of verificationism as witnessed by rearguard defenders like A.J. Ayer to exert real pressure on the wider project of analytic philosophy. That is, they give reason for doubting its claim to offer insights or increments of knowledge beyond whatever is smuggled in by way of covert premises or presuppositions.

Of course, it may be said that this argument is off the point since analytic philosophy is by no means confined to any such narrowly logicist approach. After all, the term is normally used to describe a great variety of methods, theories or programmes that range all the way from logical positivism/empiricism to various reactive movements of thought that have defined themselves largely in contrast to it, these in turn ranging from Quinean radical empiricism to sundry versions of causal realism with overt – indeed programmatic – metaphysical backup. However, as I have argued at length elsewhere, the fact that it has produced such a diverse progeny should not be allowed to disguise the deeper-lying fact that analytic philosophy has continued to generate problems and dilemmas which point back to that same inability to break the closed circle that Moore, despite his status as one of its pioneering figures, was the first to diagnose. The case has been pressed even more forcefully by those continental thinkers, like Deleuze, who own no allegiance to the 'other' tradition and who deem it inadequate for failing to ask what might lie beyond or behind the various logico-semantic structures upon which analytic philosophers typically fix their sights. Thus, in his *Logic of Sense* Deleuze launches a full-scale frontal assault on analysis of the kind epitomized by Russell's 'On Denoting' or Frege's 'On Sense and Reference' and still practised, albeit to seemingly diverse ends, by their present-day descendants. Such thinking, he maintains, is a massive evasion of that issue and involves a basic failure to grasp that the linguistic forms or propositional structures in question cannot be conceived as self-sufficient but must be thought of as depending for whatever meaning or expressive force they possess on that which *precedes and motivates* their articulation in logico-semantic (i.e. analytically specifiable) form.

Hence Deleuze's long-standing commitment to a doctrine of 'expressionism' in philosophy, as well as his above-mentioned advocacy of the philosopher's task as one of 'creating concepts' rather than subjecting ready-made concepts to analysis on likewise ready-made terms. It is much the same case that Derrida puts in his early essay 'Force and Signification' where he critiques a number of structuralist thinkers – literary critics mostly – for their constant tendency to privilege form over force, or that which most readily lends itself to treatment in structural (i.e. conceptually amenable) terms over that which eludes or exceeds the best powers of structural description. Such was the issue, as Derrida saw it, between the two most advanced philosophical movements of thought during his own intellectually formative years, namely Husserlian phenomenology and the newly emergent structuralist 'sciences of man'. Where they diverged was on the question, simply put, of which should take priority: the expressive-creative element in thought that inherently surpasses any account based on the appeal to pre-existent structures or those structures themselves as the sole means by which to conceptualize the workings of language, culture or signifying systems in general. For Derrida, as emerges very clearly in his writings on Husserl, this was a constitutive and strictly unavoidable tension – an aporia, in the proper sense of that term – which epitomized the history of Western philosophical thought insofar as 'a certain structuralism has always been philosophy's most spontaneous gesture', while conversely 'that which I cannot understand in a structure is that by means of which it is not closed'.

This desire to keep both claims in play, or not to let up on the aporetic tension between them, is perhaps the chief factor that distinguishes Derridean deconstruction from the unilateral Deleuzean stress on expression (along with difference, intensity, desire and their various cognates) as that which enables thought to hold out against the coercive and homogenizing pressure of various conceptual regimes. Still it is the case – most evidently so when one compares his texts with those of philosophers in the analytic mainstream – that Derrida, like Deleuze, is very much in the business of creating rather than merely analysing concepts. Moreover, this has crucially to do with the propriety of calling his books and essays *texts* in the distinctive or qualitative sense of that term that brings them within the ambit of 'literary' exegesis as well as philosophical analysis, commentary and criticism. Thus, they invite the kind of close-focused or intensive exegetical reading that is alert to their highly inventive modes of linguistic and formal presentation, 'inventive' (that is) in comparison with the much tighter, institutionally sanctioned modes that characterize most analytic philosophy. However – a point I make with respect to both Derrida and Badiou, albeit in different ways – there is absolutely no conflict of principle or practice between an approach to philosophical issues that insists on maintaining the highest, most rigorous standards of logical argumentation and an approach that insists on the need for maximal attentiveness to textual detail. That such attentiveness very often throws up results that create certain problems for other, more orthodox readings – and also for more orthodox (classical) conceptions of logical procedure – is likewise no reason to count it just a 'literary' fad, or a merely rhetorical simulacrum of genuine philosophy like that which Socrates reputedly saw off in his exchange with Protagoras.

My point, to repeat, is that the real issue has nothing to do with this endlessly rehearsed dialogue of the deaf between a philosophic discourse secure in its possession of a rigour unknown to its typecast irrationalist opponents and a discourse (call it sophistical, postmodernist or Rortian neo-pragmatist) that is equally convinced in advance of philosophy's inevitable failure to make good its claims. If Derrida, in his third-round rejoinder to Searle, can write of the 'determined non-encounter' between deconstruction and a certain variety of speech-act theory premised on certain highly prescriptive (and proscriptive) procedural norms, then this is not just an update or minor variation on the old Socratic scenario. Rather than playing philosophy off against anti- or pseudo-philosophy, it involves an engagement on very different terms where the issue is that between a mode of philosophizing closed to any challenge that doesn't basically conform to its own procedural norms and a mode of philosophizing that constantly raises questions not only with regard to the practices of others but also with regard to its own explicit or implicit presuppositions. Derrida has managed to combine an extreme sensitivity to linguistic detail that surpasses even that of a verbal micrologist like Austin with a degree of conceptual rigour that fully matches up to that of philosophers in the logicist line of descent.

One besetting fault of analytic philosophy is that it has somehow created this delusory fault-line between what goes on in the conduct of 'natural-language' or first-order philosophic debate and what goes on at the 'higher' level of meta-linguistic analysis. No doubt that distinction is useful, even necessary, for certain purposes having to do with the formal regimentation of language so as to avoid various problematic or paradoxical (e.g. self-predicative) upshots. All the same – and here Derrida is very much in agreement with Badiou – they cannot be laid to rest by a stipulative fiat that simply says *thou shalt not* allow any admixture or problem-generating overlap between different logico-linguistic orders of discourse. For Badiou, this means rejecting Russell's 'theory of types', that is, his flatly stated requirement that we not be permitted to construct self-predicative expressions such as 'the set of all sets that are not members of themselves', or – more famously – 'the barber who shaves every man in town except those who shave themselves' (in which case who shaves the barber?). Rather we should press on with the problem right up to but then, and on just that condition, potentially *through and beyond* the point where it poses a seemingly insoluble paradox. Only through the impetus thereby created can thought achieve the kind of decisive advance that eventually delivers a solution. What this involves is the process of 'turning paradox into concept', one most aptly figured (as we shall see) in the proleptic operation of 'forcing' by which the mathematician Paul Cohen explained the emergence of evental truths – epochal or ground-breaking discoveries – beyond anything graspable in terms of pre-existent or accredited knowledge. In Derrida, it takes the form of a deconstructive practice that likewise refuses to accept any face-saving philosophic gambit based on the enforced separation of realms between a first-order, natural-language discourse and a higher-level discourse of formal or logico-semantic analysis. Thus, philosophy is capable of *thinking through* the resultant problems and paradoxes just so long as it combines the utmost attentiveness to textual detail – including (especially) anomalous or hard-to-assimilate detail – with a due regard for the highest standards of conceptual-analytic rigour. Such is at any rate the chief contention of this book and, I hope, an adequate justification for yoking together these two most distinctive and original philosophers of recent times.

(Note: I have not provided bibliographical details for sources cited in this Introduction since they are all discussed at greater length in subsequent chapters and can be tracked down easily enough through the index and relevant chapter endnotes.)

# Diagonals: Truth-Procedures in Derrida and Badiou

## I

As I have said, Badiou's relationship to Derrida doesn't exhibit anything like the pattern of routine inter-generational conflict that has characterized so many episodes of post-war French intellectual history. Thus, it bears no resemblance to those acts of barely concealed parricidal intent by which Sartre ousted the dominant currencies of pre-war (whether rationalist or Bergson-influenced) thought, or the structuralism of Lévi-Strauss, Althusser and company purported to consign Sartrean existentialism to the dustbin of outworn humanist ideas, or structuralism in turn gave way to the combined assaults of post-structuralists, postmodernists and other such reactive movements. Indeed there is something decidedly majestic about the way that Badiou rises above such manifestations of the short-term *Zeitgeist* or sad displays of the *odium scholasticum* that all too often substitutes for serious debate. His attitude towards Derrida – as evidenced by the brief but revealing encomium collected in the volume *Pocket Pantheon* – is one of admiration mixed with a certain ironic reserve and some shrewdly aimed though far from hostile remarks about the lack of any direct activist involvement on Derrida's part in the events of May 1968.[1] Even here Badiou is keen to make allowance for the highly mediated character of 'deconstructive politics', or the need to approach that topic with a due regard for Derrida's immensely patient, meticulous and painstaking way with texts, among them (if belatedly) the texts of Marx.[2] More than that, he puts the case for Derrida as a political thinker of the first importance, just so long as we read his work with the kind of extreme attentiveness and rigour that he brings to the work of others.

So Badiou is unencumbered by any desire to stake his claim as a replacement *maître à penser* or as one who has seen through the kind of 'textualist' mystification that has often been laid at Derrida's door by Marxists, activists and – from a different though related angle – by Foucault in his early polemical rejoinder.[3] Nevertheless, I shall argue, it is a complex relationship and one that brings out some salient tensions not only between the two thinkers but also within their respective projects. Badiou's answer in the *Pocket Pantheon* essay might well be characterized as a case of interpretative 'strong revisionism' as Harold Bloom describes it, that is, a mode of commentary that aims not so much to establish a relationship of fidelity and subservience to the text in hand but rather to transform or trans-value that text in keeping with the commentator's own priorities.[4] Of course this is Badiou's regular practice in the many exegetical chapters of *Being and Event* where he takes a whole roster of the great philosophers from Parmenides, Plato and Aristotle to Descartes, Spinoza, Leibniz, Kant, Hegel and their modern progeny – along with poets such as Mallarmé and Hölderlin – and subjects them to a reading (mostly in the critical-diagnostic mode) accordant with the book's general thesis.[5] Such reading goes against the intentional grain so as to bring out those symptoms of conflict, internal contradictions or conceptual stress points that indicate the workings of a transverse or 'diagonal' logic at odds with the overt gist. This is often a matter of showing how the argument turns back against itself and can be seen to undermine its overt commitment to a plenist ontology that would, in effect, preclude any real possibility of change whether in states of mathematical-scientific knowledge, conditions of the body politic or modes of artistic practice. It involves an alertness to certain symptomatic blind spots of repression whose existence, once detected, opens the way to a radically different 'subtractive' ontology wherein that possibility not only exists but also becomes the chief motor or driving force of progress in those various domains.

My reference to Bloom on the process of creative misprision – the way that 'strong misreaders' (poets for the most part) absorb and then transform the work of their great dead precursors – needs to be qualified in one major respect. That is to say, Badiou's is a distinctively *philosophical* approach where intellectual creativity goes along with a high degree of conceptual and argumentative rigour and can therefore claim something more in the way of exegetical warrant or justification. I must defer any detailed commentary on the crucial significance of mathematics (more specifically, of developments in set-theory after Cantor) for his thinking about the dialectic of being and event, or the process whereby a given ontology or conceptual scheme comes up against that which radically challenges and eventually transforms its operative scope and limits.[6] What interests me here is the difference between Badiou's deployment of this basically dialectical (or immanent-critical) approach as applied to thinkers in the mainstream Western philosophical tradition and his particular take on Derrida's project, involving as it does a more nuanced and delicate negotiation of the differences between them. At one level, this has to do mainly with the question of political activism and with Derrida's (as Badiou sees it) very marked disinclination to advance from the stage of intensive engagement with complications in the texts of Western logocentric tradition to the stage of engagement with issues of direct or urgent political concern. At another – though closely related to that – it has to do with Badiou's ambivalent relation to just those practices of textual close-reading, surely epitomized by deconstruction, that offer what he sees as an all too handy pretext for evading or endlessly deferring issues of political commitment.

One would not expect Badiou to single out Derrida for exemption from this particular line of attack. After all, the charge of political evasiveness has very often been laid at Derrida's door by Marxists especially but also by thinkers of a broadly leftist or social-activist persuasion.[7] Moreover, it would fit readily enough with Badiou's emphatic opposition to the 'linguistic turn' in its many and varied showings over the past century.[8] These range from the Frege-Russell mode of analytic philosophy or its 'ordinary-language' (e.g. Wittgensteinian or Austinian) variants to Heideggerian hermeneutics, post-structuralism, Richard Rorty's 'strong' descriptivist brand of neo-pragmatism, Foucault's archaeologies or genealogies of discourse, and postmodernism as theorized – with snippety reference to most of the above – by a thinker like Lyotard.[9] For Badiou, what marks them all out (though some more than others) as involving a sheer dereliction of philosophy's proper role is their way of falling back on an appeal to language, discourse or representation as the ultimate horizon of intelligibility or the end point of ontological enquiry. However, as I have said, he appears to exempt Derrida from the general charge and to do so for reasons closely connected with his own project. Although these emerge plain to view only in the *Pocket Pantheon* essay – after what must seem a remarkably long period of abstention from anything like a serious or sustained engagement with Derrida – they are likely to possess a revelatory force for suitably attuned readers, and moreover to strike them as casting a powerful retrospective light on crucial aspects of Badiou's work.

At any rate he does his utmost to deflect that blanket charge of Derrida's having raised subtleties of verbal exegesis to a high point of 'textualist' mystification which in turn provides a standing excuse for the avoidance of any definite, that is, any non-deconstrucible commitment in matters of politics. Nor does he subscribe to the other, more specific version of it which holds that the deconstructionist obsession with logical-rhetorical figures such as aporia, paradox, undecidability, and so forth, is just what might be expected of a movement so determined to block any process of constructive or problem-solving thought and – beyond that – any prospect of its application to the sorts of problem confronted by theoretically minded political activists. If indeed there is a certain unwillingness to lay that commitment on the line then this should rather be attributed, as Badiou says in the passage already cited in my Introduction, to the kind of 'diagonal obstinacy' that typifies Derrida's thought, along with his clearly evinced 'dislike of abrupt metaphysically derived divisions' and the fact that his way of brooding productively on fine points of textual interpretation gives rise to a mindset 'clearly not suited to stormy times when everything comes under the law of decisiveness, here and now'.[10] Of course these phrases carry more than a hint of irony, coming as they do from one who has unceasingly upheld the good old cause of May 1968 along with the undying political significance of other 'failed' or abortive revolutions such as (pre-eminently) the 1871 Paris Commune, and addressed as they are to a thinker whose revolutionary commitments were, to say the least, a great deal more guarded and circumspect.[11] Still the irony is by no means so heavy or censorious as to cancel what is clearly Badiou's genuine appreciation of a thinker whose intellectual temperament, though very different from his own, nevertheless has a fair claim to represent one possible way that a radical intelligence might come to terms with the conflicting pressures of its own time and place.

One should also note, in that phrase 'diagonal obstinacy', a more than casual allusion to the role of set-theoretical concepts in Badiou's rethinking of the relationship between being and event, that is, the Cantor-derived technique of 'diagonalisation' as that which enables thought to conceive and then work with multiple orders or 'sizes' of infinity.[12] I shall have more to say in this connection at a later stage but will here just remark on its singular effect when drawn into a discussion of Derrida's work in relation to politics, on the one hand, and to mathematics, logic and the formal sciences on the other. Thus, it opens the way for Badiou to enlist Derrida as having arrived at something closely analogous to the formal procedure that Badiou sets out in *Being and Event* and elsewhere, albeit a procedure (that of deconstruction) that makes no explicit appeal to set-theoretical concepts and which operates more through the close-reading of philosophical and other texts. So we should, I think, take Badiou very much at his word – and not (or not merely) as conforming to the old French custom of high-toned testamentary tributes – when he declares that he will henceforth emulate Derrida's famous punning neologism *différance* (= difference/deferral/deference) by likewise substituting an anomalous *a* for the 'correct' letter *e* in the final syllable of his own key-word *inexistence*.[13] Just as *différance* functions in Derrida's texts as a signifier of that which eludes any possibility of conceptual closure or univocal definition, so also *inexistance* will function in Badiou's texts as a pointedly apt designation of that which eludes the mathematical, scientific or socio-political count-as-one. It is the term for whatever 'inexists' or finds no place within some given situation or state of knowledge, whether through being denied any form of effective political representation (like the 'paperless' North African immigrant workers in France) or through figuring nowhere in the currently accredited tally of beliefs, propositions or truth-claims.[14] Thus, for Badiou, 'the wager of Derrida's work, of his infinite work, . . . is to *inscribe the inexistent*'. If that word has acquired its deviant spelling by the end of Badiou's short essay, then this is no mere linguistic *jeu d'esprit* – any more than with Derrida's numerous inventive yet philosophically load-bearing neologisms – but a shift brought about strictly in consequence of certain precise and far-reaching analogies between their two projects.

There is further evidence of this when the passage just cited brings together a markedly Derridean inscriptionalist or textual idiom with a thoroughly Badiouan appeal to the range of conceptual resources opened up by Cantor's exemplary passage through and beyond the paradoxes of traditional thinking about the infinite. Thus, the reference to Derrida's 'infinite work' of inscribing the inexistent is no idle compliment or piece of neatly turned phraseology but rather a precisely gauged evocation of the link between Badiou's set-theoretically inspired rethinking of ontological issues and Derrida's less formally explicit but, in their own way, just as rigorous deconstructive procedures. This is most likely why Badiou exempts Derrida from his otherwise sweeping condemnation of the linguistic turn in its sundry current guises as merely an update on old sophistical or cultural-relativist themes. What is crucially different about Derrida's commentaries on canonical texts from Plato to Husserl is his relentless teasing-out of aporetic or contradictory chains of logical implication which can then be seen to pose a large problem to any orthodox or fideist account.[15] Such are those conflicts that arise between the *vouloir-dire* of authorial intent and that which a text is logically constrained to signify when examined with a readiness to track certain discrepant details that challenge or subvert more conventional protocols of reading. The result may very well go against not only our best evidence of what the writer expressly, consciously or knowingly meant to say but also the weight of received exegetical wisdom as well as, very often, our intuitive sense of interpretative validity or truth. Hence the elusive yet marked affinity between Derrida's way with texts – his 'patient deconstruction of oppositions' as Badiou puts it, not without a certain muted irony – and Badiou's approach to the various thinkers (philosophers and poets) whose work he subjects to a form of immanent dialectical critique. Where they differ is chiefly in Derrida's far greater emphasis on textual close-reading or exegesis as the means to locate those tensions, aporias or moments of undecidability when classical (bivalent or true/false) logic is forced up against its limits. In Badiou, the procedure is pursued to broadly similar ends – with a view to exposing the covert implications, the suppressed premises or (in Derrida's phrase) the 'unthought axiomatics' of a dominant tradition – but more by way of conceptual analysis than through a sedulous attention to details of the text.

# II

In this respect, Badiou may be said to stand closer to Adorno, or negative dialectics in its first-generation Frankfurt mode, than to any version of that well-nigh ubiquitous linguistic turn that has undeniably left a strong imprint on Derrida's work.[16] And yet, as emerges to striking (even moving) effect, Badiou is attracted not only by the rigour of Derrida's work but also – what might seem at odds with that – by its quest for alternative, less sharply polarized terms of address or some means to shift argumentative ground from a downright clash of contradictory logics (within the text or among its commentators) to a 'space of flight', as Badiou describes it, beyond all those vexing antinomies.

> You take, for example, the great metaphysical oppositions. We shall have to diagonalize them. Because restricting discursive space means leaving no massivity, no linear massivity. Binary oppositions cannot possibly locate the *hors-lieu* in any *lieu*. So, we will have to deconstruct them. We will have to cut across them. That is what deconstruction is. Deconstruction is, basically, the set of operations that can bring about a certain restriction of the space of flight, or of the space of the vanishing point.[17]

'Restriction', that is, insofar as it places certain definite limits on the space for manoeuvre as concerns this or that particular text, or again – more precisely – on what should count as a warranted claim with regard to those specific complications of sense, reference and logic that result from a properly deconstructive reading. Hence the well-known passages (in *Of Grammatology* and elsewhere) that find Derrida emphatically asserting the need to respect indications of authorial intent so far as possible while nonetheless remaining maximally alert to those symptoms of conceptual stress that signal the presence of a counter-logic at odds with the text's overt (intentional) purport.[18] Indeed, as Badiou very pointedly remarks, it is just this Derridean preference for re-inscribing (i.e. first inverting then displacing) certain kinds of binary opposition that is most characteristic not only of deconstruction as a formal procedure or practice of textual close-reading but also of Derrida's mode of address to political and ethical themes. So we should not take it as a cunning backhander – or a case of praising with faint damns – when Badiou refers to Derrida's having been 'kept apart from the truth of the red years between 1968 and 1976', and when he further explains that the truth in question 'spoke its name with the words: One divides into two'.[19]

No doubt Badiou is here staking his own militant distance from any such conflict-avoidance strategy, as well as signalling for those in the know that this political difference goes along with an equally decisive difference in terms of their respective commitments with regard to certain aspects of the relation between language, truth and logic. Of course it is not the case that these two utterly distinctive thinkers are at bottom saying the same thing, the one (Derrida) in linguistically oriented or 'textualist' and the other (Badiou) in mathematically derived or formalist terms. Yet one should, I think, take Badiou at his word in the *Pocket Pantheon* essay when he allows that some thinkers – those, like Derrida, with sufficient exegetical as well as political patience – can and should pursue the other, basically non-confrontational path. Moreover, one can see how this way of thinking, or something very like it, played a role in the development of Badiou's ideas from the binary-dominated concepts and categories of *Being and Event* to the more nuanced, differential understanding of the relationship between being and existence that typifies *Logics of Worlds*.[20]

> When Derrida outlines the concept of 'différance' he wants to suggest a single term that can activate the being/existence distinction in its vanishing point. Derrida *puts to flight* what remains of a metaphysical opposition in the being/existence difference in such a way that we can grasp difference as such, *in its act*. And *différance* in action is obviously that which stands at the vanishing point of any opposition between being and existent, that which cannot in any sense be reduced to the figure of that opposition. And then we have to examine the democracy/totalitarianism opposition in the same way. Or the real impact of the Jew/Arab opposition on the Palestinian conflict. When he takes a stance on the Jew/Arab opposition in the Palestinian conflict, he once again deconstructs its duality.[21]

This makes it very clear how close are the links, as Badiou perceives them, on the one hand between Derrida's early and his later (more overtly political) writings, and on the other between Derrida's work as a whole and Badiou's critical ontology – his conception of the being/event dialectic – as it moved towards the more stratified or nuanced account laid out in *Logics of Worlds*.

So we shouldn't too easily fall in with the idea that these two thinkers stand squarely apart as regards the single most divisive issue in present-day philosophy of language and logic. It is not just a matter of situating each of them at some point on a scale that runs from the language-first proposition, that is, that any critique of prevalent ('logocentric') ideas must always take account of its own embeddedness in a certain cultural-linguistic milieu or tradition to the logicist claim that such critique has to start with a strenuous rejection of the turn towards language as – supposedly – the ultimate limit or horizon of intelligibility. This is basically the same issue that divides continental thinkers of a strongly hermeneutic or language-centred orientation such as Heidegger and Gadamer from those, like Adorno or Habermas, who whatever their otherwise sharp differences agree on the need for a critical approach that holds out against received ideas and their customary modes of expression. From the latter viewpoint, it is a *sine qua non* of enlightened or progressive thought that it should always maintain the utmost vigilance with regard to those ingrained habits of belief that may always turn out to have been kept in place by the inertial force of communal usage or linguistically encoded prejudice. On this account, the true dividing-line falls not, as the textbook story would have it, between (so-called) continental and (so-called) analytic philosophy but rather between those thinkers on either side who pretty much go along with the linguistic turn for all practical purposes and those others who reject it on philosophical, political or ethical grounds.[22] Nobody who has read Badiou's *Manifesto for Philosophy* or registered the impact of his forceful reflections on the prevalence of latter-day 'sophistry' – especially where influenced by Wittgenstein – could be in any doubt as regards his deep and principled aversion to this whole movement of thought.[23] Worst of all, in his view, is the way that it precludes any substantive critique of existing beliefs, values or truth-claims by declaring that such criticism has to make sense by the lights of some communal consensus or cultural life form which would otherwise find it unacceptable or downright unintelligible.

One can therefore see why Badiou's readings of various canonical philosophers proceed more directly through a critical engagement with the conceptual and argumentative structures of their thought and not, as in Derrida, through a practice of meticulous textual close-reading. Of course, it is then open for any Derridean to ask how Badiou could possibly advance his strong-revisionist claims – for instance, his subversion of the plenist ontology or the static and immobile concept of being endorsed by thinkers from Parmenides to Spinoza – unless through a rigorous textual analysis that locates and deconstructs those specific passages where the doctrine in question can be shown to encounter certain problems unresolvable on its own express terms.[24] And indeed it is the case that Badiou arrives at his unsettling conclusions through some careful and detailed as well as critically acute and markedly heterodox readings. Still there is a difference between, on the one hand, Derridean close-reading where the problems emerge in and through a process of direct engagement with the text and, on the other, Badiou's mode of dialectical critique which takes for granted the text's having been read with adequate attention to detail and which thus – on the strength of that previous engagement – presumes the entitlement to argue its case at a certain level of abstraction from the kinds of exegetical detail required of an *echt*-deconstructive approach. One motivating factor here, as I have said, is Badiou's opposition to anything – any argument, theory, or school of thought – that goes along with the linguistic turn or the notion of language as an end-point of critical enquiry. This helps to explain his ambivalence towards Derrida's work despite their both being centrally concerned to expose the symptomatic blind-spots, aporias or conflicts between manifest and latent sense which reveal the limits of a certain restrictive ontology (Badiou) or a certain logocentric 'metaphysics of presence' (Derrida) whose liability to such disruptive effects is an index of its deeply ideological character.

This kinship emerges with unmistakeable force if one compares, say, Badiou's strongly heterodox yet rigorously consequent readings of Plato, Aristotle, Descartes, Rousseau, Kant, Hegel or Heidegger with Derrida's no less strenuously argued deconstructive commentaries on those same thinkers.[25] In Derrida, it is chiefly a matter of revealing the various deviant, non-classical or paraconsistent logics that can be shown to inhabit their texts and produce those moments of undecidability – aporias, in the strict sense of the term – which call into question certain of the author's leading premises or presuppositions.[26] If the *modus operandi* is that of textual close-reading, then this should not be seen as consigning Derrida's work to the realm of literary criticism or applied rhetoric but rather as offering the means to make that case with a high degree of demonstrative force and with reference to certain highly specific contexts of argument. In Badiou, it is chiefly a matter of showing how certain overt ontological commitments – those that endorse some version of a plenist or changeless, timeless and wholly determinate ontology – are fissured by the need to introduce an anomalous term that implicitly concedes the problematical status of any such doctrine and its covert reliance on that which it has striven to keep off bounds. This is why Badiou devotes a large portion of his commentary in the early sections of *Being and Event* to a detailed rehearsal of the issue of the one and the many as raised to intensely thought-provoking though somewhat baffled effect in Plato's dialogue *Parmenides*.[27] What emerges here is the conceptual impossibility of thinking an absolute plenitude of being – an absolute dominion of the one over the many or of the timeless and unchanging over everything subject to time and change – and hence the need (so deeply repugnant to Plato's idealist mind-set) to reckon with this in any workable theory of truth and knowledge.

Thus, Badiou sees a strong proleptic link between Plato's reflections on that topic and the subsequent history of more or less bewildered attempts, on the part of philosophers and mathematicians, to get a grip on the concept of the infinite as something more than a merely notional, virtual or place-holder term.[28] His reading of intellectual history is premised on the claim that what Cantor eventually achieved – an operational grasp of the infinite and its multiple 'sizes' or cardinalities – was there already as a readable subtext to the vexing antinomies of Plato's dialogue and was then worked out through numerous episodes in the long history of subsequent attempts to resolve them. Only with Cantor did these dilemmas, supposedly endemic to any thinking about the infinite, at last give way to a conception that would 'turn paradox into concept' or transform what had so far been a cause of intellectual anxiety into a source of knowledge-transformative insights not only in mathematics but also (so Badiou maintains) with respect to basic ontological questions across the whole range of scientific, social and humanistic disciplines. What Cantor's discovery made it possible to think was the concept (not merely the idea) that there existed multiple orders of the infinite – such as the infinity of integers and even numbers, or integers and fractions thereof, or rational and real numbers – and, moreover, that these could be reckoned with or subject to calculation in rigorous and perfectly intelligible ways. The effect was to open up a vast new region of transfinite operations that David Hilbert famously described as 'a mathematician's paradise', and which finally laid to rest those deep misgivings about the topic that had typified the response of many thinkers from Plato and Aristotle down to Cantor's more orthodox-minded contemporaries.[29] So it was that his breakthrough soon gave rise to a whole range of powerful techniques for creating (or discovering, as mathematical realists would say) new possibilities of further extending the set-theoretical domain.

Plato's worry is conveyed in the dialogue through Socrates' encounter with his senior and mentor Parmenides. It has to do with the way that reflection on the infinite tends to generate problems, dilemmas, aporias or instances of limit-point paradox which pose a real threat to the kind of thinking – the pursuit of a well-defined systematic structure for the conduct of rational enquiry – that philosophers have typically espoused. The result of this encounter is to force Socrates and his admiring, ever-faithful, yet at this point discernibly independent-minded student and chronicler Plato into a sequence of hard-pressed dialectical manoeuvres on the theme of the one and the many that leads both thinkers, like many others after them, right up to and (arguably) just beyond the point of conceptual deadlock. Thus the dialogue, at least as Plato reconstructs it, brings Socrates out decidedly at odds with Parmenides' doctrine that only the one can truly be said to exist while the multiple is merely a product of delusory phenomenal or sensuous experience. Instead it is seen to manifest an incipient grasp of the contrary truth according to which multiplicity precedes and outruns any limit arbitrarily placed upon it by this or that particular state of knowledge, ontological scheme, discursive regime or appearance of consistency brought about by some local operation of the merely stipulative count-as-one. This the dialogue achieves despite and against Plato's well-known predilection for the transcendent unifying power of that which participates in the abstract realm of the forms, or ideas, such as justice, beauty and (ultimately) goodness. In short, '[w]hat Plato is endeavouring to think here, in a magnificent, dense text, is evidently inconsistent multiplicity, which is to say, pure presentation, anterior to any one-effect, or to any structure'.[30] And again, in a pithy formulation by Badiou that very clearly credits Plato with a precocious (perhaps preconscious) attempt to make sense of that thesis: 'in the absence of any being of the one, the multiple in-consists in the presentation of a multiple of multiples without any foundational stopping-point'.[31]

'In-consists' is here used in the pointedly technical sense developed throughout *Being and Event*. What the neologism nicely and compactly denotes is that absolute precedence of the multiple over the one – or the inconsistent over the consistent – which plays a central role in Badiou's thinking not only about mathematics but also on other topics central to his work, among them most importantly politics. This he conceives as elementally a matter of the count-as-one and its exclusionary effect when deployed to distinguish some socially dominant fraction of the populace as members in good standing and to marginalize or negate some other fraction (for instance, that of the *sans papiers* or 'economic migrants') as lacking such status.[32] Nevertheless, just as Plato's 'official' (Parmenidean) doctrine of transcendental monism encountered resistance from certain inbuilt necessities of thought – a resistance that would finally give rise to Cantor's conceptual breakthrough – so likewise those oppressed or victimized minorities exert a counter-pressure at certain points in the existing body politic which at critical times may become the sites of protest, struggle and (potentially) social transformation. Thus, in terms of the more-than-analogical relation that Badiou posits between set theory and politics, any such change is likeliest to start at 'evental sites' where conditions exist for the emergence of an aberrant or 'uncounted' multiple, that is, a collectivity – something like Sartre's 'group-in-fusion' – with a shared interest in bringing it about.[33] These are subject multiples who 'belong' but are not 'included', or owing to whose conspicuous absence from the count-as-one the extant social structure can be known to 'inconsist', that is, to harbour absences (defects of adequate representation or shortfalls of accountability) that call its legitimacy into question.

This is all worked out with great precision and care for detail in Badiou's writings on the course of set-theoretical investigation after Cantor. It is expounded chiefly with reference to the work of Paul Cohen who devised (or discovered) a formal means of explaining how certain as-yet unknowable or unprovable truths in mathematics might nonetheless be implicit through their absence from the present state of knowledge and the power of that absence to generate certain specific problems and aporias.[34] Here again, as so often with Badiou, the Sartre comparison – famously exemplified by Pierre's absence from the café – is one that fairly leaps to mind.[35] I hope that by now it will be clear what I am suggesting with regard to the relationship between Badiou and Derrida. There is no doubt that Badiou is the more overtly formal thinker or the one whose work has drawn more heavily on developments in mathematics, logic and the formal sciences. There is also no doubt that Derrida is the more language-oriented or text-conscious thinker of the two, a difference that might seem to set them apart on basic philosophical grounds. However, to repeat, this impression ought to be checked by considering the well-nigh ubiquitous character of the 'linguistic turn' across numerous schools of post-1920 'analytic' and 'continental' thought. One effect of this – for thinkers not overly in hock to that typecast dichotomy – has been to question the very idea that an extreme sensitivity to linguistic nuance cannot go along with (must indeed be inimical to) an adequate power of conceptual grasp. Nor should it be forgotten, as so often it has by admiring and hostile commentators alike, that Derrida more than once invokes formal arguments such as Gödel's undecidability-theorem in order to explain what is involved in the deconstructive reading of a text.[36] This is not just a vaguely analogical or downright opportunist appeal to the presumed authority of mathematics and logic but a reference-point that precisely captures the movement – the logico-syntactic-semantic procedure – of Derrida's classic readings.

## III

My point is that Derrida's meditations on the logics of the *pharmakon* in Plato, of supplementarity in Rousseau, of parergonality in Kant or of *différance* in Husserl along with his later, more generic reflections on the aporetic logics of the gift, hospitality and auto-immunity are all essentially formal despite (or more accurately just on account of) their often starting out from some localized evidence of textual complication.[37] That is, they have to do with the scope and limits of classical (bivalent) logic – its coming up against strictly unresolvable instances of self-contradiction or aporia – and are therefore dependent on textual exegesis *only though crucially* in order to present this case with the maximum degree of evidential warrant and demonstrative (logical) rigour.

Indeed, one could plausibly interpret the development of Derrida's thought over five decades of intense activity as a shift of focus from textual close-reading as the *sine qua non* of interpretative truth or validity to a somewhat more generalized or less context-specific mode of conceptual analysis. I have ventured this claim in somewhat cautious and tentative style because it is misleading in one respect at least, namely its failure to acknowledge the wider (referential or real-world) contexts to which those later writings are very specifically addressed and to which they often respond in strongly marked ethico-political terms.[38] Here again, as with the (putative) issue concerning 'formal' *versus* 'textualist' modes of thought, if one takes due account of this dimension – always present in Derrida's work but latterly more overt and emphatic – there will seem fewer problems about finding significant points of contact between that work and various aspects of Badiou's project. It will then become clearer that their thinking converges on certain shared objectives, among them the concern to articulate a formally adequate account of the contradictions that they both find implicit across a great range of discourses, concepts, institutions, socio-political orders and practices. Moreover, they can then be seen as holding the shared belief that those contradictions have their locus of emergence only in the various specific contexts – from mathematics, logic and the physical sciences to politics, ethics and art – where thinkers and practitioners must henceforth discover the relevant validity-conditions as well as an anticipatory grasp of what would truthfully count as an advance on the present state of knowledge or current ideas of justificatory warrant.

All this was implicit in the well-known aphorism of Roland Barthes when he sought some common ground between structuralists and their Marxist or socialist-realist opponents by remarking that 'a little formalism turns one away from history, but a lot brings one back to it.'[39] What I think he had more specifically in mind – and what bears directly on our current discussion – is the difference between a wholesale version of the 'linguistic turn' (whether post-structuralist, Wittgensteinian, late-Heideggerian or Rortian neo-pragmatist) and a version that concedes the centrality of language to human thought and cognition yet also acknowledges the constraints imposed by logic on the one hand and referential ties or commitments on the other. Thus, a formalist approach is one that preserves at least this much of the classical *trivium* model with its three major disciplines of logic, grammar and rhetoric. The model was devised so as to allow rhetoric its appointed place as the study of language in its suasive or performative aspect but always within the order of priority laid down by a due regard for logic and, next to that, for grammar as the structural component of language that serves to articulate its proper relation to the correspondent structures of truth, fact or veridical knowledge and experience. It was subject to drastic revision through various programmes of reform from Ramus down and is nowadays either consigned to the intellectual history books or resurrected by boa-deconstructors like Paul de Man in order to advance a radically extended conception of rhetoric that would claim to undo – subvert or undermine – the priority of logic and grammar.[40]

Whatever may be one's assessment of de Man's somewhat wiredrawn arguments to this effect, it is clear that the *trivium* conception suffers from an overly literal understanding of the correspondence relation between logic, language and reality and a failure to conceive how that relation might be subject to disturbance by factors beyond the remit of logical or grammatical analysis. Still it is the model that looms over Wittgenstein's early Tractarian account of these matters, and also – of course – the model that he roundly rejected in the *Philosophical Investigations* and other 'late'-period writings.[41] Wittgenstein's was the most extreme – arguably the most naïve and literal-minded – of those doctrines that typified analytic philosophy in its early, predominantly logicist period. His subsequent turnaround was likewise the most extreme of those sundry reactive movements of thought which swung right across to a notion of language (language-games, discourses, phrase-regimes, descriptive paradigms, worldviews, conceptual schemes, etc.) as the furthest we can get towards a better understanding of the relation between thought and world.[42] It is in this context that Badiou and Derrida can be seen to hold out against the limiting conditions imposed on philosophy by a cyclic swinging back and forth between opposite and equally disabling doctrinal poles. Both thinkers maintain a steady commitment to standards of logical consistency and analytic-conceptual rigour along with an acute critical awareness of the ways in which certain problematic or anomalous instances – 'events' for Badiou, aporias or moments of undecidability for Derrida – may on occasion require a suspension and consequent redefinition of those same standards.

Badiou focuses on the effect of some crucial intervention in mathematics, science, politics or art which establishes a novel truth-procedure whose longer-term consequences are then worked out by 'militants of truth' – or those with the requisite degree of post-evental fidelity – and brought to the point where there occurs a decisive transformation in the existing order of knowledge, society or artistic expression. Derrida is more apt to describe such events in textual terms, that is to say, as likewise transformative occurrences but of the sort best exemplified by what happens when a deconstructive reading of (say) Plato, Rousseau, Kant, Hegel, Marx, Nietzsche, Husserl or Heidegger controverts not only the received understanding of those thinkers but also its bearing on issues in the sphere of general and regional ontology. Indeed, there are some major misconceptions about Derrida that might be dispelled by noting the salient points of convergence between his project and Badiou's more explicitly ontological approach to the ongoing dialectic of being and event. One is the old canard, still much bandied about among Derrida's detractors, that in making his notorious claim to the effect that 'there is nothing outside the text' ('il n'y a pas de hors-texte'; better rendered 'there is no "outside" to the text') he should be taken to espouse a textualist variant of absolute or transcendental idealism according to which, quite literally, written marks on the page are all that can be known to exist.[43] Another is the notion often advanced by critics on the left that when Derrida claims to deconstruct the Western logocentric 'metaphysics of presence' from Plato to Heidegger, he must have in mind some timeless and seamless structure of false consciousness – or mode of self-perpetuating error and delusion – that has remained perfectly unaffected by even the most radical interim changes of socio-political life.[44]

My comparison with Badiou may help to make the contrary point, that is, that each of those textual engagements raises a historically specific range of issues which in turn have to do with a particular form of ideological misrecognition or a distinct, politically inflected way that the logocentric prejudice has taken hold under given material and cultural conditions. In short, the main task of critical reading, as Derrida conceives it, is precisely to articulate those fault lines in the structure of metaphysical presupposition that are normally concealed by our placid assurance of knowing our way around language and the world but which show up to most striking effect when placed under deconstructive scrutiny. Nor should this for one moment be taken to suggest that Derrida is proposing linguistic therapy in the Wittgensteinian mode, that is, seeking to talk us down from the giddy heights of metaphysical abstraction and restore us to a communally sanctioned sense of what constitutes apt or proper usage.[45] One additional benefit of viewing his work in relation to Badiou's is that it shows just how far they share a decidedly anti-Wittgensteinian emphasis on the power of critical thought to question, challenge, unsettle and subvert the complacent habits of belief typically enshrined in (so-called) ordinary language.

As we have seen, Badiou offers numerous examples of the process or procedure whereby some given state of knowledge, political situation or stage of artistic advance – along with the ontology that underwrites it – is thrown into doubt or forced to the point of crisis and transformation through various strictly consequent though strictly unforeseeable turns in the logic of events. Indeed that phrase, 'logic of events', is one that neatly encapsulates the nature of this process as Badiou describes it, since the logic (or intelligible sequence of developments) emerges fully formed only 'after the event' yet with no less a sense of rigorous necessity given the new advance in knowledge, the new access to political power on the part of a hitherto oppressed group or the new possibilities of expression opened up by some breakthrough artistic achievement. In mathematical terms – always his ultimate point of reference – it involves that quintessentially set-theoretical operation of 'turning paradox into concept' or finding the resources for a radical rethinking of some presently insoluble problem which then becomes the springboard for a full-scale conceptual revolution. As paradigm cases Badiou cites the advances achieved by Cantor with his grasp of the multiple orders of infinity and by Cohen with his account of 'forcing' as that which made possible all such advances, itself included.[46] If one asks what relevance this might have to Derrida's (on the face of it) very different body of work, then the answer has to do with that jointly logical and referential dimension which, as I have argued, sets it decidedly apart from most developments in sceptically inclined philosophy of language or critical theory over the past half century.

Thus Derridean deconstruction, as distinct from its various spin-offs or derivatives, necessarily maintains a due respect for those axioms or precepts of classical logic (such as bivalence and excluded middle) that have to be applied right up to the limit – the point where they encounter some instance of strictly irresolvable aporia – if such reading is to muster any kind of demonstrative force. The same goes for those basic referential constraints on language that are built into its very nature as a mode of informative-communicative discourse and which Derrida doesn't for one moment deny even though he shows how they are subject to certain complicating factors when approached with a sufficiently nuanced sense of their involvement in larger chains of contextual and logico-semantic entailment. Moreover, the two considerations are closely intertwined since, as can be seen from debates on the topic from Frege down, there is simply no separating issues of reference from issues of truth, issues of truth from issues of (Fregean) sense, and these in turn from issues concerning the logical structure of the sentences, propositions or other such larger units of discourse within which alone terms can properly be said to refer or to possess a determinate (referentially warranted) truth-value.[47] Of course that set of claims has been subject to much debate, with some – Quine among them – criticizing Frege on radically holistic grounds for not having pressed right through with the contextualist argument and extended it beyond the sentence to the entire 'web' or 'fabric' of discourse (or currently accredited knowledge) at any given time.[48] However, this contention has been challenged in turn by those, like Michael Dummett, who object that we could never get a purchase on language – never learn to use it in the first place or manifest a grasp of its working principles – unless (*contra* Quine) we had a prior grasp of its compositional structure, that is, the dependence of language as a whole on those sentential structures that define the conditions of assertoric warrant for this or that statement or truth-claim.[49] Quite simply, we should then be at a loss to understand the most basic elements of linguistic intelligibility or to figure out other people's meanings, intentions or communicative gist on the basis of a rationally informed conjecture as to the sense (and the truth-conditions) that they are likeliest to have in mind for their discourse from one sentence to the next.

What most needs stressing against the common currency of pro- and anti-Derrida commentaries alike is that Dummett's argument is fully borne out in the case of those classical deconstructive readings that constitute the heart of Derrida's project. To be sure, there are passages, much cited in the secondary literature, where he does give every appearance of endorsing a wholesale contextualist position *à la* Quine. On this account, it must be the aim of such readings to subvert or undermine every last appeal to the 'transcendental signified', whether this be conceived in idealist terms as the ultimate reality behind sensory-phenomenal appearances or – in realist terms – as the referential point of anchorage between language and reality or word and world. However, it will soon strike any attentive reader that when Derrida writes about the logic of the *pharmakon* in Plato, or supplementarity in Rousseau, or the *parergon* in Kant, or *différance* in Husserl (etc.), he is certainly out to discredit the former (idealist) conception but by no means seeking to undermine the very notions of truth and reference. Indeed, if one wanted to characterize deconstruction in philosophical (as distinct from literary-theoretical or cultural-critical) terms, then its specific *differentia* would lie precisely in the tension – or the constant possibility of conflict – between an adherence to those 'classical' values and the kinds of anomalous or discrepant evidence that may be encountered in the course of a sufficiently intelligent, sensitive and rigorous deconstructive reading. My point, to repeat, is that Derrida shares with Badiou this desire not only to detect and locate but also, so far as possible, to *analyse and formalize* whatever creates such an obstacle or challenge to existing modes of belief. More than that, it gives rise to a truth-procedure that may for some time – like Cantor's proposals – come up against strong doxastic or institutional resistance, but which thereafter acts as a periodic spur to the activity of thought by which paradox is turned into concept.

# IV

I would, therefore, suggest that Derrida's protocols of reading, early and late, can best be understood as closely analogous to those transformative events that Badiou describes across a range of disciplines, domains or practices from mathematics to politics and which find their most rigorous formal specification in the set-theoretical procedure of forcing developed in the work of Cohen. Thus, when Badiou offers his against-the-grain readings of canonical philosophers from Plato and Aristotle to Descartes, Spinoza, Leibniz, Hegel or Heidegger, it is through a formal procedure – not merely an interpretative option – devised in order to explain how set-theoretical theorems or conjectures can be truth-tracking or sensitive to future discovery even though they exceed the utmost compass of current provability or present-best knowledge. That is to say, those thinkers can be held to have thought truer than they knew just on condition (1) that their texts are read with sufficient care and (2) that this care is directed more towards structures of conflictual logico-semantic implication than towards whatever the author may have declared with regard to their express, conscious, programmatic or manifest purport. For Derrida likewise, as explained in a famous passage from *Of Grammatology*, it is a matter of bringing out the often complex and contradictory relationship between that which an author knows or acknowledges concerning his/her writerly intentions and that which eludes their grasp precisely on account of its resisting or subverting any straightforward intentionalist approach.

This point is worth more detailed treatment since it has often been ignored or subject to misunderstanding among a sizeable number of Derrida's commentators. On the one hand, he declares, it is vital to take stock of an author's manifest intent since '[w]ithout this recognition and this respect, critical production would risk developing in any direction at all and authorize itself to say almost anything'.[50] Nevertheless – the point of departure for a deconstructive reading – 'this indispensable guardrail has always only *protected*, it has never *opened* a reading'. To suppose otherwise would be to confine criticism or philosophy to the subaltern and wholly uncritical task of 'reproducing, by the effaced and respectful doubling of commentary, the conscious, voluntary, intentional relationship that the writer institutes in his exchanges with the history to which he belongs thanks to the element of language'.[51] What deconstruction seeks to reveal, conversely, is 'a certain relationship, unperceived by the writer, between what he commands and what he does not command of the patterns of the language that he uses'. And again – as should be emphasized in view of its distorted reception history to date – deconstruction in the proper sense of that term, that is, as exemplified by Derrida's classic essays must involve not only a keen awareness of these intra-linguistic complications but also a strong analytical grasp of the logical or logico-semantic structures that are thereby subject to a dislocating torsion beyond their power to contain or control. After all, this could be the case – or register as such – only on condition that the reader is able and willing to apply the most rigorous standards of logical accountability (including the axioms of classical or bivalent true/false reasoning) and thereby locate those moments of aporia or logico-semantic breakdown that signal the limits of any such reckoning.

Hence, Derrida's doubtless mischievous but by no means disingenuous expression of outrage when John Searle upbraids him for thinking to deconstruct Austin's categorical distinctions – for example, between proper and improper speech-acts, or apt and non-apt contexts, or good-faith and insincere, deceptive or imitation speech-acts – by applying a strict bivalent logic that is simply out of place (Searle claims) in the context of everyday, ordinary, non-regimented linguistic usage.[52] The passage is worth quoting at length since it goes clean against – and helps to discredit – such a range of prejudicial ideas on the topic of Derridean deconstruction. Thus:

> [f]rom the moment that Searle entrusts himself to an oppositional logic, to the 'distinction' of concepts by 'contrast' or 'opposition' (a legitimate demand that I share with him, even if I do not at all elicit the same consequences from it), I have difficulty seeing how he is nevertheless able to write [that] phrase . . . in which he credits me with the 'assumption', 'oddly enough derived from logical positivism', 'that unless a distinction can be made rigorous and precise, it is not really a distinction at all'.[53]

Derrida's point is not so much to cock a snook at logical positivism but rather to bring home the unwitting irony of Searle's setting up as the appointed guardian of 'analytic' values and priorities while blithely recommending that they be relaxed, suspended or held in abeyance whenever (as in the context of speech-act theory) they encounter problems or anomalous instances. Here again he agrees with Badiou that thought can make progress – whether in mathematics, the physical sciences, politics, art or ethics – only so long as it persists in the effort to work its way *through and beyond* those dilemmas that periodically emerge in the course of enquiry and can later be seen to have supplied the stimulus to some otherwise (quite literally) unthinkable stage of advance. There is no direct equivalent in Derrida to the set-theoretical procedure of 'forcing' as formalized by Cohen and extended by Badiou to fields that would normally be seen as altogether resistant to any such approach. Nevertheless, as I have said, there is a more than suggestive analogy between Badiou's meticulous working-out of that procedure in its various contexts of application through a stage-by-stage sequence of mathematically based demonstrative reasoning and Derrida's likewise meticulous attention to those deviant or non-classical logics – of supplementarity, *différance*, parergonality, autoimmunity and so forth – which he finds at work in the texts of a culture that has consistently striven to conceal or efface them.

Moreover, the analogy is greatly strengthened by his telling invocations of Gödel's incompleteness-theorem at just those cardinal points – notably in his treatment of Mallarmé's paradoxical reflections on language, logic, reference and truth – where deconstruction is most deeply engaged in exposing the extent of that same concealment.[54] In Badiou's essay of tribute to Derrida, he elects to pass over the Gödelian connection and to focus instead on the link with Cantor's technique of diagonalization, that is, his proof that there exist infinite sets (like that of the real numbers) that cannot be placed in a one-for-one order of correspondence with the infinite set of integers or natural numbers, just as the power-set of any given set (the set of all its subsets) must always numerically and exponentially exceed the set itself. However, that technique was taken over and put to various other mathematical and logical purposes, among them most notably Gödel's incompleteness theorem.[55] At any rate these various connections help to explain not only Badiou's (as it might seem) curious take on Derrida in the *Pocket Pantheon* piece but also the development in his thinking – some would say the outright transformation – between the two master texts *Being and Event* and *Logics of Worlds*. After all, it is in the latter that Badiou offers his full-scale exposition of the themes that dominate his later work and which also find cryptic though eloquent expression in the tribute to Derrida. Chief among them are the ideas of *existence* (as distinct from being), *inexistence* (with its proximate source in the subtractive ontology of *Being and Event*), *degrees of existence* (these taken to vary for any given being or entity across different worlds) and the likewise differing *transcendentals* that exert their existence-bestowing effect on or in each of those worlds. 'Given a multiplicity that exists in a world, there will always be an element in that multiplicity that is a non-existent in that world. A non-existent cannot be characterised in ontological terms, but only in existential terms; it is a minimal degree of existence in any determinate world'.[56] To be sure, this conception has its ultimate source in the set-theoretical terms and procedures laid out in *Being and Event*. But they have now undergone a major shift of emphasis with the turn to a scalar (differential) account of the way that existence supervenes on being or the process by which certain beings make the passage from existing only in that 'minimal' degree to existing in a world that allows full scope to their diverse powers of thought, imagination, scientific inventiveness, political activism or artistic creativity.

It is here that Badiou locates the point of convergence between his own and Derrida's work, that is, in the latter's kindred desire to articulate those various kinds and degrees of inexistence that mark the subordinate term of any binary pair or whatever finds itself excluded or marginalized by prevalent social, political, cultural or conceptual structures. The greatest error, according to Derrida as Badiou reads him, is to confuse the order of being with that of existence, and – by the same token – to confuse inexistence with nothingness. This leads to the wholly mistaken presumption that there is no need to reckon with multiples (e.g. ethnic, social or political groups) that occupy a world wherein their existence is restricted to a bare minimum by a transcendental that rules against their enjoying a more active or effective mode of involvement. Thus, 'any multiplicity is assigned a degree of existence in the world, a degree of appearance. The fact of existing, qua appearing in a determinate world, is inevitably associated with a certain degree of appearance in that world, with an intensity of appearance, which we can also call intensity of existence'.[57] Hence, Badiou's recognition of Derrida as having raised this topic to a high point of critical visibility despite doing so in a 'textualist' register that he (Badiou) clearly finds less than appealing. Indeed, within the short compass of this *Pocket Pantheon* text, he manages to link up the major concerns of 'early' and 'late' Derrida with a force of logical (as opposed to merely suggestive or associative) argument that has so far eluded most of Derrida's commentators. In particular, he brings out the marked though elusive continuity between a mode of deconstruction primarily focused on issues of textual exegesis (albeit with large epistemological and ontological implications) and a mode of deconstruction that engages more directly with real-world problems and dilemmas.

Badiou offers a way of reading Derrida that has no problem in negotiating the passage from texts like *Of Grammatology*, *Margins of Philosophy* or *Writing and Difference* to later works where his approach is for the most part conceptual-thematic and therefore, as I have said, takes the work of textual close-reading very largely for granted. Most striking here is Badiou's brief but pregnant commentary on Derrida's *Spectres of Marx*, a text that many critics have found brilliantly inventive, passionate and ethically stirring yet oddly devoid of substantive political or theoretical content.[58] Derrida's refusal to meet those demands – to deliver some programme, formula, or theory that might be cashed out in the present – is itself a sure mark of the desire to make room for that which currently lacks any adequate means of representation or any acknowledged right to exist (in Badiou's distinctive sense of that term) under currently prevailing cultural, political or socio-economic conditions. Badiou's reading does much to redeem *Spectres* from the charge brought against it by left-activist detractors who deplore what they see as its merely gestural Marxist 'commitment' and failure to achieve any real depth of political or philosophic thought.[59] On the other hand, his reading strikes a cautionary note for those Derridean adepts overly enthused by the notion of 'hauntology', that is, the idea that Marxism ought to embrace a 'spectral' conception of political justice which accepts its endless deferral to a future of indefinite or unspecifiable since ontologically fugitive possibility. Although Derrida works this conception out with his usual inventive brilliance – and, be it said, with a charge of ethico-political passion undiminished by the book's highly speculative character – there is no doubt that it can easily serve, for others more impressed by the brilliance than inspired by the passion, as a pretext for the failure or refusal to engage with practical issues in the world outside the text.

Thus to read Marx through Derrida, or with an eye to those aspects of Derrida's Marx so adroitly drawn out by Badiou, is to see how and why these (seemingly) opposite responses both fall short of an adequate reckoning. Let me quote the most relevant passage at length since it makes this point with the inseparable mixture of passion and precision that typifies all three thinkers:

> In Marx's analysis of bourgeois or capitalist societies, the proletariat is truly the non-existent characteristic of political multiplicities. It is 'that which does not exist'. That does not mean that it has no being . . . . The social and economic being of the proletariat is not in doubt. What is in doubt, always has been, and is now so more than ever, is its political *existence*. The proletariat is that which has been completely removed from political representation. The multiplicity that it is can be analysed but, if we take the rules of appearance in the political world, it does not appear there . . . . That is obviously what the *Internationale* sings: 'We are nothing, let us be all' . . . . From the point of view of their political appearance, they are nothing. And becoming 'all' presupposes a change of world, or in other words a change of transcendental. The transcendental must change if the ascription of an existence, and therefore a non-existence or the point of a multiplicity's non-appearance in a world, is to change in its turn.[60]

This is clearly a 'creative' or revisionist reading of *Spectres* insofar as it attributes to Derrida words, phrases, concepts, ontological concerns and certain 'technical' (mainly mathematical) thought-procedures that are not to be found in Derrida's work, at least on the literal face of it. However, it can fairly be said to respect what Derrida calls the 'classical exigencies' of interpretation, that is, the conditions incumbent upon any reading that wishes to avoid the familiar charge – one often brought against Derrida himself although, I would argue, without adequate warrant – of treating the text in hand as merely a pretext for some ingenious display of self-willed 'strong' misprision. Those conditions include (though it might surprise some of Derrida's 'literary' disciples) an attitude of qualified regard for the claims of authorial intent and also – what entails that qualification – a demand that texts be read with the utmost attentiveness to their complex and sometimes contradictory structures of logical implication. Such is the requirement even, or especially, where this leads up to an aporetic juncture or moment of strictly unresolvable impasse so that the *logical* necessity arises to deploy a non-classical, that is, a deviant, paraconsistent, non-bivalent or (in Derrida's parlance) a 'supplementary' logic.[61]

However, crucially, this is not the kind of readiness to switch or revise logics at the drop of a speculative hat that has characterized a good deal of Anglo-American 'analytical' discussion in the wake of Quine's 'Two Dogmas of Empiricism' and Hilary Putnam's kindred reflections.[62] Rather it is revisionism only under pressure, that is, as the upshot of a logically meticulous reading that must be undertaken if deconstruction is not to take refuge in irrationality or even – as with certain of its US literary variants – in some specially (often theologically) sanctioned realm of supra-rational ambiguity or paradox.[63]

# V

This is the aspect of Derrida's work that has made the greatest impression on Badiou, as witness his striking re-assessment of *Spectres of Marx*. Above all, it offers a needful corrective to the widespread idea – one that Badiou, given his antipathy towards the 'linguistic turn' in its sundry manifestations, might well be expected to endorse – that Marxism 'after Derrida' is a merely textual or rhetorical affair with no purchase on issues of real-world history and politics. What counts so strongly against that charge is Derrida's sheer analytic acuity, a virtue that places him more in the company of an *echt-analytical* philosopher like Russell than exponents of the language-first, conventionalist, social-constructivist or communitarian outlook. Or again, it is Derrida's temperamental as well as intellectual affinity with a thinker like Austin who managed to combine a Wittgensteinian attentiveness to 'ordinary language' with an undiminished power of analytic thought and – owing to that – a very un-Wittgensteinian precision of conceptual grasp as applied to the finest nuances of linguistic usage.[64] Thus despite his ill fame among analytic philosophers as the *ne plus ultra* of 'textualist' (i.e. post-structuralist, postmodernist or more broadly 'continental') thinking, Derrida is much better understood as an immensely gifted close-reader of numerous philosophical texts who has also – by way of that same close-reading activity – put forward some remarkably original theses concerning the structural and historical genealogy of certain crucially load-bearing philosophical concepts. This is why Badiou can advance a speculative reading which itself goes beyond the letter of Derrida's text – beyond any 'straight' interpretation – and yet finds adequate probative warrant in aspects, features or logical dimensions of that text that lack (and may even turn out to controvert) the supposed self-evidence of direct or express authorial intent.

It is, therefore, a reading very much in line with Badiou's repeated demonstrations, both in and outside the set-theoretical context, of the way that thought typically achieves its most radical or world-transformative advances through a process either identical with or closely analogous to the formal operation of 'forcing' as defined by Cohen. The truth-procedure set to work in this particular instance of Badiou's practice as a textual analyst-commentator is the same as that brought to bear in those passages of strong-revisionist yet closely reasoned and intensely critical commentary on philosophers from Plato to Heidegger that punctuate *Being and Event*. Such, to repeat, is the process of enquiry by which certain truths can be shown to have been latent within some earlier state of knowledge and yet, at the time in question, to have exceeded any currently available means of proof, discovery or verification. This leaves Badiou flatly opposed to the strain of logico-semantic-metaphysical anti-realism that was first introduced to analytic philosophy of mathematics, logic and language by Michael Dummett and which denies on principle the objectivist (alethic realist) claim that truth might always exceed or transcend our best intellectual or cognitive powers.[65] Indeed, it is on account of their shared resistance to this and other doctrines of epistemic, linguistic or discursive constraint – doctrines which make truth coterminous with the scope and limits of human knowledge and/or linguistic expression – that Badiou can propose his heterodox reading of Derrida as nothing less than what Derrida's work requires if that work is to be read in keeping with its own critical practice. Or again, the great virtue of Badiou's brief yet piercing traversal of Derrida's *oeuvre* is that it brings out the crucial though less than obvious relationship between textual close-reading, political engagement and a formal dimension nonetheless rigorous for going by way of those essential formative and motivating 'conditions' that Badiou considers indispensable to any philosophical project meriting the name.

For it is just his point that the approach to these issues through mathematics – as the discourse of ontology *par excellence* – is uniquely revealing even when applied to thinkers who make no explicit use of it just so long as their thought is sufficiently disciplined to register the pressures and counter-pressures of a truth-oriented discourse capable of pointing beyond their present-best state of knowledge. That Derrida would accept this characterization of his own work is, I think, strongly attested by the fact that he makes such careful allowance for the constant imbrication of blindness and insight – or ideology and critical acumen – in so many texts of the Western logocentric canon from Plato to Husserl. What gives Badiou's reading of Derrida a special interest is its clear demonstration of the fact – to adapt Barthes' aphorism once more – that while 'a little formalism' may lead thought away from a sense of its larger historical and social responsibilities, the effect of adopting a more consistent and rigorously formalized approach may well be to restore that missing dimension.[66]

# Badiou: Truth, Ethics and the Formal Imperative

## I

Alain Badiou is generally thought of as an anti-ethical thinker, not least on account of his own many and often very forceful declarations to just that effect.[1] Thus, he rarely misses a chance to denounce what he regards as the collusive relationship between ethics (or the kinds of moralizing talk that typically go under that name) and various presently dominant forms of social, political, class- or gender-based and – increasingly – global-strategic interest.[2] Still we shouldn't take his disclaimers entirely at face value since they will then serve only to obscure or conceal a conception of ethics that is heterodox to the point of repudiating any such description but nonetheless cogent and (to use a clichéd but in this case perfectly apt expression) thought-provoking for that. For, whatever his scruples in this regard, Badiou has devoted a good proportion of his work to issues that possess a clearly marked ethical dimension and that figure as test-cases for the exercise of intellectual conscience. I use this phrase 'intellectual conscience' (rather than falling back to the more obvious 'moral', 'social' or 'political' qualifiers) not because Badiou's is a peculiarly rarefied or hyper-theoretical approach but rather because that work manifests an exceptional degree of dedication to the project of *thinking through* what is required by any genuine ethical commitment. It is also an apt choice of phrase insofar as he rejects any ethics that would fall short of that standard by resorting to various (as he sees them) evasive substitute appeals such as those that place their ultimate trust in consensus values, shared beliefs, communal life-forms, liberal opinion or the sphere of presumptively enlightened public opinion.

Indeed it had better be said plainly that Badiou is an anti-ethical thinker on just about every definition or conception of 'ethics' that has played a significant role in modern debate. Above all, he has resisted that Kantian conception according to which the imperatives of ethical (practical) reason are thought of as resulting from the moral agent's exercise of a purely rational, autonomous, self-legislative will oblivious to the 'pathological' promptings of appetitive desire or self-interest.[3] Nor has Badiou any time for that other, more socially grounded aspect of Kantian thinking which conceives moral values as finding their justification through the regulative idea of a truly enlightened *sensus communis* (or public sphere of open participant debate) wherein that will finds collective expression as the product of suitably harmonized values and beliefs among those best qualified to judge.[4] Moreover, and for similar reasons, he is squarely opposed to the kind of communitarian thinking – often with its source in late

Wittgenstein – that locates ethical value in the kinds of judgement upon which the members of some given community or cultural 'form of life' would most likely converge in keeping with their shared values, beliefs, commitments and priorities.[5] This latter he regards as indeed nothing more than the philosophic form currently taken by an abject readiness to throw in one's lot with some regnant ideology or received 'commonsense' doctrine. It must be seen as falling lamentably short of the critical vocation – or the prime imperative to question all such dominant views – which he takes to define the task of philosophy at any time and all the more so in an age of massively distorted since systematically misinformed consensus belief. Badiou has gone out of his way to denounce this and other variants of the presently widespread 'linguistic turn' which he sees as just a latter-day revival of ancient Greek sophistry and its resort to the arts of rhetoric or suasive language, most often deployed to irrational or downright mendacious ends.[6] It is against that pervasive doxa that Badiou brings to bear all the force of his polemical as well as his exceptionally acute analytic intelligence.

Thus, the main target of his criticism is the notion that mere consensus belief or agreement over a sufficient range of culturally salient issues might somehow offer a basis for ethical thinking. This is merely the complicitous mirror image of a Kantian-deontological approach that places moral values outside and above all the messy contingencies of historically situated human choice and which moreover (for just that reason) very often comes down – as in the thinking of liberal ideologues such as Hannah Arendt – to a counsel of contemplative detachment from the urgencies and pressures of a fully engaged practico-political life.[7] At the same time, Badiou is notably unimpressed by the various alternatives currently on view. Among them are those that seek to maintain a critical edge and avoid the charge of deep-laid conservatism often levelled at the communitarian approach by espousing a qualified version of the Kantian deontological appeal to values that transcend any merely *de facto* consensus of belief while heading off the standard range of anti-foundationalist objections by endorsing a likewise qualified version of the communitarian argument.[8] Here again the result is a compromise creed that makes room for certain local adjustments to the strength or scope of such criticism in deference to the weight of majority opinion, received wisdom or the dominant *sensus communis*. Badiou finds such notions politically as well as philosophically bankrupt since they betray or negate the potential for change – for the transformation of presently existing social realities – that provides the sole means by which to assess the validity or truth of any ethics meriting the name. Indeed one could argue with reference not only to his short, passionate and highly polemical book on the topic but also to numerous passages elsewhere in his work that Badiou – like many Marxists and others who suspect the ideologically motivated character of various quasi-universal values and principles – is 'against ethics' in just about every currently accepted sense of the term.

In which case clearly the question arises: what can he offer by way of replacement for these various failed candidates? An adequate answer to this question – one that would follow out the intricate logic of Badiou's argument across a wide range of subject areas – is well beyond the scope of this chapter. However, one can best summarize by saying that any such treatment would involve consideration of the central role played in his thinking by four such subject areas. These are *mathematics* (in particular that modern branch of it concerned with set-theoretical conceptions of the multiple and the infinite), *the subject* (especially as theorized in the wake of Lacanian psychoanalysis), *art* (where his commitments lie squarely with the more advanced or formally adventurous modes of literary, visual-artistic and musical production) and *politics* (in which regard he has kept faith with the legacy of May 1968 and continues to denounce every sign of what he sees as the 'Thermidorian' betrayal of that legacy by the *nouveaux philosophes* and other media-savvy representatives of mainstream French intellectual culture). Such are the fourfold enabling 'conditions' of philosophy which Badiou defines more broadly as science, love, art and politics with science relating to mathematics in a fairly obvious way and love by no means reducible to but finding at least one partial means of theoretical articulation in the discourse of psychoanalysis. On the other hand, crucially, philosophy must at all costs avoid becoming 'sutured' to any one of those conditions whose exclusive or single-minded pursuit is then apt to leave the philosopher exposed to the worst kinds of temptation. Here, Badiou offers the cautionary instance of Heidegger's Nazism and – albeit in a very different, less plainly disastrous mode – the strain of technocratic and un-self-critical scientism espoused by some schools of analytic philosophy.

If this all seems to leave my question hanging in the air, then perhaps that very fact – the fact that, quite simply, there is *nowhere else to look* outside or beyond those fourfold conditions for an ethical dimension to Badiou's thought – is itself the best answer. In each case his most emphatic point is that ethical choices, acts, decisions or commitments can never be subject to evaluation from any standpoint of pure (hence purely illusory) detached or contemplative reason, nor again – the most favoured current alternative – by existing communal norms. Rather, they arise at the point of collision between some prevalent state of affairs that has hitherto set the terms for what counts as a proper, valid, permissible or meaningful contribution in some specific domain and that which arrives to disrupt, challenge and transform all those pre-existent standards of validity and truth. Such is the dialectic of 'being' and 'event' that Badiou works out with extraordinary originality in his book of that title and which amounts to a radical, mathematically based rethinking of the relationship between truth and knowledge – or ontology and epistemology – across all the above-mentioned disciplines or fields of human intellectual-creative endeavour.[9] Thus, thought and action should always be conceived in terms of a specific *engagement with* or *intervention in* some particular, historically located episode of scientific discovery, artistic creation, political activity or (Badiou's favourite phrase) amorous encounter which alone provides the relevant evaluative context whereby to assess the 'truth-procedure' in question. What he is concerned above all to emphasize in relation to each of these subject-domains – even (here taking a qualified lead from Lacan's ruminations on the topic) in the case of sexual love – is the absolute centrality of truth to any adequate conceptualization of the complex, often unpredictable dynamics through which those transformative episodes come about.[10]

At stake here is the issue of continued fidelity to an 'event' whose effect has been to raise such a challenge to some well-established scientific paradigm, artistic practice, political order or other such dominant system of values and beliefs. Fidelity of this kind may often be manifest in very different ways within a single life-history, as with the two highly gifted French mathematicians Jean Cavaillès and Albert Lautman who were both Resistance members shot by the occupying German forces.[11] While their courage and sheer moral heroism are beyond doubt, they should both most aptly be seen, in Badiou's estimate, as thinkers whose deployment of rigorous, axiomatic-deductive procedures in their mathematical work was likewise displayed to striking effect in their perfectly consistent carrying-through of ethico-political precept into practice. For it is just his point – one that places Badiou very much in the company of Spinoza, despite deep disagreements between them in other respects – that ethics can best be saved from its various present-day ideological distortions and abuses by precisely this emphasis on fidelity to a truth-procedure.[12] It then becomes first and foremost a matter of rigorously consequent reasoning rather than of good faith or moral conscience in the commonplace (liberal-humanist) sense of those terms.

## II

That his two chief exemplars should both be mathematicians is yet more appropriate given the centrality of set-theoretical concepts, categories, operations and procedures to Badiou's project as a whole. In brief, his claim is that mathematics alone has the conceptual resources to provide us with a discourse capable of thinking through the various paradoxes (chiefly that of the one and the many) that have vexed philosophers from Plato down, and which have now reached the point of adequate – that is, productive and thought-provoking rather than thought-disabling – formulation only as a consequence of Cantor's epochal revolution in mathematical thought.[13] What made this possible was a working grasp of the infinite (and the infinitely multiple orders of infinity) that had once struck philosophers and mathematicians as a conceptual scandal and a breeding ground of paradox to be avoided at all costs if reason was not to find itself tied into knots of self-contradiction. Otherwise – among the more theologically or mystically inclined – it was sometimes treated as a pointer to regions of speculative thought beyond all such prosaic rational limits. Badiou's argument goes by way of an intensive critical-expository account of all the main developments in set-theoretical thinking from Dedekind and Cantor to the present. However, what gives that argument its quite extraordinary scope and reach is that Badiou conceives every major scientific, political, creative and ethical advance as brought about through just the kind of discovery that is best, most strikingly exemplified by Cantor's way of 'turning paradox into concept'. Thus, again, it is an event of that epochal order whereby what had hitherto figured as an obstacle to progress is suddenly transformed into a source of ever more productive since conceptually tensile or paradox-driven insights. In political terms, this involves a challenge to the dominant 'count-as-one', that is to say, the ideologically imposed conception of what qualifies for membership in good standing of this or that nation, ethnic group, polity or other such collective whose identity is maintained against 'alien' intrusion precisely by defining and enforcing those same membership conditions.

It is here that Badiou makes his bold and (to say the least) philosophically heterodox step from expounding certain technical developments in modern set theory to accounting for the various mechanisms of social victimage, ethnic persecution and political disenfranchisement that continue to typify the lives of many who inhabit the margins of present-day 'liberal-democratic' states. His main example is that of the French *sans-papiers* or migrant (mainly North African) workers lacking any official documentation who therefore exist in a kind of social limbo, denied recognition by the state and deprived of even the most basic citizenly rights. Their predicament is best understood, he claims, through the distinction between *belonging* and *inclusion* which, together with that between *member* and *part*, plays a crucial role in set-theoretical thinking. What that distinction brings out with a high degree of formal-conceptual rigour is the always precarious since forcibly imposed character of the count-as-one and the ever-present threat of its disruption by an errant, uncounted or anomalous multiple that finds no place – no legitimate or recognized place – within the presently existing socio-political-cultural order. Moreover, it is precisely through the pressures brought to bear by that which counts for nothing in some given situation – through the anomaly that haunts any such order on account of its excluding or working to marginalize certain multiples – that the most decisive transformations come about, whether in the history of mathematical thought or in the course of political events. Indeed the 'event' in Badiou's strongly qualitative sense of that term is just what transpires at the critical point where existing conceptual resources run out or where thinking confronts problems so far beyond its power to contain or comprehend that they must be taken to herald some imminent challenge to its most basic structures and presuppositions.

Such is the structural correspondence, as he sees it, between signal advances in the realm of set theory and signal events in political history – sometimes 'failed' or as-yet unfulfilled revolutionary portents – which likewise require that we distinguish what 'counts' as a matter of official, text-book record from what genuinely counts as a matter of human liberatory potential. Hence Badiou's stress on the need for a 'subtractive' rather than a positive ontology, one that would register the symptomatic stress-points or 'evental sites' where some newly emergent conflict or anomaly might yet turn out – for the issue is never decided in advance of its ultimate working-through – to have marked the inception of a 'truth-procedure' with momentous consequences. This may take the form of a logical paradox or dilemma such as those that both vexed and fascinated the ancient Greek thinkers and which continued to play a tantalizing role throughout the long centuries of baffled reflection on the infinite when, for most philosophers and mathematicians, it seemed to pose a massive threat to the coherence or integrity of their enterprise.[14] Or again, it may arise from within the very system which it then forces to the verge of conceptual ruin, as famously occurred when Bertrand Russell discovered the paradoxes of self-predication ('the set of all sets that are not members of themselves', etc.) and thereby jeopardized his own great project of placing mathematics on a perfectly consistent since purely logical basis.[15] However – as Badiou is keen to establish with reference to certain historical events – one can see the same process working itself out at just those crucial junctures when new socio-political forces emerge, most often at an unexpected moment or a 'site' far removed from what appears (to contemporary observers and perhaps to mainstream chroniclers thereafter) as the most significant or world-transformative episodes.

An event in this authentic or qualitative sense is what typically occurs when some existing situation is suddenly brought to crisis-point by the coming-to-light of a hitherto suppressed anomaly, injustice, conflict of interests or instance of exclusion from the tally of those who legitimately count according to prevalent (e.g. liberal or social-democratic) notions of inclusivity. At such moments, only a 'subtractive' (rather than a positive) social ontology can tell us what transpired since it alone makes adequate sense of the way that certain oppressed, disregarded or disenfranchised minorities may nonetheless come to exert a force of political leverage denied to community members – those included in the dominant count-as-one – whose status denies them any such role. As with mathematics and the physical sciences, so likewise in the political sphere, it is at just these 'evental sites' that the requisite conditions may be seen to have existed for a breakthrough discovery or a radical challenge to dominant social structures. On the other hand there is absolutely no guarantee at such times that the chance will be taken or the moment seized in such a resolute, committed and clear-sighted way as to enable its effective carrying-through to the end-point envisaged by those who first responded to its call. Hence Badiou's close attention to 'failed' revolutions or to episodes, like the 1871 Paris Commune (as well as the 'events' of May 1968), that have since gone down among thinkers on the Left as terrible setbacks or as melancholy witness to the folly of premature, ill-organized revolt.[16] For him, conversely, they figure as touchstone events insofar as their very falling-short or the distance between their aims and their outcome is a test of fidelity for those who inherit both the problems and the promise of their so far unredeemed political legacy.

To phrase it like this is perhaps to risk leaving a false impression of his thinking since the language of fidelity – or of keeping faith with those who suffered such defeats – might seem within reach of that liberal-humanitarian talk or all-purpose rhetoric of 'human rights' to which Badiou is so strongly averse. At best, so he argues, such language merely serves as a means of concealing the massive gap between what is commonly touted (for home consumption or for export) as 'representative democracy' and the actually existing version of it along with all its manifold exclusions, distortions, structural inequalities, maltreatment of target minorities, etc. At worst it does duty as a pious smokescreen for the kinds of marauding interventionist foreign policy that seek to pass off their real motives of economic and military-strategic self-interest under the cover of a human rights doctrine with emphatic (but in this context entirely specious) universalist appeal. As Badiou notes in his book *The Century*, with reference to the invasion of Iraq and other recent episodes, such talk is all too readily co-opted to the service of a hegemonic liberal creed with decidedly illiberal designs on the liberty of those who might presume to resist its more forceful blandishments.[17] All the same, as we have seen, fidelity is a core value in Badiou's ethical thinking even if it is often defined more by standards of logical consistency and rigour – even by those of axiomatic-deductive reasoning – than through any direct appeal to ethical (least of all Kantian) grounds.

Nor should we conclude from his attack on the fake universalism invoked by politicians who abuse the rhetoric of human rights that Badiou must in that case belong to the company of those who adopt a flatly opposed, that is, a radically particularist or anti-universalist stance. They are thinkers – nowadays a large and diverse company – for whom 'difference' (whether ethnic, cultural, linguistic or gender-related) is a notion often raised, ironically enough, to the status of an absolute or *a priori* principle and one that is taken to trump any appeal to the typecast delusive 'Enlightenment' idea of shared, for example, cross-cultural or trans-gender interests and values.[18] Indeed Badiou is among the most vigorous defenders of a true universalism – as opposed to the mendacious rhetoric currently peddled in that name – which would allow human beings to transcend rather than annul, suppress or forcibly subdue the various differences that stand in its way. Hence the remarkable diversity of thinkers and activists whom he is able to recruit in the process of explaining this on the face of highly paradoxical or even downright contradictory relationship between fidelity and universalism. At its most extreme, the paradox is pushed to the point where Badiou – an avowed atheist – can take St Paul not only as an exemplar of fidelity to the event of Christ's life, death and resurrection but also as an early exemplar of universalism insofar as he insisted (albeit to the tolerant amusement of his Greek interlocutors) that in Christ there could be neither Jew nor Greek but only the single overriding question of acceptance or non-acceptance concerning that event.[19]

Given the dire historical consequences of Paul's religious dogmatism – which, after all, far outweighed any benefits conferred by his highly selective 'universalist' stance – one may reasonably think that Badiou is here over-indulging his own somewhat Pauline taste for a challenging paradox. However, his general point comes across clearly enough: that difference-thinking of the kind promoted by a great many present-day 'advanced' or 'radical' thinkers on the cultural left is in truth a politically and ethically retrograde movement of thought which serves only to block any prospect of achieving genuine (revolutionary) social change through the recognition of shared human interests above and beyond the divisions, disparities and conflicts of interest that presently obstruct such change. It is primarily in order to make this point – to emphasize the human universality of any truly progressive or emancipatory politics – that Badiou stakes his claim for mathematics as the discipline best suited to provide that project with an adequate conceptual and social-ontological grounding. It is also why he comes out so strongly against every version of the turn to language or discourse (together with their various surrogate terms such as 'paradigm', 'framework' or 'conceptual scheme') as the furthest that philosophy can possibly go in the quest for truth. This can be seen to have followed straight on from Kant's self-avowed 'Copernican revolution' which declared ontological issues strictly off-bounds by giving epistemology pride of place and defining its proper remit in representational terms, that is, with reference to the scope and limits of the human capacity for bringing intuitions under concepts.[20] It went along with his idea – one to which Badiou is likewise strongly, even fiercely opposed – of practical (moral) reason as best exercised in the mode of detached or contemplative judgement rather than through those forms of direct activist engagement that Kant equated with merely impulsive behaviour or with the worst, most destructive kinds of revolutionary zeal.[21] For Badiou, on the contrary, ethical commitments involve both a readiness to act decisively in response to specific pressures of circumstance and also – quite compatibly with that – a willingness to apply the most rigorously consequent standards of reasoning to any decision and course of action thus arrived at.

## III

Hence Badiou's invocation of those two mathematician-*résistants* as exemplary figures in this respect, a reference that gains additional force from his showing in meticulous detail how certain mathematical, especially set-theoretical procedures of thought have a valid application in our thinking about issues of social justice. Hence also his emphasis on the ethico-political as well as the formal or logical force of a truth-procedure that starts out from the three main precepts of set theory. First is the irreducible multiplicity of being, that is, the ontological priority of the 'inconsistent' multiple over every application of the count-as-one that seeks to contain that unruly excess by reducing it to a mode of consistent, paradigm-preserving since paradox-avoiding conceptualization.[22] This is why Badiou devotes considerable efforts to revealing the inadequacy of various attempts to cope with the endemic problems and aporias of set-theoretical thought by adopting some stopgap (pseudo-)solution that resorts either to a preconceived formalism or, as in Bertrand Russell's Theory of Types, to a stipulative rule that simply excludes them for reasons of intellectual hygiene.[23] Second, and closely related to this, is the power-set axiom according to which there is always – as a matter of the strictest formal or logical necessity – an excess of subsets over sets, of inclusion over belonging, or of parts over elements, an excess that of course surpasses all the limits of finite reckoning or calculation once thinking enters the realm of infinite multiples. Third is the concept of the void, or the null set, as that which must be thought of as included in each and every other set and as the locus of that same ubiquitous lack, that structural absence or subtractive dimension whereby any given ontological order might always be subject to disruption by anomalous events beyond its utmost power to comprehend. So much has been evident at least since Plato and the troublesome upshot of his dialogue *Parmenides* which demonstrates, albeit against its author's will, that 'the one is not' and therefore that any appearance of consistent multiplicity must always involve the concealment or suppression of an inconsistent multiplicity that would otherwise exceed and destroy that appearance.[24]

This applies most strikingly to cases where the multiples in question are of the transfinite order that Cantor opened up to mathematical thought through his discovery – against all the odds of intuitive and, as it had seemed, conceptual or logical self-evidence – that it was possible (indeed necessary) to conceive the existence of different 'sizes' of infinity. Thus, mathematics provides what Badiou finds woefully lacking across the whole range of post-structuralist, postmodernist and other such linguistically oriented discourses. What he finds so utterly implausible is their claim to radicalize the currency of the human and social sciences through their challenge to the mode of signification – the naturalized tie between signifier and signified – upon which (according to these 'superstructuralist' theories) can be seen to rest the entire apparatus of late-capitalist cultural and social hegemony.[25] Only through the turn to mathematics as a needful corrective to that earlier linguistic turn can philosophy regain something of its true vocation. This he equates with its critical power to challenge or resist those various forms of ideological misrecognition that are scarcely disturbed – rather confirmed or left securely in place – by the notion of language (in whatever theoretical guise) as the ultimate horizon of thought. However, Badiou is just as critical towards the kinds of approach that are nowadays dominant among both working mathematicians and mainstream philosophers of mathematics. They must likewise be seen to sell themselves and their discipline short by disowning any wider ontological ambitions or any idea that mathematics might provide a more exacting conceptualization of issues in the extra-mathematical (especially the social or political) domain.[26] For it is precisely his leading claim – one that enables the otherwise improbable, even absurd conjunction of set-theoretical with political-activist concerns – that quite simply mathematics *is* ontology insofar as it provides our best, most practically efficacious as well as conceptually rigorous means of thinking our way through and beyond a great variety of real-world problems, issues, conflicts and dilemmas.

Badiou is thus using the term 'ontology' in a sense that ranges over the abstract (mathematical), the physical (including natural-scientific) and the socio-political domains. It is a term that applies – on his understanding – just to the extent that they each raise issues having to do with the relationship between what is *actually the case* with regard to some present stage of scientific advance or state of social being and what *might conceivably become* the case through some signal transformation the advent of which can as yet be discerned only through the localized emergence of stress-points, anomalies, recalcitrant data or signs of increasing conceptual or social-political strain. This realist commitment keeps Badiou well clear of deploying that term in a Heideggerian or depth-hermeneutic sense, or to anything like the ontological-relativist effect that has become almost *de rigueur* among many analytic or 'post-analytic' philosophers after Quine.[27] For him, as for other recent thinkers of ontology who resist what they see as that damaging misconception, it is prerequisite to any ontological project meriting the name that it should not let go of those crucial distinctions between knowledge and truth, belief and knowledge or 'the real' as it figures in our present-best or even best-attainable states of understanding and the real as it exists quite aside from all such epistemic considerations.[28] Indeed, it is on this account chiefly that Badiou takes his stand against Heidegger concerning the ancient Greek philosophical instauration which Heidegger declares to have occurred through poetry – that is, through philosophy's primordial encounter with a distinctively poetic, hence culture-specific and linguistically rooted mode of thought – while Badiou locates its emergence in the challenge posed to philosophy by mathematics with its various problems and paradoxes, most notably that of the one and the many.[29] Thus, Heidegger's preferred point of origin presages a history of cultural-linguistic particularism, along with the need for a hermeneutic project which aspires (and necessarily in some degree fails) to achieve understanding across all the consequent deep-laid differences of worldview or horizon. Badiou's, on the contrary, presages a history wherein misunderstandings, conflicts and breakdowns of cross-cultural communication have indeed been endemic but wherein they can best be accounted for precisely as so many failures to achieve the universality to which thinking properly aspires despite and against those forces of entrenched prejudice and mutual incomprehension.

This in turn requires a conception of truth as inherently transcending both the scope of knowledge at this or that particular temporal stage of human cognitive advance and the sundry disagreements concerning truth between various parties or claimants to knowledge across different paradigms, conceptual schemes, theoretical frameworks, life-forms, discourses and so forth. Here I should acknowledge that Badiou is careful to mark his distance from a fully fledged Platonist outlook as concerns mathematics since he thinks that unless we take due account of the methods, techniques and proof-procedures by which mathematical knowledge accrues, we shall fall back into just the kinds of stale and unprofitable wrangling that have typified so much analytic debate between hard-line realists or objectivists on the one side and anti-realists or constructivists of various technical persuasion on the other.[30] However he is also very firm in maintaining that those methods and procedures would make no sense – that we could have no grasp of what a 'proof' consisted in or what counted as valid axiomatic-deductive reasoning – were it not for our prior grasp of the necessity that truth should be conceived as verification-transcendent, or as always potentially surpassing the limits of human knowledge. Otherwise, in the formal as in the physical sciences, there would simply be no accounting for our knowledge of the growth of knowledge or our capacity to understand how it is that our present best conceptual or explanatory powers might fall short of truth in just the same way that we can now see other thinkers to have fallen short in the past. What gives Badiou's thought its extraordinary depth and speculative reach is the way that he extends this crucial insight from the realm of mathematics where truth can be attained only by means of formal (axiomatic-deductive) proof-procedures to the domain of politics and social ethics – despite his avowed antipathy towards such language – where those procedures find a more than merely suggestive application.

The most obvious point at which the set theory and the politics converge is on the fact that there exist certain hard-to-quantify but objectively existent numerical disparities between the sum-total of human beings in a given society quite aside from any ethnic, socio-economic, gender-related or other 'identifying' traits and the sum of those who count for electoral, welfare or educational purposes by the lights of a prevailing 'social-democratic' order. Several main components of Badiou's thinking come together in making this case. They include his aversion to the idea of 'difference' or radical 'otherness' that has lately acquired such a cachet – no doubt as the structural complement of identity-politics – and also his insistence on a purely extensionalist approach to set-theoretical procedures, that is, one that treats all the parts or elements of a set as strictly indistinguishable one from another for formal-operational purposes.[31] In this he stands opposed to those mathematicians (or more often philosophers of mathematics) who adopt an 'intensionalist' approach whereby there are significant distinctions to be made in terms of qualifying attributes or membership criteria.[32] It is not hard to see how Badiou's preference in this respect – although firmly based on formal, that is, mathematical and logico-semantic considerations – goes along with his commitment to a standard of social justice conceived in strictly egalitarian terms. This is also why he is strongly opposed to that otherwise diverse range of doctrines in recent philosophy of mathematics – anti-realist, nominalist, formalist, intuitionist, fictionalist, instrumentalist and so forth – which respond to the much-touted problem with objectivism (that it appears to place truth forever beyond reach of human knowledge) by veering to one or another of those overly reactive fallback positions. Thus, he has no time for the sorts of discussion carried on by analytic philosophers who start by posing the issue as a flat dilemma – *either* objective (verification-transcendent) truth *or* knowledge within the compass of human epistemic grasp – and who then most often go on to endorse some third-way alternative, such as 'truth' by the standards of this or that recognized expert community, which in fact comes down to anti-realism under a more emollient description.[33]

What Badiou sets in place of this deadlocked and largely sterile debate is a detailed account of various signal episodes in the history of mathematical thought, especially those – from Parmenides and Plato to Dedekind, Cantor and beyond – when knowledge came up against the limits imposed by its failure to grasp the further implications of some previous discovery that left it facing an as yet irresolvable paradox. Hence his focus on precisely what occurs at the breakthrough stage when 'paradox is turned into concept' and when, as happened in exemplary fashion with Cantor's revolution, thinking is irresistibly drawn or impelled into a whole new realm of conceptual-ontological enquiry that had hitherto been marked off-bounds on account of its presenting such a downright affront to commonsense intuition or accepted ideas of rational procedure. It is by way of this ongoing dialectic – this recurrent pattern of advances that expose some hitherto unsuspected paradox which in turn becomes the driver of another such advance and thereby the source of another such productive since thought-provoking paradox – that Badiou is able to achieve what many analytic philosophers deem impossible, that is, to maintain a robustly realist conception of truth while nonetheless making adequate room for the various discovery-procedures involved, along with their development to date. Thus, he lays fair claim to have overcome not only the set-piece analytic dilemma as characterized above but also its 'continental' near-equivalent, that is, the antinomy of structure and genesis which has dogged epistemology from Plato to Descartes and thereafter (in a yet more insistent and vexing form) from Kant to Husserl and beyond. Here it concerns the problem – some would say the strictly insoluble problem – of reconciling truth conceived in terms of absolute ideal objectivity with the idea of truths as having been arrived at through certain appropriate (knowledge-conducive) means by certain thinkers chronologically located at certain crucial stages of discovery or progress within a certain intelligible history of thought.[34]

Thus when Derrida, in his early writings on Husserl, remarks that this problem is nowadays most sharply posed by the encounter between structuralism and phenomenology he is not taking a narrowly 'presentist' view but, on the contrary, treating those movements as the latest heirs to a deep-laid conflict of philosophic aims and priorities.[35] What Badiou brings out through his focus on various landmark advances in the scope and power of mathematical thought is the way that a 'subtractive' conception of truth on the set-theoretical model allows us to conceive it *both* as transcending or surpassing any given state of mathematical knowledge *and* as a conceptual lacuna, anomaly, paradox or other such defect that figures nowhere in the current state of positive knowledge yet the existence of which may signal the path to some decisive future advance. This is the point at which Badiou manages that switch of ontological domains from mathematics to politics or from the formal to the social and human sciences that will surely strike many philosophers – at any rate those in the analytic camp – as a category-mistake of the first order or a gross confusion of properly distinct, even strictly non-communicating realms. However they would, I think, be hard put to show just where in Badiou's often highly complex but always meticulously reasoned process of argument (one that derives its validity-conditions from mathematics and the procedures of axiomatic-deductive thought) this flagrant error is supposed to have occurred. Indeed he is well able to turn back charges of this sort by remarking – sometimes in disdainful fashion – that the kinds of territorial imperative that most often give rise to such objections are also those that have driven much recent analytical debate into the dead-end of realism *versus* anti-realism conceived in merely abstract terms quite apart from any detailed working-through of particular problematic episodes. For it is Badiou's claim that recent approaches in the analytic vein have often condemned themselves to tedious irrelevance by endorsing the altogether false idea that insofar as mathematics aspires to a condition of formal rigour, it cannot be conceived as offering any points of conceptual-exploratory purchase for disciplines 'outside' or 'beyond' its specialist domain.

# IV

His emphatic rejection of this whole way of thinking appears most plainly in Badiou's concept of the count-as-one as an imposed or purely stipulative limit on the range of multiples that meet the conditions to qualify for membership (to count as properly, legally belonging) under some given dispensation. Thus, he devotes a good deal of complex and demanding argument to explaining just how it is that certain epochal transformations come about – whether in the mathematical-scientific or the socio-political spheres – through a process that involves two crucial concepts (those of 'forcing' and the 'generic') that Badiou derives from set theory and, more specifically, from the work of the mathematician Paul Cohen.[36] In brief, they have to do with the precisely specified conditions under which a given situation or state of knowledge may turn out to contain or to generate anomalies that are not just easily corrigible errors owing to some localized breakdown or lapse of logical grasp. Rather they function – at whatever latent or so-far unacknowledged level – as an index of the failure to follow out the further implications of a previous discovery and hence, when viewed from the standpoint of a more advanced stage of knowledge, as having effectively (or symptomatically) pointed a way forward through the very fact of their falling short in some crucial and now specifiable respect. Badiou devotes a good deal of highly concentrated logico-mathematical commentary to Cohen's formal demonstration that thinking is indeed possessed of this capacity to go beyond the limits of conscious (let alone self-conscious or reflective) awareness and register the existence of truths that surpass its present-best power of conceptual articulation.[37] This it is able to do in virtue of the way that certain unresolved and even as-yet unrecognized problems can exist within the state of mathematical knowledge at any given time and exert a nonetheless powerful destabilizing force, that is to say, a pressure upon thought to elaborate new methods and truth-procedures whereby to bring those problems more clearly into view and then seek out solutions to them. Thus '[t]he term "generic" positively designates that what does not allow itself to be discerned is in reality the general truth of a situation, the truth of its being, considered as the foundation of all knowledge to come'.[38]

Nor should it appear so very paradoxical to claim that thinking may often press ahead of what is accessible to consciousness or grasped as a matter of knowledge, understanding or epistemic warrant. That appearance is merely the result of philosophy's having so long been in thrall to the presumption – one that found its classic statement in Descartes but was already there in Plato and became pretty much common coin among rationalists, empiricists and epistemologists from Kant on down – that thought and consciousness are so closely bound up each with the other as to make them joint conditions (along with truth) for knowledge on any adequate account. Yet it is clearly the case that any radical new departure in thinking whether as concerns mathematics, physical science, politics, ethics or the creative arts will at some stage require a decisive movement of advance beyond what is currently available to consciousness in terms of established procedures or accustomed ways of carrying on. In which case – a conclusion that Badiou fully accepts – philosophy has long been kept in ignorance of its true ontological-mathematical vocation by those various false turns (from the rationalist/empiricist 'way of ideas' to its present-day 'linguistified' spin-offs) that have all in some way fallen prey to this error, even where they have seemed to react most vigorously against it. On this view, the Wittgensteinian/Heideggerian notion of language as the end-point of all human enquiry is just another showing of that same old reactive pattern whereby the sophists squared up to Socrates in defence of rhetoric *versus* the claims of purebred rationalism, or thinkers such as Herder and Hamann rejected what they saw as the groundless and overweening claims of Kant's critical philosophy.[39]

However, Badiou's chief point is that this false identification of the scope and limits of thought with the scope and limits of consciously available knowledge has often placed a drastic and disabling restriction on philosophy's grasp of how thinking proceeds at its moments of most significant creative, intellectual and ethico-political advance. It is for this reason also – rather than any great attachment to the therapeutic virtues of psychoanalysis – that Badiou sets great store by Lacan's 'structuralist' reading of Freud along with his insistence on the need to conceptualize Freud's discovery of the unconscious and its complex topological features in rigorously formal, indeed mathematical (or quasi-mathematical) terms.[40] Here again what Badiou most wishes to stress is the relative paucity and limited remit of conscious, self-conscious or reflective thought when compared with the kinds of intellectual breakthrough or creative-exploratory advance that thinking is able to achieve at a level well 'below' that Cartesian threshold. On the other hand, as becomes clear in his joint reading of Lacan and Descartes, Badiou is very far from endorsing the now distinctly *passé* post-structuralist/postmodernist doctrine according to which nothing could be salvaged from that old figment of the bourgeois-humanist-rationalist imaginary, the Cartesian subject-presumed-to-know.[41] For it is his contention that if we look elsewhere than to the *Meditations* for Descartes' most important contributions – if we focus rather on the *Discourse on Method* and *Rules for the Direction of the Mind* – then we shall see that his own thinking exemplified the same capacity for running ahead of any conscious grasp or apodictic self-evidence that Badiou considers the precondition for genuinely groundbreaking or innovative thought.[42] It also helps to emphasize his cardinal point: that processes carried on outside or beyond the spotlight of phenomenological awareness – whether these count as 'unconscious' or 'preconscious' according to the standard distinction – will often far surpass those carried on under the spotlight in terms of their complexity, formal rigour and conceptual as well as creative or imaginative reach.

Thus Badiou goes along, at least up to a point, with Lacan's claim that Descartes' arguments were subverted by Freud's discovery – that instead of '*cogito, ergo sum*' we should rather say '"*cogito ergo sum*" *ubi cogito, ibi nonsum*' ('where I think "I think, therefore I am", that is just where I am not').[43] However, he is just as keen to insist that what is thereby very partially exposed to view is a range of thought-processes, operations and procedures that may be unconscious not so much on account of their belonging to some realm of repressed or subliminal mentation but rather on account of their so far exceeding our present-best powers of conceptual or logical grasp. This is why Cohen's ideas of 'the generic' and 'forcing' are of such crucial significance to Badiou's project. What they allow him to express with maximum formal precision is the always conceivable surpassing of knowledge by truth and of conscious knowledge by a preconscious grasping-in-thought of that which has yet to be recognized as belonging to the range of accredited truths but which nonetheless exerts a transformative force – a persistent and at times disruptive pressure – through its very failure to do so. Thus there are certain anomalies or fallings-short of a consistent and maximally adequate system of thought that can be seen (no doubt with benefit of hindsight but then, as Badiou might reasonably say, how stupid to deny ourselves that) to have served in just such a thought-provoking and knowledge-conducive role. Indeed it is precisely his point in stressing the priority of inconsistent over consistent multiplicity – and the problems faced by proponents of the opposite thesis from Plato down – that this has been the great driver of progress not only in mathematics and the formal sciences but also in areas of human thought and activity that might seem as far as possible removed from any such notionally 'abstract' or specialist sphere.

Hence the many reproachful, even exasperated passages where Badiou takes issue with those who harbour such a false idea of mathematics, thus closing their minds both to its extraordinary scope of conceptual creativity and – by no means incompatible with that – its unrivalled degree of rigour and precision in the seeking-out of truths unavailable to other, less formally disciplined modes of knowledge.[44] If there is one main presumption that has characterized debates concerning the relationship between the formal and the social sciences – especially that between mathematics and ethics or politics – it is the fixed idea that, quite simply, they belong to different spheres of understanding and therefore that any attempt to bring them together will involve some flagrant category mistake or failure to maintain an important set of boundary markers. Joshua Gert puts this case most concisely in a recent essay on the topic of *a priori* knowledge and response-dependence. Since 'the difference in subject matter between mathematics and ethics is very great', therefore '[i]t is safe to say that no one has provided any powerful reasons to suppose that the same capacities that allow us to know truths of the former domain could also be responsible for our knowledge of the latter'.[45] However, it is worth noting that the confidence with which this verdict is delivered – its air of stating what amounts to a matter of self-evident or even (on the terms here established) of *a priori* truth – results in large part from the author's subscribing to a philosophical agenda that ultimately takes its lead from Kant's epistemological project, in particular, the role of judgement (that most problematical of Kantian notions) as a mediating function or agency between sensuous or phenomenal intuitions and concepts of understanding. Beyond that, more explicitly, it comes out of the current debate around response-dependent (or response-dispositional) properties which has itself grown up chiefly in consequence of the ongoing effort, by analytic and continental thinkers alike, to find some viable third-way alternative to the realist/anti-realist stalemate.[46]

I have argued elsewhere that this alternative is really no such thing but rather a fuzzily conceived and highly unstable compromise 'solution' that can be seen to lean over in one or the other direction – towards truth as objective and recognition-transcendent or 'truth' as epistemically constrained – according to the theorist's own predilection or the area of discourse under review.[47] My point here, more specifically, is that any proposal (like Badiou's) that we should think of mathematics and of ethics or politics as subject to equally rigorous standards of investigative thought is apt to strike many as misconceived on account of its wilfully collapsing both the Humean fact/value dichotomy and the far more elaborate system of distinctions grounded in Kant's doctrine of the faculties. Either that, or it will most likely suffer by association with the above-mentioned types of argument from response-dependence and their far from convincing claim to have established a common scale upon which can be ranged – albeit at opposite ends – both a truth-oriented discipline such as mathematics where there might just be room (to this way of thinking) for appeals to best judgement or expert opinion and a variety of subject areas, such as prototypically colour-perception, where the usual approach has been through some version of the Lockean appeal to 'secondary qualities'.[48] In these latter sorts of case, the furthest one can get towards trans-individual standards of assertoric warrant is widespread agreement among those whose responses qualify as normal by (what else?) commonly accepted standards and whose perceptual judgements are elicited under likewise normal (non-distorting or natural) ambient conditions.

## V

I have taken this brief detour through Kant and the travails of present-day epistemology in order to bring out by sharp contrast the perfect indifference that Badiou displays towards all such (in his view) grossly inadequate and misconceived approaches to questions of truth, knowledge and responsibility. What they typically serve to promote or sustain is that Kantian idea of the subject – whether the epistemological subject-presumed-to-know or the deliberative subject of practical reason – as properly deploying its capacities and powers in a mode of detached or contemplative judgement that is exercised at the furthest possible remove from the pressures and temptations of real-world political engagement. It is this conception of subjectivity, in no matter what 'transcendental' register, that Badiou sets out to contest and repudiate by every means at his command. Chief among them is his own radically opposed definition of the subject as 'any local configuration of a generic procedure from which a truth is supported', or of 'subjectivization' as 'that through which a truth is possible, [since] it turns the event towards the truth of the situation for which the event is an event'.[49]

It is in this sense – and in this sense only, as distinct from other, less discriminate (e.g. post-structuralist) versions of the thesis – that Badiou seeks to demote the subject from its erstwhile privileged status as arbiter of truth in its various modalities.[50] That is to say, the concept remains very much at the heart of his thinking but only insofar as it pertains to the agency of some particular subject in achieving or promoting some particular advance within some particular field of endeavour at some crucial point in its field-specific history of changes, developments or transformations to date. Of course this is not to exclude the possibility (indeed, in social or political terms, the near-necessity) that such a role will be assumed not by an individual but rather by some collectivity of like-minded subjects – a Sartrean 'group-in-fusion' – brought together by an exceptional sense of shared predicament and purpose.[51] Thus, Badiou's operative notion of the subject is one that depends upon his Cohen-derived concepts of 'forcing' and 'the generic' since it refers not to any conscious, transparent, self-reflexive or transcendental locus of knowledge but rather to a certain power of 'indiscernment' – roughly paraphrased: a preconscious grasp of the defects and anomalies that mark an existing state of knowledge or social relations – which thereby potentially opens the way to some as yet ill-defined or barely conceivable advance. Above all, as Badiou stresses in his reading of Descartes, this requires that we avoid the perennial confusion between *consciousness* and *thought* that has so long bedevilled philosophy and continues to exert a distorting influence on a great many current debates in epistemology, cognitive psychology and philosophy of mind. Its main effect is to skew the issue so that 'conscious' becomes more or less synonymous with 'advanced', 'progressive', 'knowledge-conducive', 'self-critical' or 'illusion-free' while anything conceived as lying outside or beyond the focus of conscious thought is treated as by very definition 'unconscious' and hence as prey to all the 'commonsense' errors that result from accepting the naïve self-evidence of first-hand intuitive belief.

To be sure, Badiou is as emphatic as any of the seventeenth-century rationalists in maintaining that knowledge arrived at through the exercise of reason or critical intellect can and must be regarded as properly possessing a decisive power of veto over arguments that can claim no better warrant than the appeal to sensory-intuitive witness. In this respect, his thought pays constant homage to that distinctive critical-rationalist strain in French epistemology and philosophy of science which has its source in the 'other', scientifically oriented aspect of Descartes' thinking and which descends through Bachelard and Canguilhem to certain highly qualified yet nonetheless recognizable manifestations in Foucault and Derrida.[52] However, it is also important to see that the kinds of truth-procedure here in question – whether as concerns mathematics, the physical sciences, politics or ethics – are in no sense beholden to the subject conceived as a conscious or reflective knower. Nor again should we think of them (absurdly) as belonging to the 'unconscious' in anything like the received psychoanalytic, that is, pre-logical or sub-rational sense. After all, the procedures in question here are those that have produced – among other things – some of the most advanced and sophisticated theorems and proofs in mathematics, as well as a range of comparable achievements across various seemingly remote but (as Badiou would have it) closely analogous subject-domains. As regards this latter phrase, we should remark how the term 'subject' denotes not only some particular topic-area but also, to his way of thinking, the fact that the subject (= thinker or agent) is so much a part – both producer and product – of the relevant truth-event as to have no existence, at least for present purposes, outside the particular episode wherein or whereby they achieved that status.

It is in just this sense that we should understand the complex relationship between psychoanalysis, mathematics, politics and truth as Badiou conceives it. If his conception is maximally remote from any vulgar-Freudian idea of the unconscious as a repository of repressed and inarticulate desires, then it is just as far from that chiefly US-acculturated ego-psychological approach – much reviled by Lacan and his acolytes – that would treat the talking cure as primarily a matter of bringing such repressed material back into the daylight realm of conscious, reflective, self-controlled and hence (so these critics maintain) socially conformable thought and conduct. 'What localizes the subject', Badiou writes, 'is the point at which Freud can only be understood within the heritage of the Cartesian gesture, and at which he subverts, *via* dislocation, the latter's pure coincidence with self, its reflexive transparency'.[53] That is to say, there is no possibility of thinking to any purpose about these issues except on the basic premise that the unconscious is indeed accessible to reason or to a discourse (whether of the practising psychoanalyst or the philosopher) which claims a validity beyond that of instinctual or commonsense belief. Nevertheless, and just as importantly, this rational discourse is itself at any given time subject to certain limiting conditions that can emerge or be revealed as such only by exposure to that which lies beyond the utmost limits of its present conceptual or explanatory grasp.

This is why Badiou devotes the final section of *Being and Event* to a closely worked demonstration of how Lacan's supposed radical break with the heritage of Cartesian rationalism is in fact something more like an unresolved and indeed unresolvable tension between those two premises. It is also why he has kept so carefully defined a distance between his own thinking and that of the more dogmatic or card-carrying post-structuralists – whatever their proclaimed sources in Lacan, Althusser, Foucault, Barthes, Derrida or elsewhere – who would regard 'the subject' as a figment of the bourgeois or liberal-humanist imaginary fit only for deconstruction by the standard range of theoretical moves.[54] What Badiou brings out to such powerful effect in every aspect of his work – whether those parts of it addressed to technical issues in mathematics or those passages concerning the history of political events – is the illusory nature of subjectivity when conceived in humanist or Kantian-autonomist terms but also its absolute indispensability as a means of explaining how knowledge and political history could ever achieve any kind of advance against all the odds of entrenched prejudice, 'commonsense' belief or intuitive self-evidence. This was always the chief stumbling block for post-structuralist theory insofar as it espoused a thoroughgoing version of linguistic-discursive-cultural constructivism and thereby invited the twofold charge of reducing truth and knowledge to a dead level of ideological (mis)recognition and depriving human agency and thought of any power to intervene or affect the course of events.[55]

Thus Badiou is fully justified – in ethico-political as well as mathematical and scientific terms – in roundly rejecting such blanket denunciations of 'the subject' and insisting that it offers the only means to explain how such advances might come about. All the same this is not to invoke anything like its traditional role as presumptive locus of autonomous selfhood or as the seat of those various constitutive attributes (thinking, reasoning, judging, willing and acting) that between them supposedly define what it is to be human. Rather, it is a question of just that precisely specifiable margin of choice which opens up before suitably placed subjects at just that critical stage in some ongoing project – whether of advanced mathematical enquiry or resistance to the dominant structures of socio-political power – when they can either respond as 'militants of truth' and press on with that project through commitment and fidelity to previous such events or else (more often) seek refuge in adherence to existing, conformist modes of thought and conduct. What is most important to grasp about Badiou's heterodox conception of the subject is that he always deploys it with specific reference to some given juncture in the history of concepts or political events, and that for him its chief task is to explain how revolutions can occur despite and against the massive weight of received belief, orthodox thinking or ideological consensus. Thus 'the subject', in Badiou's usage of the term, is by no means just a theoretical place-filler but precisely his term for that which drives forward the kinds of signal advance here in question. It is what impels the process through which mathematics periodically succeeds in 'transforming paradox into concept', or through which a history of failed or abortive revolutions (such as the events of 1848) can at some later date – with the advent of that which it strove to achieve – come to assume a strongly proleptic or prefigurative role.[56] To just this extent – since Badiou is not given to over-stretched or vaguely suggestive analogies – mathematics and politics are capable of treatment in formally homologous terms. A failed revolution has the virtue of defining, in and through its very failure, what might have been and therefore has yet to be accomplished, just as a long-disputed theorem or conjecture in mathematics – one for which no adequate proof was available – may at length (after decades or centuries) attain such proof and henceforth be admitted to the class of known mathematical truths.

This comparison is all the more pointed for the fact that committed anti-realists most often extend their basic precept to all three disciplines or areas of discourse (mathematics, history and ethics) that are under consideration here. Thus, for a thinker like Michael Dummett, it makes absolutely no sense to say of some unproven mathematical theorem that it is either true or false – objectively so – even though we cannot yet and might never come up with an adequate formal proof; or again, to assert of some well-formed and truth-apt historical conjecture that the episode in question either occurred or didn't, despite our total lack of documentary evidence; or again, to claim that 'Jones is courageous' despite Jones having so far led a very quiet life which placed no demands on him in that respect and therefore offers no grounds for judgement. Any theorems, conjectures or hypotheses ventured in any of these domains must be thought of as falling into the 'disputed class' of statements that are neither true nor false since truth is epistemically constrained – or subject to the scope and limits of attainable knowledge – and hence better redefined in terms of 'warranted assertibility'.[57] As we have seen, Badiou comes out very strongly against this whole anti-realist line of argument and goes some highly complex and ingenious (chiefly set-theoretical) ways around in showing how truth can indeed transcend the bounds of existing knowledge or accomplished provability and yet not leave the realist or objectivist committed to a doctrine that ineluctably leads to an ultra-sceptical upshot. On his account, unknown truths can exert a palpable pressure for change – a sense of their ultimate potential to remove some presently existing anomaly, paradox or conceptual shortfall – which avoids the absurd anti-realist conclusion that all truths are either known or knowable. If mathematics is the focus of Badiou's most intensive and complex as well as most formally elaborate passages of argument, then it should also be realized just how close is the connection in his thinking between mathematics (as the primary means to conceptualize the relationship of being and event) and politics (as the domain wherein that relationship discovers its most important field of application). It is here that we can best get a grasp of the kindred process by which certain historical events can be seen to have occurred in response to some presumptive anomaly – some absence, non-occurrence, symptomatic lack, unresolved tension, or failure – that left open a space of possibility for what nonetheless arrived as a largely unexpected or downright unpredictable occurrence.

# VI

So there is a great deal riding on the issue between realism and anti-realism as Badiou construes it, that is, in terms of the event as that which transcends the limits of any given conceptual scheme (or extent of so-far achieved ontological grasp) while nonetheless making its absence felt – and thereby obliquely manifesting itself – through symptoms of unresolved paradox, aporia, logical tension or conceptual strain. That this must always be the case if one presses thought to those limits and beyond, as in the long pre-Cantorian history of puzzling over the infinite, is a central claim of *Being and Event*. It is made good through a critical-diagnostic reading of all those philosophers, mathematicians and political thinkers – from Plato and Aristotle to Leibniz, Spinoza and thence all the way to Dedekind and Cantor – who have either emphatically rejected such a notion as contrary to every dictate of reason or embraced it up to a certain point where their thinking can be seen to have shied away from its more radical implications.

Such is Badiou's claim, to repeat, that 'consistent multiplicity' always results from a restrictive operation of the count-as-one in its various modes and object-domains whose effect is to repress, dragoon or dissimulate the 'inconsistent multiplicity' which – as a matter (at least since Cantor) of formally demonstrable truth – necessarily both precedes and exceeds it.[58] It is by way of that claim along with its set-theoretical elaboration that Badiou is able to press his case for the pertinence of mathematics to every area of ontological enquiry, including the socio-political, where there exists a more or less drastic non-equivalence between members and parts, belonging and inclusion or the 'state' and the 'state of the situation' as he defines these pointedly contrasted terms. Here again, it is a matter of that structure of exclusion by which certain elements remain uncounted, in this case a structure that can best be grasped – along with the potential sources of resistance to it – through the aforementioned analogy with Cantor's power-set theorem concerning the excess of subsets over sets.

Thus, it offers a sharp since mathematically specifiable means of explaining why any acknowledged, that is, state-recognized collectivity will include certain parts, like the *sans-papiers*, who quite literally count for nothing in respect of civil, electoral or social-communal standing. If there is, as I have argued, an ethical core to the work of this philosopher who has set his face so firmly against most varieties of present-day ethical thought it is to be found in just that remarkable combination of high formal rigour with strength and depth of political commitment.

Perhaps the most striking instance of this is the fact that Badiou's mathematical and social ontologies are alike dependent on his maintaining the axiom of double-negation-elimination, that is, the principle that 'two negatives make a positive' or that – as a matter of strict logical necessity – the conjunction of two 'nots' is equivalent to a straightforward affirmative statement of the thesis or proposition concerned. From which it follows also – crucially for his entire project – that certain truths can be established through arguments by *reductio ad absurdum*, or by showing how one runs into trouble (i.e. into contradiction, absurdity or self-evident falsehood) if one affirms their negation or the contrary thesis. Thus: '[t]he strict equivalence of $A$ and $\sim\sim A$ – which I hold to be directly linked to what is at stake in mathematics, being-qua-being (and not sensible time) – is so far removed from our dialectical experience, from everything proclaimed by history and life, that ontology is simultaneously vulnerable in this point to the empiricist and the speculative critique'.[59] This principle is a mainstay of classical, that is, bivalent or true/false logic and is also of the utmost importance for defenders of a realist approach to the formal and physical sciences since it underwrites the basic realist premise that truth may be located in that which exceeds – indeed, that which negates or contradicts – the verdict of present-best knowledge. Moreover, it has the added significance, for Badiou's purposes, of granting a decisive truth-telling role to those various modes of negation whose effects may be analysed not only in the discourse of mathematics, logic and the formal sciences but also insofar as they leave their mark on the dominant structures of socio-political existence. If he takes them to operate in a realm quite apart from that of 'sensible time' or from any self-evidence of the kind 'proclaimed by history and life' this does not in any way conflict with his claim concerning the significance of mathematical discovery-procedures for our thinking about those other kinds of issue. Rather it has to do with the former's pertaining to an order of verification-transcendent truth that cannot be conceived – in intuitionist or anti-realist fashion – as dependent upon (or as brought into being by) the various particular, temporally indexed processes of thought through which they have been produced by human individuals in likewise specific kinds of mind-state or epistemic circumstance.[60]

That is to say, mathematics is best conceived, in realist terms, as embarked on the progressively further-reaching exploration of a pre-existent and as yet very largely unexplored ontological domain and not as somehow creating that domain or making it up in the course of enquiry. All the same their discoveries do have the power of revealing just how those structures of exclusion have left their mark on human intellectual, scientific, political and socio-cultural history. That mark may most often be humanly degrading, as Badiou makes clear in his passionate address to the plight of those confined to the margin – or ejected into the wilderness zones – of 'representative' democracy as it has come to function in present-day France and elsewhere. Yet it is also, on occasion, the mark of an 'evental site' where the resultant conflicts and anomalies are brought to a head or become so acutely overdetermined as to throw those dominant structures into sharp relief and thereby induce a legitimation-crisis that might be resolved only by some epochal change in the order of thought or the order of socio-political representation. Such has indeed been the central aim of Badiou's project: to locate with maximum formal precision (i.e. by way of a mathematically based ontology) the points at which thinking is forced up against its limits of conceptual, descriptive or explanatory power and obliged to concede the exorbitant character of certain events – in whichever sphere of theoretical or practical endeavour – that inherently surpass those limits.

What is so remarkable about his work, at least when set against the ruling conventions of present-day analytic thought, is its readiness to transgress all manner of established and by now deep-laid categorical distinctions. Among them are disciplinary boundary markers such as that between the formal sciences where supposedly there is no room for matters of 'extraneous' empirical or (still less) socio-political concern and the social or human sciences where formal rigour is either thought out of place or introduced merely as a useful means of regimenting otherwise unruly or recalcitrant material. For Badiou, on the contrary, it is only by pressing so far as possible in that direction and respecting the claims of a formal ontology to limn the very structure and content of reality that we can think the occurrence of a truth-event, as yet incapable of more precise or substantive specification, that would bring about some decisive advance beyond our present state of knowledge or socio-political stage of life. That is to say, it eludes our conceptual grasp since its future advent – one that cannot be securely predicted by any available proof-procedure or means of practical implementation – will at length turn out with benefit of hindsight to have revealed some crucial anomaly or shortfall in that previous condition. This type of future-anterior construction ('will turn out to have', etc.) is one that Badiou frequently deploys and that derives its formal as well as substantive warrant from those various otherwise unaccountable advances – in set theory and elsewhere – for which Cohen's concepts of 'forcing' and the 'generic' provide the only adequate means of theorization. To repeat, 'forcing' denotes the crisis-indicative yet anticipatory-progressive movement of thought whereby an existing though as yet scarcely registered obstacle to progress is nonetheless enabled to register as such at whatever subliminal or preconscious level and thus provide the needful incentive to move through and beyond some current impasse. In conjunction with this, the 'generic' denotes that which belongs to all multiples in a given situation and which therefore admits of no distinctive features – no membership-criteria based on their possession of certain identifying attributes – that would mark them off from other such parts. In Badiou's words, '[a] generic multiplicity is an "anonymous" part of this world, a part that corresponds to no explicit predicate'. And again: '[a] generic part is identical to the whole situation in the following sense: the elements of this part – the components of a truth – have their being, or their belonging to the situation, as their only assignable property'.[61]

As I have said, this is why Badiou adopts a strictly extensional as opposed to intensional understanding of set-theoretical ontology, one that treats sets, subsets, multiples and elements solely in terms of their numerical values as defined across a strictly undifferentiated object-domain. It is thus concerned with objectively specifiable relations of inclusion, exclusion and belonging or non-belonging rather than with taking account of certain intrinsic or differential features such that the possession or non-possession of them would effectively decide the issue of membership from case to case. If thought is to achieve real progress – whether in mathematical, scientific, ethical or political terms – then it will need to apply this principle with maximum rigour and deny itself the recourse to any such imputed distinguishing traits or means of discriminative treatment. These have been deployed most often by way of conserving old theories and their favoured ontological commitments in the face of some radical challenge, or providing a handy rationale for discriminatory practices of various sorts, or enforcing selective procedures whose effect is to perpetuate existing forms of social injustice. Only by espousing a purely extensionalist approach – one that is perfectly indifferent to whatever might otherwise be deemed to constitute grounds for inclusion or exclusion – can thought remain open to the challenge of that which doesn't fall under its presently existing concepts and categories. It will then be more alert to just those signs of emergent conflict that most often exert their subtractive force at some eventual site where the count-as-one is exposed to the challenge of whatever it pre-emptively and arbitrarily excludes or where the dominant order of socio-political representation likewise encounters a check to its claims of justice or universality.

It is solely on condition of maintaining that commitment to a strict extensionalist ontology that the sciences, both formal and physical, have managed to achieve a series of decisive breaks with the order of received or commonsense-intuitive ideas. Moreover, it is by means of an analogous advance that political thought has also been enabled – albeit (to date) within certain clearly marked limits – to make real progress beyond various forms of racial, ethnic, class-based or gender-related prejudice. This in turn comes about through a perceived conflict between the claim to inclusiveness advanced on behalf of some existing social order and the fact of exclusion that can be shown to inhabit all systems of political representation. It emerges with the greatest demonstrative force when these are subject to formal analysis and also to the kind of immanent critique – or measuring-up against rigorous standards of validity and truth – that Badiou finds most strikingly exemplified in the history of mathematical thought. In motivational terms, that force derives chiefly from a dawning recognition of the gaps, absences, irruptions of the void or other such symptoms of looming crisis – whether in scientific discourse or the discourse of some dominant social ideology – that point towards a truth beyond their present power to contain or comprehend. Hence Badiou's stress on the need to reformulate issues from a range of (on the face of it) heterogeneous topic-areas in ontological and therefore – so far as they allow – mathematically formalized, that is, set-theoretical terms. This he takes to offer a uniquely powerful grasp of the means by which epochal changes most often come about, whether in the scientific domain (where they may well be subject to a stage-by-stage formal or rational reconstruction after the event) or in the ethico-socio-political sphere (where they are naturally more resistant to such understanding even though there exists a close analogy between the kinds of procedure involved).

What emerges through analysis along these lines is the continuing and open-ended dialectic that repeatedly forces thought to the limit of some given conceptual scheme and then – as a result of the tension or torsion induced by a truth beyond present reach – serves as a kind of subliminal prompt or oblique means of orientation towards precisely that region of as-yet unexplored ontological terrain where the truth in question awaits discovery. Clearly there is a sharp conflict of views between Badiou's realist conception of mathematics as engaged in exploring features of a landscape that possesses those features quite aside from how it is represented or projected to the best of our mapping ability and, on the other hand, that range of current doctrines (anti-realist, constructivist, instrumentalist or conventionalist) that would, in effect, give cartography the last word concerning such matters. Philosophically speaking, these latter movements of thought find support not only from Dummettian anti-realism but also from the widespread acceptance of Quinean-Kuhnian ideas about ontological relativity according to which 'truth' should be thought of as internal to this or that paradigm, framework or conceptual scheme.[62] Indeed it is a chief motivation of Badiou's whole project to challenge what he sees as the strictly preposterous or back-to-front order of priorities that finds no place for ontology except as a derivative or secondary field of enquiry subject to the scope and limits of human epistemic grasp, and which then looks to language – very often conceived in radically holistic or cultural-contextualist terms – as the ultimate horizon of knowledge or intelligibility. In this respect at least (and despite some otherwise deep differences of view) he is at one with the rationalist Spinoza as regards the absolute precedence of truth over everything pertaining to language and the chronic liability of language – even when used with maximum care – to confuse or obfuscate the deliverance of truth.[63]

It is also, of course, what puts him markedly at odds with that whole broad swathe of present-day thinking in philosophy and the human sciences which promotes just the opposite thesis, that is, the precedence of language or discourse over everything pertaining to knowledge and truth. Badiou sees no hope of significant advance in any of those disciplines except by rejecting the linguistic turn in whichever guise and instead pursuing the claim of mathematics to provide a uniquely qualified account of the being/event dialectic, that is, the unpredictable yet rigorous process of discovery whereby some current-best state of ontological grasp is subject to challenge by that which eludes and exceeds the count-as-one in its various modes. That such considerations might have an impact far beyond the logico-mathematical domain – that they might bear crucially on issues of social and political justice – is Badiou's most strikingly heterodox claim by normal philosophic lights, and one that will conjure bafflement among the great majority of analytic thinkers. After all, it seems to be in flagrant contravention of at least two major precepts – the fact/value dichotomy and the separation of first-order ('material') from second-order ('formal') modes of discourse – that have between them characterized a good deal of work in that 'other' line of descent. Still it is worth noting, in this connection, that the post-analytic drift toward notions of truth as relative or internal to some given 'ontological scheme' is one that started out in reactive fashion from Quine's famous demolition-job on just the kind of thinking classically exemplified by Carnap's logical-empiricist programme for policing the boundary in question.[64] What Badiou's work offers, in sharp contrast, is an intricately reasoned account of the relationship between truth in its logico-mathematical and its material (e.g. socio-historical as well as natural-scientific) modes which sacrifices nothing in formal rigour to the prime imperative that thinking keep faith with the interests of justice or emancipatory critique.

# VII

It is on just these grounds and in just this sense that Badiou comes out against ethics, or – more precisely – against the kind of thinking that most often goes under that name nowadays and which offers yet another symptomatic instance of the polarization that afflicts so much present-day analytic philosophy. Here it is the rift between ultra-formal (meta-ethical) concerns and a first-order discourse that frequently equates what's right or just with what counts as such by the lights of some given communal practice or acculturated way of life. Again this rift seems to have its source in a reactive pattern of thought whereby the unyielding formal imperatives of Kantian moral autonomy on the one hand suffered a further process of analytical rarefaction and on the other gave rise to a strong counter-movement, that is, a communitarian rejection of any such abstract or rigourist demands.[65] So there is clearly more than one reason for Badiou's aversion to Kantian ethics and, even more, to the political doctrine that Kant derived (albeit by some highly circuitous routes through his aesthetic notions of the sublime and the beautiful) from his cardinal precept of subjective disinterest as a touchstone of ethical virtue.[66] This was his idea of great events – like the French Revolution – not as calls to active intervention among those who came later and took them as a source of political impetus but rather as topics for a mode of contemplative, that is, non-interventionist thought that would deploy the faculty of reflective judgement as a salutary check upon the will to act or as a means to hold out against the standing temptation of just such precipitate conduct.[67] Moreover, when defenders of the liberal-democratic status quo cast around for some kind of philosophical support, the result is most often a vague amalgam of Kantian notions with the pragmatist or communitarian outlook which in turn displays a strong elective affinity with those Wittgensteinian and other variants of the 'linguistic turn' that Badiou takes so strongly to task.[68]

Thus he devotes a good deal of polemical as well as philosophical energy to denouncing what he sees as the Potemkin façade of a social order that exploits such ideas as a part of its legitimizing rhetoric. They typically serve as a smokescreen behind which to conceal the massive disparities of economic, political, social and cultural power that exist – and encounter very little in the way of effective 'ethical' resistance – under currently prevailing conditions of capitalist liberal democracy. Here again, many philosophers– especially those of an analytic persuasion – would object that Badiou is playing fast and loose with a range of categorical distinctions as between the sorts of questions properly addressed on terms laid down by ontology or epistemology (taking these to be importantly distinct but also importantly related areas of concern) and the sorts of questions properly addressed by ethicists and some, not all, political philosophers. What complicates matters yet further is the fact that Badiou is very far from going along with that present-day fashion – in whichever quarter of the postmodern-pragmatist-post-analytic-Wittgensteinian-Rortian-constructivist trend – that would dismiss such objections as merely a symptom of continuing attachment to various deluded since plainly obsolete markers of expert or specialist competence in this or that discipline. After all, as Rorty is fond of pointing out, this road of thought is one that tends to point the traveller firmly in a certain direction and which makes any preference for stopping short or desire not to press right through to its ultimate conclusion look more like a fudge than a principled philosophic stance.[69]

Hence Badiou's absolute insistence on respecting those basic distinctions – like that between being and event or ontology and whatsoever comes to disrupt and reconfigure any presently accepted ontological scheme – in the absence of which we could have no grasp of the process whereby revolutionary changes come about, whether in politics or in the history of the formal, natural or social sciences. However, as should also be clear by now, it is a vital part of Badiou's project that the reader should be brought to the point of rethinking other deep-rooted philosophical beliefs, chief among them the idea that formal rigour of a certain kind – that which has its home ground in mathematics and logic rather than the maxims and imperatives of Kantian practical reason – is *ipso facto* devoid of any possible bearing on matters of ethical moment. Indeed his work mounts a constant challenge to those two components of the academic-philosophical mindset whose effect has been mainly to obstruct any closer, more active engagement between the various modes of enquiry whose present-day compartmentalization found something like its inaugural template in Kant's doctrine of the faculties. On the one hand is that prejudicial way of thinking that has resulted in the failure of mathematicians, logicians and exponents of the formal sciences to pursue ontological (including social-ontological) issues beyond what these thinkers take as their self-prescribed specialist domain. On the other it has prevented thinkers in politics, ethics and the social sciences from forming any conception of how a mathematically based ontology might lead them to the point where that model runs up against its own presently existing conceptual limit, that is, where it confronts the event as that which intrinsically eludes any such prior specification.

It should be clear by now that on both counts – as in other salient respects examined in this chapter – Badiou's thinking runs squarely athwart some of the deepest-laid premises or governing conventions of philosophy from Kant to the linguistic turn in its sundry analytic or mainland-European guises. This applies above all to his heterodox conception of ethics and his acidulous view of what currently passes under that name – whether in academic discourse or in the state-sanctioned and media-sponsored rhetoric of liberal, centre-left, social-democratic or 'progressive' reformist policy – as merely so much window-dressing designed to avert the public gaze from those flagrant instances of social exclusion that would otherwise be seen to constitute a massive anomaly and hence a standing provocation to other, more militant or activist modes of involvement. However, the fact that Badiou's project is philosophically as well as politically and ethically so much at odds with all the major currencies of nowadays accredited thought is surely no reason – prejudice apart – to ignore its singular challenge.

3

# Deconstruction, Logic and 'Ordinary Language': Derrida on the Limits of Thought

## I

Over the past few years I have argued the case for Derrida as a realist in matters epistemological and a stickler for the requirements of classical (bivalent) logic despite his frequent – almost trademark – aptitude for showing how that twin commitment comes up against its limit in various specific contexts.[1] If this has been decidedly uphill work, then the gradient has been set more by the weight of received opinion concerning his work, among disciples and detractors alike, than by anything about that work that bears the stamp of anti-realism or a lack of concern (let alone a quarrel) with standards of truth and falsehood classically conceived. Indeed, were it not for his honouring these commitments in practice as well as in his various statements of principle, then deconstruction could not make good its claim to demonstrate the moments of aporia induced by a classical-realist philosophy of language, logic and representation when confronted with certain problematic passages in certain philosophical and other kinds of text. That is to say, those aporias can only show up against a default presumption that language does (normally) fulfil its expressive and communicative role in a jointly referential, truth-functional and hence for the most part knowledge-conducive way.

Thus it is a precondition for Derrida's meticulous tracings-out of the deviant logics of supplementarity, différance, parergonality and so forth that they register primarily by contrast with – or as deviating from – those same referential and logical norms that alone provide the necessary backdrop to a deconstructive reading.[2] Nor is this, as opponents like Searle would have it, just another clear sign that Derrida is out to subvert every standard of serious, reputable philosophic thought by affecting to turn on their heads a whole bunch of self-evident normative distinctions (literal versus figural sense, concept versus metaphor, 'serious' versus 'non-serious' discourse, sincere or genuine speech-acts versus those cited, spoken in jest or uttered out of context) while surreptitiously taking for granted the necessity of making those distinctions along with their standard normative force.[3] On the contrary, what Derrida brings out to remarkable effect is the way that the exception neither proves nor disproves the rule but shows up with sufficient regularity and rule-questioning or rule-complicating force as to require a careful reconsideration of how we should think about particular rule-governed (e.g. referential or logical) modes of discourse and representation.

Like Austin and Ryle – the two 'analytic' philosophers with whom he evinced the greatest degree of intellectual as well as temperamental sympathy – Derrida takes it that supposedly marginal cases (whether speech-acts or passages in texts) might turn out upon closer inspection, and approached without the customary kinds of prejudice, to have a far from marginal, and perhaps philosophically crucial, significance.[4] Hence his affinity with those two doyens of the post-war Oxford scene. All three take the view that analysis may have its most rewarding work cut out in beating the bounds of intelligibility, or in trying to show just why – by what seemingly perverse but far from idle or trivial compulsion – philosophy is so often driven to query its own more settled or routine habits of thought.[5]

Where Derrida differs from them is in his always, rather than occasionally, allowing for the extent to which so-called ordinary language may exhibit quite extraordinary powers of inventiveness, creativity or resistance to treatment in a systematizing manner. This goes a long way towards explaining his *Ausseinandersetzung* with Searle and also his sense of a genuine, even in some ways a deep but nonetheless distinctly qualified kinship with Austin and Ryle.[6] Most significant here – and what explains this complex interplay of kinship and difference – is Derrida's rare ability to combine passages of analysis that display the utmost degree of formal, conceptual and logical precision with passages of textual exegesis that exhibit the utmost acuity in matters of linguistic implication and nuance. Thus Searle got the picture exactly upside-down when he charged Derrida with invoking rigorous criteria of bivalent logic merely in order to show how 'ordinary language' (and 'ordinary language philosophy') failed to meet such wholly inappropriate since non-context-sensitive standards of performative warrant or 'felicity'. So it was – again according to Searle – that Derrida could claim the liberty to play fast and loose with Austinian distinctions such as those between constative and performative speech-acts, sincere and insincere professions of intent, or good-faith perfomatives uttered in the appropriate (uptake-conducive) kinds of circumstance and those uttered in various sorts of non-standard and hence invalidating context. Yet it would take a fairly cloth-eared or linguistically unresponsive collocutor either to deny the force of those examples that Derrida adduces in support of his case or else to disregard his further point about the vocabulary of speech-act theory itself. For that lexicon includes a number of crucial terms – among them 'performative' and 'speech-act' – that partake of a curious ambivalence between actually 'doing' and rehearsing, citing, mimicking, feigning or more or less 'sincerely' imitating things (deeds) with words.[7]

Nor is this, as critics like Searle would have it, just the sort of muddle that is sure to result if one mixes a strain of ethical nihilism ('promises have no binding force') with a likewise far-gone strain of epistemological and logico-linguistic relativism. For it is just Derrida's point, here as elsewhere, that we shall make no progress in the attempt to think through the classical antinomies of free-will and determinism, or – what might be deemed another formulation of the same basic problem – moral autonomy and moral obligation, unless and until we take adequate account of the aporias that tend to arise with particular force in the context of Austinian speech-act theory.[8] Moreover, if those problems are going to receive anything like an adequate treatment, then they will need to be approached on some basis other than the strict demarcation between natural-language utterance and formal (speech-act theoretical) discourse that passes pretty much without question on Searle's account. All of which compounds the irony when Searle makes that point about Derrida's having revealed his proclivity for playing frivolous games at the expense of serious (reputable) philosophic argument by dragging in examples of deviant, fictive, contextually inept, 'parasitical', 'etiolated' or otherwise non-standard speech-acts by way of support for his deconstructive project. Where Searle's assumptions most conspicuously come to grief – most clearly run up against the line of counter-argument suggested by his and Austin's working terminology as well as by their choice of examples – is through the constant tendency of language to 'go on holiday', as Wittgenstein put it, or to throw up the kinds of anomalous or deviant case that resist the best efforts of categorization by tidy-minded speech-act theorists. In this respect, Austin is much closer to Derrida than to Searle since he not only makes allowance for that element of unruliness in language – his own language included – but also seems to take pleasure in its power to unsettle the best-laid plans of those, like him, who also have a taste for taxonomies.

Thus it is a fair (if not quite a safe) bet that Austin would have found himself more in tune with Derrida's theoretically informed but far from system-bound approach to topics in philosophy of language than with Searle's resolute efforts to keep the vagaries of performative utterance from working their mischief on the constative discourse of a well-regulated speech-act theory. Still I should not wish to exaggerate the depth of this kinship or the likelihood that, had Austin not died so young, there might have developed an *entente cordiale* rather than the current almost routine state of hostilities between analytic philosophy and everything 'French', or anything coming out of France that doesn't make a point of disowning that stereotyped label. In Austin, there is still a certain conflict of allegiance between his outlook of principled and no doubt genuine respect for the claims of everyday usage or commonsense wisdom and the way that those claims – and the verbal usages wherein they find their most natural expression – tend to come under strain when subject to the pressures of conceptual analysis.

The former leaning is most apparent in that well-known passage from his essay 'A Plea for Excuses' where he writes that 'our common stock of words embodies connections and distinctions [that are] likely to be more numerous, more sound, since they have stood up to the long test of the survival of the fittest, and more subtle, at least in all ordinary and reasonably practical matters, than any that you and I are likely to think up in our armchairs of an afternoon – the most favoured alternative method'.[9] The latter inclination comes out in an earlier passage from the same essay where Austin seems to take a far more instrumentalist view of language and one that would seem to have more in common with the other, *echt*-analytic line of descent from logic-first or language-reformist types like Frege and Russell. Thus:

> words are our tools, and, as a minimum, we should use clean tools: we should know what we mean and what we do not, and we must forearm ourselves against the traps that language sets us. Secondly, words are not (except in their own little corner) facts or things: we need therefore to prise them off the world, to hold them apart from and against it, so that we can realize their inadequacies and arbitrariness, and can relook at the world without blinkers.[10]

Austin appears either not to have noticed this conflict of aims or to have thought it quite possible to switch perspectives as and when required without compromise to either. However, there is a real problem here for anyone, like Searle, who wants to tidy up Austin's loose ends and put speech-act theory on a systematic footing while nonetheless professing a due respect for the authority of 'ordinary language'.

As concerns Ryle, the equivalent tension is that which will strike any reader of *The Concept of Mind* who notes its rhetoric of commonsense, person-in-the-street appeal – most of all when it pillories philosophers from Descartes down for endorsing that absurd idea of the mind as an immaterial 'ghost in the machine' – while itself promoting a massive, philosophically inspired revision of what, for better or worse, is just the kind of moderate dualist outlook that most non-philosophers take pretty much for granted.[11] Of course, this is not to say that they (the persons-in-the-street) are right in so believing and that philosophers should put aside their copies of Ryle – along with their copies of Wittgenstein and numerous other subscribers to the nowadays standard anti-dualist line – and revert *en masse* to Cartesian ways of thought. Rather it is to say that Ryle, like Austin, is caught up in that same tension between a will to analyse, criticize or correct the deliverances of ordinary language or commonsense doxa and a belief that, since philosophy has got us (philosophers) into this mess, we had better look outside the seminar room for alternative, better sources of guidance. Nor is that problem by any means confined to the discourse of 'ordinary language' philosophy or the sorts of issue that typically arise when philosophers bring their specialist interests to bear on non-specialist topics or modes of expression. In fact, as Richard Rorty remarked in his Foreword to a 1967 anthology of essays, it marks the fault line that has run through successive phases of the broadly 'analytic' enterprise and which separates logicists and language reformers on the one side from appealers to the bedrock of commonplace usage on the other.[12]

Still one may accept Rorty's diagnosis of this dilemma at the heart of analytic philosophy as practised then and since without for one moment endorsing the solution that he first sketched out in that Foreword and went on to elaborate in various writings over the next four decades.[13] In particular, two aspects of his project offer a useful contrastive index to the chief significance of Derrida's work in the present context of discussion, that is, its capacity to point a way beyond the stalemate predicament that Rorty pinpoints yet fails to resolve in any adequate manner. First is his well-known neo-pragmatist recommendation that philosophy should learn the lesson of its failure to clear up any of the big problems that had dogged it from Descartes down and had merely taken a more technically geared up or linguistically formulated guise among successive schools of analytic thought. Much better it should now desist from any attempted revival of its old claim to raise questions of a distinctly 'philosophical' character and to furnish them with answers or putative solutions of a likewise distinctive kind. Rather it should try to be as inventive, creative, provocative, edifying or life-transformative as possible while turning its back on all those vain attempts – from Descartes, through Kant, to the analytic mainstream – to carve out a region of special expertise where philosophers alone may tread without fear on account of their privileged access to a range of uniquely privileged intuitions, concepts, categories, grounds, 'conditions of possibility' and so forth. Only thus could it escape the self-imposed isolation into which it had been driven by those narrowly specialized concerns and hence have a decent claim to rejoin the wider 'cultural conversation of mankind'.

Along with this – second – goes his widely influential view of Derrida as a writer who at best exhibits all the above virtues but who at worst manifests a sad tendency to slip back into bad old 'philosophical' habits of thought. Even though he gives them a negative spin – as by using terms like *différance* or 'condition of *impossibility*' – nevertheless they are the sorts of metaphysically loaded vocabulary that he should have left behind once and for all through his own demonstration of the benefits on offer from treating philosophy as just another strictly non-privileged 'kind of writing'. It seems to me that Rorty gets things wrong by adopting – and also foisting onto Derrida – a basically defeatist strategy in order to avoid that same dilemma that he pinpoints so shrewdly in the discourse of late-sixties analytic philosophy. Where his 'solution' is simply to give up on it and herald the advent of a different, radically transformed, 'post-philosophical' culture, Derrida's response is to think the dilemma through with maximum conceptual and logical rigour though always with a readiness to accept that *at the limit* – at the point where thought is driven up against certain classically intractable blocks or aporias – it may need to adopt some alternative, for example, non-bivalent or 'deviant' logic.[14]

This is not the place for a detailed rehearsal of the various forms that it takes, or the various kindred logics of the *pharmakon*, 'supplementarity', 'parergonality', *différance* and so forth, that Derrida discovers in (rather than projects or foists onto) the texts of Plato, Rousseau, Kant, Husserl and a good many others.[15] Suffice it to say that his readings – and the arguments conducted in and through his practice of intensely close-focused textual exegesis – are such as to discountenance any interpretation of Derrida, like Rorty's, that takes him to have come out on the far side of those old-style philosophical concerns. Thus, where Rorty sees him as showing the way towards a post-philosophical culture where notions like truth, knowledge or logic are traded in for the idea of self-renewal through the endless powers of creative 'redescription' offered by language, Derrida conversely insists on the need for maximal rigour and conceptual precision in our dealing with philosophic texts. Indeed, he would fully subscribe to Paul de Man's precept that '[r]eading is an argument . . . because it has to go against the grain of what one would want to happen in the name of what has to happen; this is the same as saying that reading is an epistemological event prior to being an ethical or aesthetic value'.[16] Moreover that claim holds good even if, as de Man goes on to say, '[t]his does not mean that there can be a true reading, but that no reading is conceivable in which the question of its truth or falsehood is not primarily involved'.[17]

Every word of these carefully phrased sentences has a direct bearing on Derrida's work and, more specifically, on the various ways that it resists assimilation to the jointly neo-pragmatist, postmodernist and pan-textualist movement of thought that Rorty is so keen to promote. The resistance comes chiefly from that formal or logico-syntactic dimension of Derrida's readings that enables him – again like de Man though unlike post-structuralists and others who adopt a radically language-first approach – to register the kinds of anomalous, discrepant or aporetic detail that run counter to normal, acculturated habits of expectation and hence require some more or less drastic change of interpretative tack. Even if (in de Man's qualifying clause) there is 'no true reading' in the sense, as I take it, no reading that could truly or justifiably claim to have got the text right once and for all, that doesn't in any way conflict with his subsequent dictum that there cannot be a reading – at any rate one conducted according to his own (and Derrida's) stringent protocols – 'in which the question of its truth or falsehood is not primarily involved'. Thus truth-values will always be in play, along with an appeal to the standards of classical (bivalent) logic, as soon as it is allowed – in keeping with the basic deconstructionist premise – that texts beyond a certain level of semantic and logico-syntactic complexity may well turn out through immanent critique to generate resistance to readings of a routine, fideist, orthodox, over-simplified, doctrinally driven or ideologically collusive character. Otherwise, were it not for that possibility, there could be no question of detecting and pursuing those various deviant or non-classical logics that Derrida brings out to such striking effect.

What typifies his mode of engagement – and gives his writing a peculiar pertinence *vis-à-vis* the split that Rorty identifies within the analytic tradition – is its way of combining an Austinian acuteness and sensitivity to the nuances of (so-called) 'ordinary language' with a high degree of logical-conceptual precision in the analysis of philosophic texts. This is why he is fully justified in taking Searle to task *both* for the latter's over-readiness to lift or relax the requirements of bivalent logic in the context of speech-act theory *and* for his failing to acknowledge how far such a theory must negotiate unlooked-for complicating factors – especially concerning the categorization of speech-act types and modalities – that may very well create problems for any attempt to achieve a clear-cut, definitive or logically regimented theory.[18] Despite their seemingly disparate or downright contradictory nature, these criticisms both find warrant in Derrida's ability to do otherwise, that is, to read not only Austin's but also a great variety of philosophical texts in such a way as to explore both their furthest, very often most deeply problematic logical entailments and their subtlest nuances of verbal implication.

# II

Here again de Man puts the case programmatically in terms that Derrida could pretty much accept as describing his own deconstructive project and, more specifically, his aims in seeking to rescue Austin from the kind of systematizing approach brought to bear by a speech-act theorist like Searle. Thus, when de Man writes of the 'resistance to theory' in his essay of that title, he alludes to the way that a close rhetorical reading of certain texts may 'disturb the stable cognitive field' that is classically taken to extend from logic, through grammar, to epistemology conceived as providing a securely grounded 'knowledge of the world'.[19] What he has in mind is the tendency of theory to self-deconstruct or, more precisely, to reveal complexities of verbal implication or logico-semantic sense that find no place within its own categorical mapping of the field. This process is best helped along, so de Man argues, by an attentiveness to the rhetorical dimension of texts that takes the term 'rhetoric' not in its drastically restricted or diminished present-day sense but rather as specifying that element, aspect or constituent factor in language that resists accommodation to prevalent ideas of coherent or acceptable sense.

Thus: '[t]o empty rhetoric of its epistemological impact is possible only because its tropological, figural functions are being bypassed'. And again: '[i]t is as if . . . rhetoric could be isolated from the generality that grammar and logic have in common and considered as a mere correlative of an illocutionary power'.[20] His main point here is to rescue the concept of rhetoric from those, like Rorty or (de Man's more immediate target) Stanley Fish, who would treat it as wholly and exclusively a matter of language in its suasive or performative aspect.[21] For them it functions as a means of pressing their neo-pragmatist case against theory or philosophy insofar as those disciplines purport to transcend such 'merely' rhetorical devices and thereby offer access to truths above and beyond the currency of in-place communal belief. For de Man and Derrida, conversely, the 'resistance to theory' is something that arises only in consequence of theory's having been pursued with the greatest dedication right up to that point in the reading of a text where it encounters certain rhetorical complexities beyond its power of conceptual resolution. It is at this point also that logic runs up against moments of aporia beyond its capacity to order or contain within the classical (bivalent) calculus of truth-values.

Nothing could be further from that Rortian notion of Derrida as one who practises philosophy as just another 'kind of writing', and whose best efforts in this post-philosophical vein are those that most thoroughly renounce the old craving for method, logic and truth.[22] Of course – as he readily concedes in his rejoinder to Searle – a deconstructive reading would scarcely count as such if it didn't raise certain problematical issues or discover (rather than create or invent) certain far-reaching questions with regard to the scope and limits of logic as classically conceived. However – to repeat – this questioning should in no way be taken to indicate a Rortian attitude of indifference, disdain or just plain boredom as regards such erstwhile core philosophical concerns. Thus, in Derrida's words, '[n]ot only do I find this logic strong, and, in conceptual language and analysis, *an absolute must (il la faut)*, it must . . . be sustained against all empirical confusion, to the point where the same demand of rigour requires the structure of that logic to be transformed or complicated'.[23] One is tempted to remark of a clarion statement like this that any background rumbling the ear may catch is most likely the sound of whole schools of Derrida interpretation collapsing as the impact spreads. Among them are the two, as it might seem antithetical modes of response – exemplified by Searle and Rorty – one of which reviles him for having rejected or betrayed the baseline standards of philosophical debate while the other holds him up as a culture-hero on the same account. What they have in common is a failure to perceive (or reluctance to conceive) how writing of so markedly idiosyncratic and 'literary' a kind can nonetheless exhibit an acuity of logical-conceptual grasp fully equal to that which analytic philosophers take as their governing ideal.

Between these extremes are other, more temperate responses which again divide between those who find some (but not enough) of the 'analytic' virtues in his work and those – very often philosophically minded literary types or philosophers of a more 'continental' persuasion – who stop well short of Rorty's position but still tend to fight shy of Derrida's more 'technical' early books and essays. However, these commentators – both sorts – can also be said to get him wrong insofar as a distinctive and, I think, a strongly motivating aspect of his work is just that combination of keen analytical insight with a high, indeed a preternatural degree of linguistic inventiveness or creativity. This is perhaps the best way to understand what de Man means, in the above-cited passage, when he disavows the claim that 'there can be a true reading' but insists all the same that 'no reading is conceivable in which the question of its truth or falsehood is not primarily involved'. On the one hand, it is wholly unsurprising that he like Derrida – not to mention the great majority of present-day literary critics and theorists, along with not a few philosophers – declines to endorse the kind of ultra-conservative hermeneutic creed that would view the interpreter's proper task as that of divining, ascertaining or recovering the work's true (i.e. authorially intended and aboriginally fixed) import.[24] On the other, what sets him and Derrida apart from the company of post-structuralists, postmodernists and celebrants of open-ended textual 'free-play' (together with its usual corollary, the 'death of the author') is that countervailing stress on the absolute necessity that truth-values – criteria of truth and falsehood – be recognized to play an adjudicative role in every case where there occurs some doubt as to the purport, meaning or significance of some particular passage.

It is precisely this emphasis, I would claim, that marks the crucial (philosophical) distinction between deconstruction as exemplified primarily by Derrida's canonical texts and those other, broadly postmodernist schools of thought with which it is so often and damagingly confused.[25] There is a much-quoted passage from *Of Grammatology* that states the case with such crystalline clarity and precision that I cannot forebear citing it yet again here. To deconstruct a text, Derrida writes:

> obviously cannot consist of reproducing, by the effaced and respectful doubling of commentary, the conscious, voluntary, intentional relationship that the writer institutes in his exchanges with the history to which he belongs thanks to the element of language. This moment of doubling commentary should no doubt have its place in a critical reading. To recognize and respect all its classical exigencies is not easy and requires all the instruments of traditional criticism. Without this recognition and this respect, critical production would risk developing in any direction at all and authorize itself to say almost anything. But this indispensable guardrail has always only protected, it has never opened, a reading.[26]

What 'opens' a reading, as we are able to conclude from an attentive perusal of Derrida's texts, is exactly that vigilant awareness of conflicts between overt and covert or express and logically implicated sense that requires the possession in equal measure of a fine sensitivity to verbal nuance and a keen power of conceptual or logico-semantic analysis. The nearest thing to this within the broad confines of analytic philosophy is Austin's singularly well-attuned ear for the subtleties (and often the vagaries or dubieties) of what ordinarily passes for 'ordinary language'. If Derrida is able to press beyond Austin's typical appeal to the tribunal of everyday or commonsense linguistic judgement it is, I think, mainly through his bringing to bear a critical perspective informed by the 'conflict of interpretations' that loomed so large over his early intellectual development, namely that between phenomenology and structuralism.[27]

This conflict he saw as by no means confined to its modern (mainly French post-1960) manifestation but rather as having been a constant feature of philosophical thought wherever – as for instance in Plato, Rousseau, Kant, Hegel, Husserl or

Saussure – it encountered certain recurrent since deep-laid antinomies, chief among them those of genesis and structure, diachrony and synchrony or language in its expressive-creative and its purely indicative aspects. Hence Derrida's otherwise puzzling, not to say perversely anachronistic claim that 'a certain structuralism has always been philosophy's most spontaneous gesture', and moreover that 'what I can never understand, in a structure, is precisely that by means of which it is not closed'.[28] Here we should recall his equally cryptic assertion, in the above-cited passage from *Of Grammatology*, that the 'indispensable guardrail' of a decent respect for authorial intention and the protocols of scholarly method 'has always only protected, it has never opened, a reading'. 'Phenomenology' and 'structuralism' are for him not simply the names of two, well-defined and geo-chronologically located movements of thought but rather, beyond that, a pair of terms that between them capture the single most pressing and perplexing aporia confronted by philosophy of mind and language. They evoke the problem that arises – at least for the more linguistically sensitive or self-aware practitioners of these disciplines – when philosophers seek both to specify the structural determinants or conditions of possibility for thought, language and experience in general and somehow to convey or articulate that which by very definition transcends any such account. This is not, as Rorty would have it, because philosophy is played off the field by any showing of linguistic creativity but rather because such language belongs to a pre-predicative or expressive dimension beyond the grasp of those structural concepts that analysis requires in order to achieve some kind of descriptive or explanatory purchase. What thinking comes up against here is the root dilemma of any philosophy that would claim to delve back into the *sources and conditions* (taking each of those terms in a carefully specified sense) of our being-in-the-world as sentient, sapient, linguistically creative and humanly responsive subjects.

This is the same dilemma that Kant shied away from when he followed Aquinas in saying that even if angels might be thought of as possessing a singular and undivided faculty of 'intellectual intuition', then certainly this lay beyond the cognitive powers of mere human mortals. For the latter, subject as they are to the scope and limits of a physically embodied intellect, knowledge must always involve the more prosaic since indirect or non-immediate process of bringing sensuous (phenomenal) intuitions under concepts of understanding.[29] As it happens, a number of analytic philosophers, notably John McDowell, have lately homed in on other passages of Kant's First *Critique* where the pesky dualism of intuition and concept – the source of so many subsequent problems for thinkers from the German idealists to the logical positivists – assumes the more harmless-sounding guise of a distinction between 'spontaneity' and 'receptivity'.[30] McDowell spends a good deal of time trying to persuade us that any appearance of a sharp dichotomy here, or any notion that these terms might be mere stand-ins for 'intuition' and 'concept', is unwarranted since Kant himself insists on their absolute, in-principle inseparability and on his having resorted to such misleading dualist talk only as (so to speak) a *faute de mieux façon de parler*. However, as I have argued in detail elsewhere, this reassurance is somewhat undermined by the fact that McDowell (like Kant) cannot do without that particular line of talk and in this respect seems to be in much the same position as those – logical positivists and their varied progeny – whose predicament he claims to have escaped or transcended by the switch of elective vocabulary.[31] My point is that analytic philosophy even in its less hidebound or more speculative, that is, 'continentally' oriented forms still bears the mark of that dualist mindset which after all – by a curious twist of reception-history – it inherits from none other than Kant. Indeed another shift of perspective from the German to the French line of 'continental' descent – taking phenomenology from its Husserlian source to its subsequent encounter with Saussure through Merleau-Ponty and Derrida – might help analytic philosophers to think their way beyond the dilemma still visible in those, including 'post-analytic' types like McDowell, who perpetuate the old dualism in notionally different terms.

This would emphasize first the missing dimension of bodily and affective experience so central to Merleau-Ponty's re-envisioning of Husserl's 'intellectualist' project, and second a more productive and creative way of approaching the antinomy of genesis and structure, or the problem of steering a philosophically viable course between diachronic and synchronic modes of understanding.[32] Along with this very often goes the further problem of doing justice on the one hand to language and thought in their creative-expressive-inventive aspect and on the other to those powers of conceptual grasp that have for so long – and especially in the context of 'analytic' *versus* 'continental' debate – been taken to characterize a sharply opposed conception of philosophy's proper role. That difference is one that goes all the way back to Plato's wielding of the philosophic cudgels in what he already saw fit to describe as the 'ancient quarrel' between philosophy and poetry. More recently, it surfaced once again with a kindred force of entrenched disciplinary prejudice in the logical-positivist case, most forcefully championed by A.J. Ayer, against 'literary' (pseudo-)philosophers like Sartre and Camus who were supposedly making dramatic or emotive capital out of certain elementary confusions with regard to basic matters like the fact/value distinction.[33] Where that attitude shows up as a product of narrowly parochial thinking is in the failure to conceive that such issues might not have been resolved or effectively laid to rest with anything like the conversation-stopping finality envisaged by hardline logical positivists such as Ayer. Nor do they show much sign of disappearing when approached by thinkers on the opposite wing of the broadly analytical approach, that is, by therapeutically minded followers of Wittgenstein who seek nothing more than to cure us of all those needless philosophical worries by supplying a deflationary dose of commonsense linguistic medicine.[34] What stands in the way of these putative solutions – or dissolutions – of the concept/intuition or structure/genesis antinomy is their failure to engage philosophical issues at the level of creative, linguistically self-conscious, but also analytically acute and conceptually resourceful investigation exemplified by Derrida's best work.

Again, it is Austin who at times comes closest to achieving that particular combination of virtues, although in his case it results more from a somewhat quirky intellectual temperament – one that combines a certain hankering for system and method with a certain resistance to it in the name of 'ordinary language' – than from the kind of intensely theoretical reflection that Derrida deploys in addressing the issue between phenomenology and structuralism. What distinguishes these otherwise close-kin thinkers is the way that Derrida, unlike Austin, manages to do both things at once, that is, exhibit a singular gift for catching at the subtlest nuances of verbal implication even while he raises issues of a far-reaching philosophical character. He is able to do so mainly through practising a mode of intensely close-focused and self-reflexive commentary on the texts of philosophers, from Plato to Husserl, who may not have brought those issues so sharply into focus – who might indeed have been largely or wholly unaware of the logico-semantic complexities involved – yet whose texts all the same bear striking witness to Derrida's claims. Oddly and tantalizingly enough, it was Austin who coined the term 'linguistic phenomenology' as a handy description of his own approach to philosophical issues through a constant hearkening to 'ordinary language' and its endlessly varied shades of implication.[35] However, he used that phrase only once and in a typically offhand, noncommittal way which reveals something of his general discomfort around the more openly speculative tendencies of (typecast) 'continental' thought. Derrida takes the approach to a different level through his deployment of an 'answerable style' – Geoffrey Hartman's useful term – in which, through which, and with the creative-exploratory aid of which he brings to light linguistic-conceptual implications that would otherwise escape notice.[36] They are simply inaccessible to any way of reading, like Searle's, that treats speech-acts as falling into certain categorically distinct types, genres or classes and therefore as coming with clearly marked felicity-conditions or standards of appropriate usage attached. Such a theory is bound to ignore or unwittingly suppress the more complex, ambiguous or problematic instances of performative as well as constative utterance insofar as it is heavily mortgaged in advance to some particular conception of what counts – properly, sincerely, aptly, successfully, paradigmatically counts – as a normal or genuine case of the kind.

# III

In an interview entitled 'That Strange Institution Called Literature', Derrida remarks that '[g]ood literary criticism, the only worthwhile kind, implies an act, a literary signature or countersignature, an inventive experience of language, in language, an inscription of the act of reading in the field of the text that is read'.[37] Of course it might be said – almost certainly would be said by the majority of analytic philosophers – that even if this goes for literary criticism, or for some (perhaps stylistically overweening) kinds of literary criticism, then it doesn't or shouldn't go for philosophy, at least insofar as philosophers retain a sense of their proper calling. From their viewpoint, it is precisely the hallmark of philosophical discipline and competence that it keeps a tight check on any such untoward tendencies by ensuring that its own discourse should observe certain standards of conduct or certain kinds of self-denying ordinance. Among the most basic is just that demand that it not give way to the seductive possibilities of a language – in the strictest sense, an idiomatic language – that would lack the conceptual power or the generalized scope to count as properly philosophical. Nor is this aversion to excessive 'creativity' by any means confined to thinkers who identify with the *echt-*analytical branch of analytic philosophy, that is to say, the line of descent from Frege and Russell which is often thought of – and thinks of itself – as holding fast to the values of logic and method against the adepts of an 'ordinary language' approach with its source in Wittgenstein or Austin. After all, Wittgenstein in his later writings was just as suspicious of the waywardness of language once allowed its creative-expressive head or once permitted to 'go on holiday' – his own curiously disapproving phrase – and exploit the full range of its metaphoric or other such 'literary' resources.[38]

Indeed, Wittgenstein's notorious failure (or refusal) to see what it was that people so admired in Shakespeare appears to have stemmed very largely from this deep-laid suspicion – one that he shared with, among others, a conservative classicist like Dr Johnson and a finger-wagging Christian moralist like the aging Tolstoy – that when language got out of touch with everyday or 'common-sense' usage, then nothing good could possibly result.[39] As I have said, Austin was much more alive to those aspects of the extraordinary that inhabit (so-called) ordinary language when approached with an ear well attuned to its less obvious, at times distinctly problematic or paradoxical implications. Still he stopped far short of any allowance that philosophy of language, or speech-act theory, might continue to do its work – to cast a revealing *analytical* as well as appreciative light on our modes of verbal-communicative practice – if it allowed those 'deviant' implications to count on a par with the evidence supplied by various instances of straightforward, 'normal', or everyday usage. It is just this claim that Derrida makes when he shows how far the actual (logico-semantically specifiable) meaning of a text may diverge from its manifest purport, or again, how deep the fault line may run between what an author expressly means to say and what he or she ends up by saying as a matter of logical entailment despite and against that overt intent. Where Derrida goes beyond Austin is in raising this issue to a high point of visibility – through the encounter staged in his work between phenomenology and structuralism – while nonetheless remaining closely in touch with those idiomatic nuances or unlooked-for turns of semantic implication that likewise go beyond anything accountable *either* by the recourse to system or method *or* by the appeal to established or accustomed ('ordinary') usage.

This is why '[r]eading,' as Derrida says, 'must give itself up to the uniqueness [of the literary work], take it on board, keep it in mind, take account of it. But for that, for this rendering, you have to sign in your turn, write something else which responds or corresponds in an equally singular, which is to say irreducible, irreplaceable, "new" way: neither imitation, nor reproduction, nor metalanguage'.[40] What so divides his commentators, at any rate the philosophers among them, is the question as to whether this kind of responsive-creative or critical-creative-exploratory writing has its place – a proper or legitimate place – in philosophy as well as in the more hermeneutically adventurous modes of literary criticism. To *echt*-analyticals and Wittgensteinians alike, although for somewhat different reasons, it has to appear a dereliction of philosophy's primary concern with the business of resolving those various problems or dilemmas that mostly arise through our allowing language to lead us off the path of logical rigour, conceptual clarity, or plain commonsense wisdom. Where they differ, of course, is with regard to the issue of how philosophy can best hope to remedy that potent source of confusion or whether (as the former party would have it) such deliverance might come through a more exacting logical analysis of the various muddles that typically result from an over-reliance on everyday language or unaided linguistic intuition. For thinkers of the latter type, conversely, it is just that overweening idea of philosophy's corrective, prescriptive or legislative role that has created those problems in the first place by encouraging philosophers to use words in non-customary, overly technical ways and thus lose touch with the sense-making virtues of ordinary usage.

My suggestion, in short, is that Derrida's work responds to this (as he would see it) pseudo-dilemma not so much by seeking to split the difference and offer some notional third-way alternative but rather by pressing as far as possible with the project of conceptual or logico-semantic analysis while also deploying his remarkable powers of linguistic inventiveness or creativity in order to explore where that project might encounter certain limits to its scope of consistent application. Thus, when he writes of the 'singularity' of literature as that which cannot be subjected to any 'metalanguage', his comment no doubt refers primarily to those formalist or structuralist schools of literary criticism that have indeed sought, from Aristotle down, to devise some means of placing that enterprise on a more systematic or scientific footing. However, it can also be taken, in the present context, as alluding to that which distinguishes literature from philosophy, literary criticism from philosophical commentary or – perhaps closer to Derrida's thinking – the most aptly responsive and 'answerable' way to read literary texts from the most fitting, that is, analytically acute as well as hermeneutically sensitive way to read those texts that belong to the genre of philosophy. Nor is this merely a matter of convention or of what just happens to count as such according to a range of historically and culturally shifting generic markers. For it is very much Derrida's *philosophic* point in an essay like 'White Mythology' that there will always turn out to be something strictly nonsensical or self-refuting about any claim to supplant or supersede philosophy, as for instance by pressing the vulgar-deconstructionist idea that (quite simply) 'all concepts are metaphors' and hence all philosophy just another 'kind of writing' or sub-genre of literature.[41] Then again, as he argues in 'The Supplement of Copula', the same problem arises for a linguist like Emile Benveniste who seeks to put philosophy in its proper (subaltern) place by arguing that ever since Aristotle it has constantly derived its most basic logical concepts and categories from the range of syntactic and other resources available within this or that particular natural language.[42]

In the first case, promoted most vigorously by Rorty, philosophy's role and its erstwhile prestige as a discourse of truth-seeking enquiry would at last give way to the alternative, un-self-deluded since non-truth-fixated discourses of literary and cultural criticism or – better still – of poetry and fiction.[43] In the other, philosophy would yield to linguistics as the discipline best equipped to make sense of those various sense-making forms, structures, codes and culture-specific conventions which constitute the bottom-line of enquiry for every branch of the human, the social and (what is centrally at issue here) the formal sciences.[44] This doctrine of cultural-linguistic relativism, along with the kindred notion of radical inter-lingual or inter-cultural 'incommensurability', has been subject to a good many pointed critiques, among them Donald Davidson's telling if oddly laconic argument that they themselves fail to make sense by the most basic standards of conceptual and logical accountability.[45] However what is not so widely known – whether among analytical philosophers or deconstructionists of a more 'literary' bent – is that Derrida argues a similar case in the two above-mentioned essays and indeed goes yet further in exposing the self-contradictory or self-refuting character of claims to discredit philosophy by exposing its reliance on linguistic, metaphorical, narrative or suchlike (supposedly) prior constituents of every philosophical thesis or truth-claim. For if one point emerges with maximal force from these and other writings of Derrida's early period, it is the fact – not merely a contingent fact about human thought and language but a condition of possibility for all productive enquiry into the relationship between them – that proposals concerning that order of priority *cannot but* go by way of a discourse deeply beholden to philosophical concepts and categories. Thus it must take a proper critical account of the issues that have received their most adequate treatment in the texts of theorists, from Aristotle down, whose ideas in this regard belong squarely to philosophy or to the history of varied conceptualizations that philosophy has brought to bear on such topics.

So when Nietzscheans, Foucauldians, post-structuralists, postmodernists, Rortian neo-pragmatists, Wittgensteinians and others propound their kindred theses with regard to the precedence of language over thought – or of various other disciplines over philosophy – they cannot but be closing their minds to the crucial role played in their own arguments by modes of reasoning that in turn cannot but draw upon distinctly philosophical resources. The force of those repeated 'cannot buts' is of course the kind of force that these thinkers typically claim for their discipline or discipline-constitutive ways of proceeding, and will therefore strike the above-mentioned range of opponents as nothing more than a particularly blatant way of finessing the main issue. However, it is just Derrida's point in the above-mentioned essays – and also implicitly throughout his work – that thinking cannot possibly abandon (or affect to abandon) those basic protocols of right reason or logically articulated thought without thereby falling prey to some demonstrable form of aporia, paradox or downright self-contradiction. I place these terms in ascending order of negative-demonstrative power since 'aporia' is clearly, on Derrida's (as likewise on Kant's) reckoning, a condition that certain kinds of speculative reason are intrinsically prone to, while paradox claims (but had perhaps better not be granted) special exemption from the ground rules of rational thought, and self-contradiction only gets by if one adopts a dialethic or paraconsistent logic that rejects what most philosophers – revisionists like Quine included – would accept as the *sine qua non* of rational thought.[46] For it is only by espousing that radical alternative – denying the principle of non-contradiction, albeit with certain caveats attached – that one can deem Aristotle to have got it wrong when he declared this to be a nonsensical or self-refuting position, since any endorsement of a statement and its contrary entailed the simultaneous truth and falsehood of any other statement whatsoever.

My point is that Derrida operates with a strong sense of the distinction between these three kinds of challenge to the dictates of classical or bivalent logic. Moreover, it is precisely by so doing – by maintaining a keen and context-sensitive awareness of their different conditions of applicability – that he achieves the combination of logical rigour with extreme responsiveness to nuances of natural-language implication that has proved so elusive (and such a dividing-point) for thinkers in the mainstream analytic line of descent. Derrida holds out against any (e.g. postmodernist or post-analytical) claim to have done with the standards or constraints of classical logic while nonetheless testing that logic against a whole range of particular cases – arguments, concepts, idioms, passages, texts – where it comes up against different degrees or strengths of contestation. What he never sees fit to endorse is the kind of wholesale revisionist outlook with respect to those standards or constraints that is a notable feature of thinking across some large tracts of philosophical country, large enough (that is) to accommodate thinkers of an otherwise thoroughly diverse set of persuasions. Least of all would he yield any ground to the argument, put forward by Quine and Putnam among others, that classical 'laws' such as bivalence and excluded middle might – indeed should – be deemed revisable if they get into conflict with the evidence produced by the physical sciences or if they can be squared with that evidence only by means of a more or less drastic revision.[47] For in that case, as with his objection to Searle, one has effectively renounced any claim to decide on rational or logically accountable grounds just what sorts of evidence might warrant such a change, or what sorts of change to the (supposed) logical ground-rules are required in order to put right the anomaly in question.

Besides, on the epistemological view taken by Quine and his successors, there is a basic problem about maintaining this logical-revisionist doctrine which could only be avoided by doing what even he considers well beyond the pale of rational acceptability, that is, renouncing the law of contradiction and going dialethic *sans* all the customary caveats. Thus the argument runs (to repeat) that empirical evidence might conceivably trump the axioms of classical logic along with any other such well-entrenched commitments, among them those normative constraints that lie so deep as to pass for *a priori* 'laws of thought' or even – as these thinkers are willing to allow – the most seemingly secure or unquestionable 'laws' of the physical sciences.[48] Yet this sits uneasily with another main plank in their argument, namely the so-called Duhem-Quine thesis according to which theories are always 'underdetermined' by the best evidence to hand while the evidence is always 'theory-laden' and hence not available for the kind of work here envisaged, that is, that of putting up resistance to received modes of theoretically informed observation or conceptually structured perceptual experience.[49] That is to say, the Duhem-Quine thesis, if valid, is enough to rule out any notion of sensory inputs or physical stimuli – to adopt Quine's favoured ultra-behaviourist terms – as having anything like that decisive capacity to challenge, resist, obstruct or controvert the deliverances of logic or physical theory. Indeed, as I have argued elsewhere, this basic contradiction is enough to capsize a whole raft of strong-revisionist or paradigm-relativist doctrines, many of which have their source in Thomas Kuhn's working-out of the Quinean thesis in the context of a more thoroughly historicized approach to the process of scientific theory-change.[50] For it is here more than anywhere – in the kind of thinking typified by present-day 'science studies' or the strong sociology of knowledge – that one finds this curious failure to remark how flatly inconsistent are the two chief premises (radical empiricism and theory-ladenness) that purportedly constitute its chief philosophical (or anti-philosophical) pillars.[51]

Yet it is here also that the programme comes up against two major difficulties, namely (1) the normative deficit entailed by its having relativized logic and reason to an ill-defined notion of empirical, observational or (in post-Kuhnian versions) linguistic and socio-cultural warrant, and (2) the fairly blatant self-contradiction that results if one takes that claim in conjunction with the Duhem-Quine thesis. Derrida is fully alert to both problems and to the fact that any argument premised on the relativity of logic to language or of truth-conditions to conditions of assertoric warrant in this or that context will end up by confronting both in the form of a disabling or self-stultifying paradox. Moreover, his response to Searle makes it clear that Derrida rejects any notion of logic as subject to certain empirical constraints or as needing to be somewhat relaxed, adjusted or rendered more context-sensitive in response to its various (e.g. natural-language-applicable) modes of deployment. Nor is this merely, as might be thought, a result of his adhering to the well-known prejudice of French philosophers – even those who most vigorously claim to have thrown off the heritage of Cartesian rationalism – against any version of that other, typically British, empiricist way of thought which they tend to regard as naïve or downright anti-philosophical. On the contrary, for Derrida, as likewise for a thinker such as Deleuze, it is just that predominant rationalist bias in so much of the philosophy that defines their national as well as the wider (mainstream-European) tradition of thought which enables empiricism – or a certain kind of empiricism – to take on a radically heterodox or contestatory character.[52] However that kind has nothing in common with the inertly behaviourist, phenomenalist or sense-data-based conception that leaves the Quinean approach so strikingly bereft of both normative resources and a logically cogent or consistent basis for its own more extravagant revisionist claims. Rather it involves the typically Derridean way of reading texts with maximal regard to their long-range as well as localized structures of logico-semantic implication but also with a highly receptive, responsive or sensitive awareness of problematic details opaque to any reading premised on conventional ideas of what counts as a faithful or competent philosophical account.

A fairly obvious candidate for next position in the adjectival series 'receptive, responsive, or sensitive' is perhaps 'creative', which Derrida's literary disciples would no doubt embrace with great fervour, along with those on the analytic-philosophical wing who would take it as an adequate and welcome reason to ignore his work, or those (like Rorty) who wish to recast the entire philosophical enterprise in a style very much like that promoted by the literary types. It seems to me that 'creative' is an adjective that properly applies to Derrida's work just so long as one bears in mind the degree of logical, analytic and conceptual acuity involved in a practice of textual close-reading that is able to expose such a range of hitherto occluded meanings – most often unexpected twists of logico-semantic entailment – beyond the grasp of any reading premised on conservative ideas of exegetical fidelity or truth. Perhaps the term 'inventive' is a better alternative not only in so far as it carries an echo of 'invent' in the ancient rhetoricians' usage of that term, that is, 'discover', 'happen upon' or 'find out' through procedures that require a certain creativity (call it 'ingenuity') but also as regards its attentiveness to that which shows itself ready or apt for the purpose. It is here – with respect to what supposedly offers itself as a matter of empirical self-evidence – that Derrida's thought goes furthest towards deconstructing the root presuppositions that have held the philosophical project together across and despite all its sundry fallings-out to date. 'Empiricism', as Derrida construes it, is once again a matter of heightened receptiveness to details that remain invisible to other, less alert modes of reading or analysis.

To be sure, these are usually textual details in the first instance but 'textual' in precisely the expansive, world-involving sense that Derrida has so often stressed in response to his critics. On this account, texts – or those that lend themselves most aptly to deconstructive treatment – must be taken to possess a referential bearing and an implicative reach that give deconstruction its critical purchase on various issues of a real-world pertinence or (often) urgent topicality. Hence, I would suggest, the impression so often given by deconstructive readings of literary (fictive or poetic) texts that there is ultimately nothing at issue here – that they lack any such purchase – since it scarcely needs showing that although these texts may indeed create a sense of verisimilitude or logical argument, we should nonetheless always make adequate allowance for their belonging to a different, generically distinct, non-truth-functional mode of discourse.[53] For there is, to say the least, something rather off-the-point about the regular practice among Derrida-influenced literary critics of displaying such extreme ingenuity in order to reveal, over and again, how the texts in question can be seen to self-deconstruct – to lay bare their own rhetorical structures or forms of narrative contrivance – and thereby implicitly subvert or disown any such realist illusion.[54]

# IV

Indeed, I would go so far as to claim that this is what constitutes the chief difference between deconstruction, properly so called, and those varieties of post-structuralist and postmodernist thought with which it is very often lumped together by proponents and detractors alike.[55] No doubt it is a defining feature of deconstructive readings that they involve the discovery of certain referential or logical aberrations, and moreover that this discovery comes about through a mode of textual close-reading that has to do with rhetoric in one standard sense of that term, that is, the analysis of language in its tropological or figural dimension. Still it is equally important to recognize that rhetoric in this sense – what de Man terms the 'epistemology of tropes' – is a critical enterprise fully responsive to the requirements of logical reasoning and also fully cognizant of the extent to which language must, if it is to serve any useful purpose, have a referential function or point beyond itself to a real-world object domain. For de Man, the best way to retain this sense of the centrality and also the problematic status of reference is by returning to the classical model of the *trivium*, the inherently unstable or problematic meeting point of those three disciplines – logic, grammar and rhetoric – that made up the core of a traditional humanistic education.[56] Where the model most notably serves his deconstructive purpose is in allowing for the role of rhetoric, that is, of rhetorical theory and analysis as that which discovers certain complicating factors that prevent any smooth or self-assured passage from the structures (propositions) of formal logic, through their analogue in the sentences of well-formed grammar, to veridical states of affairs. Only by ignoring those disruptive factors – or by treating them as 'merely' rhetorical and void of epistemological import – can language be thought of as affording an altogether reliable, precise, logically exacting or referentially dependable source of knowledge.

There is no problem for this basic conception of language, logic and truth so long as 'rhetoric' is taken in the narrow and often derogatory sense of that term which equates it exclusively with the arts of persuasion or with the non-cognitive aspect of discourse where values of truth and falsehood simply don't apply. On that convenient assumption, as de Man puts it, 'grammar stands in the service of logic which, in turn, allows for the passage to knowledge of the world'.[57] And again, with particular reference to Kant's variation on the theme: what we find in this model is 'a clear instance of the interconnectedness between a science of the phenomenal world and a science of language conceived as definitional logic, the precondition for a correct axiomatic-deductive, synthetic reasoning'.[58] However, the model turns out not to function so smoothly when that narrow and prejudicial understanding of rhetoric is exchanged for a more adequate sense of its epistemo-critical dimension. What then becomes apparent is the standing possibility that certain kinds of text – those that engage such issues with the greatest insight or power of analytic grasp – will turn out to contain passages that resist assimilation to any straightforward or problem-free conception of language, truth and logic. For, according to de Man, it is the peculiar virtue of readings in the deconstructive mode to show just where and how this resistance occurs and also to point up its crucial bearing on various, often deeply entrenched ideologies which derive much of their suasive force from a naturalized or 'commonsense' version of the scholastic model described above. 'To empty rhetoric of its epistemological impact is possible only because its tropological, figural functions are being bypassed. It is as if rhetoric could be isolated from the generality that grammar and logic have in common and considered as a mere correlative of an illocutionary power'.[59]

Thus, the term 'rhetoric' has to be conceived as involving two functions or aspects – on the face of it sharply distinct but in truth strictly inseparable – and no longer thought of as restricted to a persuasive or 'merely' rhetorical role. On the one hand, rhetorical theory exerts a power of epistemo-critical grasp resulting from the rigorous analysis of linguistic effects that might otherwise exert a misleading, seductive or downright pernicious influence on our thinking in various subject-domains. Literary theory may achieve such a grasp but only insofar as it opens into regions of enquiry that extend from philosophy of language and logic to epistemology, ethics and political theory. On the other hand, that very rigour may always prove to be in some sense its own undoing or – not to belabour the paradox – lead up to a point where thinking encounters the need to question or qualify (rather than reject or abandon) some of those precepts that have so far acted as rules or directives for its own proper conduct. Hence de Man's double-aspect theory of rhetoric as that which raises the critical power of thought to its highest degree yet at the same time reveals the liability of thought *even then* to suffer forms of ideological delusion or misrecognition that can be rectified only through a further, more strenuous effort of analysis. Thus, the ultimate insight of deconstruction 'may well concern rhetoric itself, the discovery that what is called "rhetoric" is precisely the gap that becomes apparent in the pedagogical and philosophical history of the term. Considered as persuasion, rhetoric is performative but when considered as a system of tropes, it deconstructs its own performance'.[60]

What I wish to emphasize is the extent of convergence between Derrida's and de Man's projects, at least as regards this shared insistence on the epistemological dimension of rhetoric and the error of supposing that 'rhetoric' denotes an aspect, component or modality of language that eludes any kind of rigorous analysis since it has to do only with 'persuasion' or 'performative' (illocutionary) force. De Man makes the point by contrasting the potential of a deconstructive reading in this critical-rhetorical mode –

its power to expose blind spots of prejudice or deep-grained 'commonsense' ideology – with the 'dreary prospects of pragmatic banality' opened up by an impoverished notion of rhetoric that acknowledges only its performative aspect and thereby results in 'the equation of rhetoric with psychology rather than epistemology'.[61] Here, his chief target is Stanley Fish and the 'against theory' school of thought which takes a lead from Fish in arguing – or urging – that arguments or reasons can never be more than persuasive since rhetoric (persuasion) goes all the way down.[62] From this it follows that theories or principles are merely otiose when it comes to winning people over, and hence that a thinker like de Man must be sadly deluded when he tries to make the case that rhetoric possesses that other, more searching or rigorously consequent epistemo-critical dimension. Indeed, it is a main plank in Fish's programme to show that theory is wholly inconsequential since it can have no consequences – no results brought about by some additional measure of logical, rational or argumentative force – beyond its straightforwardly suasive efficacy.[63]

Moreover, this applies not only to the kind of 'positive foundationalist theory-hope' displayed by those who think to justify their favoured beliefs by appeal to various grounding precepts or principles but also to 'negative anti-foundationalist theory-hope', as with the deployment of theory-talk by Marxists, feminists and deconstructionists in order – so they fondly suppose – to lend their discourse a greater degree of mind-changing or world-transformative leverage. Neither project has the least chance of success, he asserts, since both stake their claim on the twin delusion first that rhetoric might be theorized in such a way as to engender resistance to its own suasive effects, and second that this theory might amount to more than just another kind of rhetorical persuasion that wraps itself in theoretical colours as a source of – what else? – enhanced persuasive power. No theory whether positive or negative can avoid the need to seek assent among a certain group of readers – an 'interpretative community', in Fish's phrase – who will either endorse or reject its claims but will do so out of a predisposed leaning in either direction or through their having come to it in a frame of mind that renders them sufficiently attentive and engaged to respond in a sympathetic or an adverse way. On this neo-pragmatist view, it is nonsense to think that any theory could possibly change anyone's mind about anything or – to state his case more exactly – that it could do so *through and by means of* theory rather than through a rhetorical-suasive strategy that falls back on theory-talk as a handy resource when addressing those with a taste for such things.

So for Fish there can be no question but that negative theory-hopers like Derrida and de Man are kidding themselves and others when they claim such a radically transformative role – such a power to resist received or naturalized ways of thought – for what is, in the final (rhetorical) analysis, just another instance of more or less well-judged suasive rhetoric. For them, on the contrary, it is no exaggeration to say that the whole point of reading and the very possibility of thinking to any critical (positive or negative) effect about what one has read depends upon Fish's being wrong in all this and on theory's possessing just the kind of critical and mind-changing power that neo-pragmatism rules out of court. De Man makes the point in his customary tight-lipped, rigourist style when he lays down the deconstructive requirement that textual exegesis not go the way of a rhetorical reading in the Fishian performative or illocutionary mode. Rather it should take the more difficult path of an engagement that resists those seductive options – those various well-tried means of fulfilling the interpreter's desire for a perfect, unimpeded, problem-free communion with the text – which typify mainstream philosophical as well as literary-critical practice.

Thus (to repeat): '[w]hat makes a reading more or less true is the necessity of its occurrence, regardless of the reader's or of the author's wishes . . . . Reading is an argument . . . because it has to go against the grain of what one would want to happen in the name of what has to happen'.[64] This can occur only on condition that rhetoric be thought of as manifesting that crucial duality between language in its suasive-performative mode and language as the register of logico-semantic tensions, conflicts or aporias that demand a more strenuous activity of critical thought – of reading as 'argument', in de Man's laconic formulation – than finds any room in Fish's account. Moreover, the resistance to simplified, naïve or ideologically complicit ways of reading can itself take rise only through the break with that notion of a seamless continuity between logic, grammar and rhetoric which, according to de Man, finds its perfect (though ultimately unrealizable) formula in the model of the classical *trivium*. Thus, '[d]ifficulties occur [for this model] only when it is no longer possible to ignore the epistemological thrust of the rhetorical dimension of language'.[65] This would be the point at which Fish's idea of reading as always, inevitably bound to follow the dictates of in-place conviction or communally shared belief comes up against a countervailing need to explain how we could ever, in that case, achieve any kind of intellectual advance or succeed in breaking with routine, habituated modes of thought. What enables us to do so – and shows the neo-pragmatist/'against-theory' line to lack credibility – is the fact that reading can indeed be an 'argument' or (the same thing if translated out of that deconstructive-textualist idiom) that thinking can indeed muster critical resources against the effects of doctrinal adherence, ingrained prejudice, or sheer cultural inertia.

This is not at all a trivial matter or, as some philosophers would have it, merely the kind of problem thrown up when literary theorists – along with theory-obsessed anti-theorists like Fish – indulge their penchant for affecting to doubt all manner of otherwise obvious or commonsense truths about language. These would include, at the most basic, its referential capacity for putting us reliably in touch with a great range of real-world objects and events and also its power to put us in touch with each other through various modes of inter-personal discourse involving the conveyance and uptake of speakers' (and authors') intentions. Of course, this presupposes that the speech-acts in question are uttered and interpreted under normal conditions, 'normal' then requiring – for philosophic purposes – some contrastive spelling-out of what might on occasion get in the way of such a smooth communicative passage, as for instance through certain irregularities of context or purport that render the utterance abnormal. Nor would Derrida for one moment deny that this is the case, or that language does – at any rate for the most part – function in just such a well-regulated way with the parties to any given speech-act possessing a reasonably clear sense of the difference between normal and abnormal instances of the kind. However, as we have seen, he also makes the point *contra* Searle that philosophy – philosophy of language more specifically – can and should bring its critical focus to bear on a range of complex, difficult, borderline, marginal, disputed or exceptional cases. For these can then serve both to challenge our more settled or complacent habits of thought and to sharpen our sense of the complicating factors that might always turn up in the course of what had seemed perfectly normal or straightforward verbal transactions.

Hence no doubt the widespread interest in deconstruction among critically minded legal scholars who likewise take it that 'hard cases', that is, those with no clear case-law precedent or unambiguous provision in statute law are sometimes the best spurs to reflection on the sorts of complexity that might lie concealed in other, supposedly routine instances where such reflection seems uncalled for.[66] When I said that these are not trivial matters, I had in mind chiefly this question as to whether, how far, and by what means it is possible for thought to exercise its critical powers *despite and against* the normalizing force of received ideas, consensus belief, commonsense judgement or other such conformist and criticism-stifling forms of the Fishian 'interpretive community'. I was also picking up on the particular issue between de Man and Fish as regards the possibility – the impossibility, as Fish thinks it – that reading might indeed be 'an argument' insofar as it goes against the grain of existing interpretative norms (and even against the persuasive force of certain passages of the text in hand) and claims to discover the source of such resistance in a counter-logic intrinsically at odds with the text's manifest purport.

Such, as we have seen, are Derrida's deviant or paraconsistent logics of 'supplementarity', 'différance', 'parergonality' and so forth, all of them emergent from a close-reading that nowhere renounces the most exacting standards of bivalent (classical) reasoning but the upshot of which is to show how their application may run into problems that cannot be resolved on classical terms. Although he doesn't make explicit reference to the *trivium* model, his entire approach is premised, like de Man's, on the standing possibility that rhetoric may create problems for logic and for any theory of knowledge entailing some version, however qualified or nuanced, of the idea that mind becomes acquainted with world through a straightforward structural correspondence between thoughts, propositions (or statements) and veridical states of affairs. So there is a need to recognize how rhetoric may work to disrupt the 'stable cognitive field' that supposedly grounds the isomorphic relation between logic, grammar and the structure of phenomenal appearances. Yet there is also the need for an epistemology of rhetoric – a rigorous accounting for that same disruptive force – that is able to reveal its critical power as an undoer of various highly appealing yet false or tendentious ideologies that often take effect through a seductive assimilation of thought and language to notions of organic or quasi-natural development and growth.[67] It is through analogies like this, according to de Man, that the *trivium* model in its naïve, literalist or dogmatic form comes to dominate a good deal of 'common-sense' thinking about language and also to leave its distinctive stamp on some highly influential (and in one case catastrophic) ideas of the intimate and privileged link between language, culture and national identity.[68]

# V

However, my main concern here is not with these overtly political dimensions of de Man's thought but rather with its relatively 'technical' bearing on issues in philosophy of language and epistemology. For in fact, as he remarks with a sidelong glance at certain

Marxist critics of deconstruction, '[w]hat we call ideology is precisely the confusion of linguistic with natural reality, of reference with phenomenalism'. From which it follows that 'the linguistics of literariness is a powerful and indispensable tool in the unmasking of ideological aberrations, as well as a determining factor in accounting for their occurrence'.[69]

If the latter assertion seems like a piece of wilful paradox-mongering, then that impression may be lessened by recalling the double-aspect character of rhetoric as de Man conceives it. Such is also the ambivalent status of literature – along with the 'linguistics of literariness' – insofar as it represents on the one hand a potent source of cultural-ideological mystification and on the other, conversely, a powerful means of undoing or resisting the effects of that widespread 'aesthetic ideology' that became the chief focus of his critical attention in the essays of his final decade. Hence, de Man writes:

> [T]he need for a phenomenalized, empirically manifest principle of cognition on whose existence the possibility of such an articulation [that between mind and world or thought and reality] depends. This phenomenalized principle is what Kant calls the aesthetic. The investment in the aesthetic is therefore considerable, since the possibility of philosophy itself, as the articulation of a transcendental with a metaphysical discourse, depends on it.[70]

This is why the epistemology of rhetoric (or tropes) comes to occupy such a privileged place – or to bear such a singular weight of critical responsibility – as regards the 'unmasking' of certain 'ideological aberrations'. For it is de Man's express view, and one implicit throughout Derrida's work, that these latter achieve their greatest since most natural-seeming effect through a failure, on the part of readers and thinkers, to exercise the kind of vigilant attentiveness to the workings of rhetoric in its suasive aspect that is exemplified in their own deconstructive readings.

Such vigilance acts as a salutary check on the tendency – the 'eudaimonic' tendency, as de Man puts it in his markedly ascetic or Kantian-rigourist tone – to simply go along with those seductive opportunities that language offers for avoiding the labour of critical thought. That is to say, they provide an escape-route from the effort of analysis required to keep thinking alert to the various pitfalls that will otherwise leave it prey to forms of ideological bewitchment. It will then be prone to indulging the false sense of transcendence that results from the seductive (rhetorically insinuated) claim to overcome the various prosaic dichotomies of subject and object, mind and world or phenomenal experience and that which purports to lie beyond the bounds of mere sensory cognition. For de Man, as likewise for Derrida, this is one of the respects in which present-day philosophy – 'continental' and 'analytic' alike – is still striving to work its way through a good many problems and challenges bequeathed by Kant. In particular, it has yet to settle accounts with the legacy of unresolved issues in Kantian epistemology that were first raised in the *Critique of Pure Reason* but then re-addressed, albeit more obliquely, in certain passages of the *Critique of Judgment*. These were issues that Kant regarded as falling safely on the side of humanly attainable knowledge – or the bringing of sensuous intuitions under concepts of understanding – but which also involved, problematically, an appeal to certain knowledge-transcendent 'regulative ideas' that took thinking beyond that relatively secure epistemic ground into speculative regions where knowledge could achieve no cognitive purchase.[71]

De Man pursues the resultant problems through a strenuous critique of that 'aesthetic ideology' which he takes to have exerted a powerful and, in many ways, a powerfully distorting impact on subsequent thought about mind, language and representation. In Derrida's case, they are taken up into a project that again has much in common with various strands of recent analytic philosophy since it can basically be seen as translating the metaphysical and epistemological themes of Kant's original enterprise into a linguistic or logico-semantic register that yields fewer hostages to sceptical fortune. These are essays that pursue an inventive, speculative, highly original yet cogently argued path through that Kantian 'conflict of the faculties' which effectively mapped out in advance a whole range of present-day disputes around the issue of disciplinary competence or whether any one discipline can or should claim priority over others that are then taken to lie within its juridical domain.[72] More specifically, it is an issue as to how far other disciplines should be held accountable to standards of truth or logical rigour laid down by and for philosophy, or how far other branches of philosophy should themselves be subject to the sorts of constraint laid down by the ground rules of formal logic.

The writings of Kant in question range over various boundary disputes – principally between the 'higher' faculties of law, theology and medicine and the 'lower' faculty of philosophy – that need not concern us here save to note that philosophy preserves its right to raise questions of the deepest import with respect to every aspect of human existence just so long as it refrains from asserting any kind of executive warrant or seeking any kind of direct influence over those charged with exerting such power.[73] This trade-off – construed by analogy with Austin's distinction between constative and performative speech-acts – is one that Derrida subjects to an intensely critical yet far from dismissive or condemnatory treatment.[74] For present purposes, its chief relevance is that Kant here rehearses a version of the issue between reason in its 'pure', that is, circumstantially unencumbered exercise, and reason in its various practically engaged, hence more socio-politically powerful and yet – in 'purely' philosophic terms – less accountable modes of deployment. The conflict thus works out as a close analogue – not just a fanciful allegory – of the sorts of dispute that typically arise when it is a question of the relative priority between logic and common sense, or analytic philosophy in its purebred Russellian form and the claims of 'ordinary', natural or everyday language.

Derrida's point is that analysis will get us nowhere if it doesn't remain closely in touch with the various real-world contexts of enquiry that alone provide a basis for its equally various projects of investigation. That those contexts must be thought of as *jointly and inseparably* textual-linguistic-discursive on the one hand and material-concrete-experiential on the other – that it is an error and the source of endless philosophical bewilderment to suppose otherwise – is the true (intended) sense of that notorious but widely and mischievously misconstrued passage where he declares that 'there is nothing outside the text' (more precisely: that 'there is no "outside" to the text').[75] What must otherwise sound like a far-out textualist variation on Kantian idealist themes can then be understood rightly, that is, as a thesis that stands squarely opposed to any such doctrine since it holds on the contrary that thought and language cannot be conceived as developing, functioning or possessing any of their properly distinctive attributes except on condition that they do refer to such (for the most part) mind- and language-independent realities. So much is plain enough if one considers the variety of referential-thematic concerns – so many as to overstretch the capacity of even his most devoted exegetes – that Derrida took up across four decades of intensely productive writing. Any notion of his having gone along with the wilder claims of post-structuralist theory and elected (impossibly) to sever the tie between signifier and signifier or, more aptly, sign and referent comes to grief on the plain evidence that Derrida is writing very pointedly and forcefully *about* these topics, issues and events. Moreover, his way of doing so is one that discovers certain problematical aspects of them that are not (*pace* Searle) just so many products of an errant or perversely skewed deconstructive approach but which pertain to the matter in hand as a matter of strict demonstrative warrant.

In short, deconstruction engages with language in a productive and critical way *just to the extent* that language is taken to possess a referential function simply in virtue of its normal informative-communicative power. However, it must also be taken to possess a power of revealing the symptomatic blind spots or aberrant passages where that function is subject to logical-conceptual strain by an emergent disparity between what the author manifestly means to say and what the covert logic of their argument constrains them obliquely to acknowledge or concede.[76] This makes it necessary that any properly deconstructive reading – any reading with a claim to adequate conceptual rigour – will likewise acknowledge the binding force, at least up to a point, of theoretical (constative) criteria whereby both to specify the relevant norms of veridical discourse and to pinpoint the stage at which those norms encounter a textual-thematic crux that resists being held to a classical account or brought within the compass of a bivalent true/false logic. The criteria in question have to do with truth-conditions or standards of validity for the conduct of rational enquiry that can be relinquished only at the cost of inviting the above-mentioned charge of manifest self-refutation. Yet, they are also prerequisite to the business of showing how certain kinds of text – ranging all the way from Husserl's meditations on the origins of geometry to writings of a primarily historical, ethical or political character – may generate extreme complications of sense that could not be discovered or even entertained as a matter of conceptual possibility without their having first been subject to the most exacting process of analysis on bivalent terms. Quite simply, any striking out into country beyond the safe confines of classical logic will need to do so from the relatively secure base-camp of a first reading – or a first stage in the reading-procedure – that accepts those terms not only as its point of departure but also thereafter as its constant point of reference. They act as a salutary check against the possible temptation of an ultra-textualist (whether Rortian or 'literary') approach that would exploit the hermeneutic or interpretative freedoms opened up by the lifting of such logical constraints but would thereby forego any genuine claim to conceptual, philosophical or critical insight.

Here we might recall that well-known passage from *Of Grammatology* where Derrida reflects on the way that deconstruction is obliged to take stock of an author's express or implied intent while nonetheless allowing that texts may harbour some deviant or 'supplementary' logic that blocks any straightforward appeal to intention as the lodestone of responsible commentary. Thus '[t]o recognize and respect all its classical exigencies is not easy and requires all the instruments of traditional criticism. Without this recognition and this respect, critical production would risk developing in any direction at all and authorize itself to say almost anything'. However, as the passage very pointedly goes on, 'this indispensable guardrail has always only protected, it has never opened, a reading'.[77] The same passage could just as well apply to the role of bivalent logic insofar as it functions not merely as a handy heuristic device or methodological convenience but rather as the sole means by which deconstruction is able to establish both the way that certain texts disrupt or complicate that logic and its own entitlement – or working credentials – as a discourse equipped to reveal just how such anomalies occur. So there is nothing in the least contradictory about Derrida's maintaining a principled regard for the requirements of classical truth/falsehood while discovering bivalence to meet its limits and give way to more complex ('deviant', 'paraconsistent', 'supplementary' or 'parergonal') logics when confronted with various problematical passages in texts.

Here it is worth noting – by way of close analogy – that one major development in modern mathematics and logic involved the seemingly bizarre combination of extreme formal rigour with an upshot that pointed to the inbuilt limits of any such reasoning. This was Kurt Gödel's famous undecidability theorem to the effect that any formal system of sufficient complexity to generate the axioms of (say) elementary arithmetic or first-order logic could be shown to contain at least one axiom which could not be proved within that system or by using its own logical-conceptual resources.[78] What is strange about this is that the theorem is itself set out and proved by means of a highly complex and extended formal-logical sequence of argument which cannot but depend upon just those resources that it shows to fall short of such probative warrant or ultimate demonstrative force. Gödel espoused an objectivist and classical – in this context what amounts to a Platonist – approach since he thought that it offered the only way to save his argument from just that charge of manifest self-refutation as well as affording the only adequate ontology and theory of truth for mathematics and the formal sciences. Unless it were the case that there existed truths beyond the limits of purely formal demonstration or proof, and unless our minds could have access to them by some non-empirical means, then there could be no accounting for our grasp of a theorem which requires such a highly elaborate structure of logico-mathematical argument yet the truth of which, on its own submission, cannot be derived by any purely axiomatic-deductive or rigorously formalized means.

This Platonist claim has been widely discussed by logicians and philosophers of mathematics, and is very far from enjoying general acceptance. However, it is one that has a clear advantage over rival (e.g. intuitionist, formalist, constructivist or fictionalist) accounts according to which mathematical 'truth' is best treated as merely a convenient *façon de parler* or else most plausibly construed in anti-realist terms as coming down to a matter of epistemic warrant or whatever lies within the scope and limits of our current-best methods of proof.[79] That advantage lies in realism's making due allowance for the always possible discrepancy between truth and knowledge, a discrepancy to which we can find ample witness by consulting the entire history to date of advances in knowledge – that is, of progressive approximations to truth – in every discipline where the question arises as to whether what presently counts as knowledge is objectively or veridically so.[80] It is here, with respect to the primacy of truth and the formal procedures thereby entailed, that we can best understand the elusive yet profound kinship between Derrida's and Badiou's projects. Indeed, I would venture to define this as the hallmark of a properly deconstructive reading as opposed to one which exploits a vaguely Derridean rhetoric of *différance* or, on occasion, a quasi-Gödelian rhetoric of undecidability. The former kind of reading entails a claim to discern or detect certain non-manifest textual structures – most often logico-semantic structures leading to a point of classically irresolvable aporia or contradiction – that are demonstrably there in the text under scrutiny even though they had hitherto passed unnoticed when subject to other, less exacting modes of analysis. The latter kind, conversely, makes liberal use of those terms and their various cognates but does so in a loose and approximative way, or through a broadly analogical (even metaphoric) mode of thought that lacks anything remotely comparable to Derrida's practice of close-reading as a form of immanent critique.

Of course its proponents could object on the grounds that Derrida has surely shown, in 'White Mythology' and elsewhere, how the distinction between concept and metaphor – along with those between reason and rhetoric, philosophy and literature and sundry affiliated pairs – falls prey to a deconstructive reading that would challenge philosophy's self-appointed role as a discourse uniquely privileged in virtue of its logical probity and truth-telling warrant.[81] However, quite apart from his numerous avowals of unswerving commitment to philosophy as a vocation and discipline of thought, it is also very clear from an attentive reading of 'White Mythology' that Derrida in fact goes out of his way to disown or repudiate any such account of his work. So far from simply 'deconstructing' the concept/metaphor distinction – at least in the vulgar-deconstructionist sense of 'inverting', 'rejecting' or just plain 'rubbishing' – his essay goes a long and highly complex argumentative way around to make the point that we should have no critical resources for raising this question of metaphor's role in the texts of philosophy were it not for philosophy's having provided every last concept and category whereby to raise it or render it a topic capable of intelligent, focused and productive discussion. Indeed, there is an obvious affinity between the travesty of Derrida's essay which takes him to hold that 'all concepts come down to metaphors', that 'logic is just a sub-species of rhetoric', or that 'philosophy is just another kind of literature' and the Fish-derived or Rortian neo-pragmatist idea of rhetoric which recognizes only its persuasive (illocutionary) aspect and not its other, epistemo-critical dimension. It is here that Derrida is most closely in accord with de Man's cardinal precept: that reading be conceived as a process of 'argument' with, in and through the text that is being read and also – strictly correlative to that – with, in and through the text that is being written by way of critical exegesis.

Such a reading is possible only on certain rather stringent conditions which are most clearly and strikingly exemplified in Derrida's early and middle-period work. Among them is that finely held, sometimes tensile or knife-edge balance between a genuine respect for the demands of scholarly, philological and interpretative rigour – along with a due regard for whatever can be fairly conjectured in respect of authorial intentions – and the need for that precise degree of exegetical departure from orthodox (fideist) protocols of reading which opens the way to fresh sources of critical insight. This in turn involves a certain implicit ontology of the text or conception of its rightful claim on the reader-interpreter, one that holds out (again *contra* Fish) for its capacity to mean something other than that which might be wished upon it by the reader or his/her 'interpretive community' and which thus maintains that crucial margin wherein deviant or non-canonical readings can establish their claim to attention. Here we should recall that a concern with such questions of textual ontology was something that Derrida imbibed early on from the intense studies of Husserlian phenomenology that figured centrally in his unfinished doctoral thesis on 'The Ideality of the Literary Object' and that continued to occupy his thinking despite – or more likely by reason of – the complications that arose through its subsequent exposure to deconstructive analysis.[82] What is most relevant in this context is the fact (one that Derrida often states as a matter of principle but which is also borne out in a practical way through the detailed conduct of his readings) that texts make certain demands upon those who would claim to comprehend, interpret or indeed deconstruct them and moreover that the kinds of constraint in question are none the less stringent when the upshot is to challenge or contest some mainstream-orthodox mode of understanding.

In which case there is clearly an onus on any competent, qualified or good-faith interpreter to acknowledge the text – if not perhaps the 'work', since by now that term is often thought to bear unwanted connotations – as a multiplex, challenging, often contradictory, ontologically elusive but nonetheless *independently existent* verbal construct that cannot be wished away through some assertion of creative autonomy on the reader's part. Such assertions have been issued with great regularity in recent years and range all the way from Roland Barthes's celebration of the 'death of the author', through Foucault's more historically nuanced reflections on the shifting role of 'the author' as a function of various discursive regimes, to Stanley Fish's dissolution of text and author alike into mere products of this or that 'interpretive community' which will always willy-nilly project them in its own image.[83] That Derrida comes out firmly against this relativization of textual meaning to readerly or interpretative predilection is one sure sign of his standing apart from those post-structuralist, postmodernist or neo-pragmatist trends that have worked so hard to promote it. To that extent his is an objectivist conception of the text – of its status and demands on the reader – which does have significant features in common with a realist ontology in the physical or formal sciences, despite all the caveats that need to be entered when proposing an analogy between such otherwise disparate orders of discourse.

# VI

In philosophy of science, this whole line of argument can be turned around, as it often is by anti-realists, and refurbished as the so-called sceptical meta-induction according to which it is the merest of delusions to suppose that science is closer to truth now than at any stage in its previous history.[84] After all, so it is said, if we are now apt to think that scientists have been either flat wrong or very partially informed with respect to the vast majority of theories, hypotheses and even confident truth-claims put forward throughout the history of the physical sciences to date then how can we suppose – without manifest hubris – that our own situation is decisively different? To which realists just as often respond that this argument is self-stultifying since the sceptical meta-induction depends upon our now having adequate warrant to claim – as a matter of rationally informed hindsight – that those previous beliefs didn't amount to knowledge or that the earlier state of knowledge was limited in certain to us now manifest respects. Besides, they may add, were it not for this character of science as a cumulative, truth-oriented and (for the most part) epistemically progressive enterprise, we should have to count the various working technologies that it has hitherto managed to devise as so many products of 'cosmic coincidence' or sheer serendipity.[85]

Of course, this disagreement goes as deep as any in epistemology and philosophy of science and is therefore unlikely – as with most such disputes – to achieve resolution through the sudden arrival of some knock-down argument on either side. Still, it is one that at any rate divides the contending parties along clear-cut philosophical lines and thus allows for meaningful debate not only in those disciplinary quarters but also with regard to the deconstructive claim, as stated most forcefully by de Man, that 'reading is an argument . . . because it has to go against the grain of what one would want to happen in the name of what has to happen'.[86] Moreover, in his carefully specified terms, 'this is the same as saying that reading is an epistemological event prior to being an ethical or aesthetic value. This does not mean that there can be a true reading, but that no reading is conceivable in which the question of its truth or falsehood is not primarily involved'.[87] These statements make the point in a typically forthright, even (some would say) authoritarian or doctrinaire style. All the same they can be seen as asserting what is likewise implicit throughout Derrida's work, in particular, those earlier writings where the emphasis falls more squarely on just how it is that texts can be found to put up resistance – formal, structural, logico-semantic and conceptual resistance – to readings that would seek, wittingly or not, to conceal or dissimulate the various anomalies revealed by a deconstructive account. It is here that issues of interpretative theory join up with those debates in epistemology and philosophy of science that turn on the question whether truth can be conceived, in realist terms, as always potentially surpassing or transcending our present-best or even best attainable state of knowledge. Or again, it is the issue – much discussed by philosophers in recent years – as to whether it can make any kind of sense to think of some optimum achievable state of knowledge as nonetheless potentially falling short of, or coming apart from, objective (i.e. mind-independent or recognition-transcendent) truth.[88]

One useful way of linking up those debates with the kinds of issue typically posed by the deconstructive reading of texts is to consider the role played by thought-experiments, that is to say, by fictive or imaginary goings-on in the 'laboratory of the mind'.[89] These are procedures that can act not only as handy 'intuition-pumps' (in Daniel Dennett's equally handy phrase) but also, on occasion, as the means of some decisive conceptual advance that could not at the time have been achieved by any other method. Such instances range historically all the way from Galileo's classic refutation of the received (Aristotelian) doctrine that the rate of gravitationally induced free fall would vary proportionately with the weight of different bodies to those thought-experiments conducted by Einstein in order to establish the theories of special and general relativity, or those devised by Einstein, Bohr and Schrödinger to investigate the implications of quantum physics.[90] What they all have in common – a feature exemplified most strikingly in Galileo's case – is the deployment at some crucial stage of a *reductio ad absurdum* argument which shows the existing or prevailing (soon-to-be-rejected) doctrine to harbour a pair of contradictory entailments which, once revealed, are sufficient to discredit that doctrine and open the way to its plainly superior since non-self-contradictory successor.

We have seen already how this mode of thought is integral to Badiou's deployment of set-theoretical resources, as well as his commitment to a realist (or anti-constructivist) conception of truth in mathematics and elsewhere. It is also identical, in point of formal argumentative structure, to the strategy adopted by de Man in his various critiques of 'aesthetic ideology', or the way in which non-natural structures like those of language, culture or society are passed off under metaphoric cover of a naturalized (quasi-organic) process of growth and development.[91] That is to say, such resistance here takes the form of a critical rhetoric – an 'epistemology of tropes' – that derives its deconstructive or demystifying force from the discovery of textual contradictions, aporias or logical non-sequiturs that had hitherto passed unnoticed through the power of received ideas to impose their own, canonically endorsed or conformist habits of response. So likewise with Derrida's practice of drawing attention to the various kinds of anomaly, discrepancy, paradox or suchlike indices of deep-laid logico-semantic tension that are there to be exposed – 'there' in the text, as he is keen to establish, rather than projected onto it – through a sufficiently alert deconstructive reading.

Here we might recall that crucially important passage in *Of Grammatology* concerning what he sees as the complex, over-determined, sometimes conflictive yet at just those moments symptomatically revealing order of relationship between author's intent and textual meaning. Thus, to repeat, 'the writer writes *in* a language and *in* a logic whose proper system, laws, and life his discourse by definition cannot dominate absolutely' since '[h]e uses them only by letting himself, after a fashion and up to a point, be governed by the system'.[92] Nevertheless, as Derrida also makes clear, the scope of that linguistic or discursive governance can be grasped only insofar as we register the countervailing degree to which an author's expressive or purposive intent is able to work both *within and against* the 'system' and thereby convey something not laid down in advance, or not always already to be found among the standing beliefs of some existent Fishian 'interpretive community'. Hence his stress on the requirement that a deconstructive reading be at least as respectful of authorial intention as those other, more orthodox or fideist readings that are naturally apt to proclaim their superior credentials in this respect. Thus '[t]o recognize and respect all [these] classical exigencies is not easy and requires all the instruments of traditional criticism'. However the effort is strictly indispensable since '[w]ithout this recognition and this respect, critical production would risk developing in any direction at all and authorize itself to say almost anything'.[93] Here one might note the implicit rebuke to any line of thought, like that of Barthes and his post-structuralist disciples, that plainly rejoices in the 'death of the author' and – what is taken to follow from this – the reader's being henceforth 'authorized' to assume just the kind of creative-expressive license that once belonged strictly to the author *ipse* as source and guarantor of meaning.[94]

As I have said, it was Derrida's intensive early engagement with issues on the disputed border between phenomenology and structuralism that seems to have left him with a sharpened awareness of this question concerning the scope and limits of interpretative freedom or, more precisely, the kind and extent of that margin for an immanent (deconstructive) critique that both respected and went beyond the requirements of a strict regard for authorial intent. Indeed, the ambiguity of the phrase 'went beyond' in that last sentence – as between 'exceeded or surpassed according to the same criteria' or 'established other, more exacting or rigorously critical standards of right reading' – is one that perfectly catches the double (though by no means contradictory) claim implicit throughout Derrida's work. The above-mentioned passages from *Of Grammatology* have been cited to various effect by commentators with equally various ideas about the scope and limits of legitimate interpretation.[95] What emerges clearly enough – *contra* the adepts of infinitized 'freeplay' or unrestrained hermeneutic license – is Derrida's conviction that truly productive critical reading can take place only on condition of respecting those 'classical exigencies' that must be thought to include a certain, albeit qualified regard for the claims of authorial intent and a readiness, where needed, to employ the best 'instruments' of philology or textual scholarship. However what the passage also evokes – unavoidably so if one construes it in relation to his *modus operandi* in this most ambitious and tightly organized of Derrida's early texts – is the jointly constraining and liberating power of those structural, conceptual and logico-semantic complexities that a deconstructive reading seeks to reveal.

Taken out of context it might well appear to be the statement of a cautious, even shuffling and evasive middle-ground position. Thus it seems delicately poised between a somewhat conservative hermeneutic outlook acknowledging the need to respect authorial intentions up to a point and, on the other hand, a likewise moderate or qualified endorsement of the new-found interpretative licence on offer from a typecast deconstructive (for which read 'textualist' or wholesale libertarian) stance. But when its context is taken more fully into account – that is, its very pointed relevance to Derrida's subsequent readings of Rousseau, Saussure and Lévi-Strauss in *Of Grammatology* – then this imputation becomes hard to sustain. Instead, one is likely to conclude that it is not so much the 'indispensable guardrail' of straightforward respect for authorial intent that keeps interpretation from going wildly astray but rather – as those readings show with such consummate subtlety and skill – the complex intertwining of overt and covert sense, manifest and latent implicature, or intentional purport and counter-intentional import. The 'indispensable guardrail' of authorial *vouloir-dire* is best envisaged as a kind of protective barrier standing well to one side of a zone within which the most significant constraints are those that define exactly that margin of play – in the high-precision engineering-related rather the pseudo-deconstructive ludic sense – which engenders the kindred Derridean logics of supplementarity, parergonality, *différance* and their various cognates. Thus it simply refuses the terms laid down by that all-too-familiar notion of a choice between respecting authorial intention as a kind of quasi-Kantian injunction to treat the text as an end-in-itself rather than a means to the interpreter's revisionist self-gratification and rejecting that idea *tout court* in favour of an outlook of free-for-all hermeneutic license.

However what chiefly concerns us here is not so much Derrida's way of re-conceiving this particular false dilemma but rather his address to a distinct though closely related issue. This is the question of just how it is that critical reading can discover truths about a text – and also truths about that which the text takes as its topic-domain – that may potentially transcend both anything plausibly attributable to the author's conscious intent and anything that has yet figured in that author's reception-history. Here again there is a more than suggestive link with the epistemological issue between realism and anti-realism or the current debate – most often addressed in logico-semantic terms – as to whether truth can possibly transcend the compass of expert opinion, optimal judgement or best attainable knowledge.[96] Moreover, it suggests another main reason for Derrida's outraged response to Searle concerning the latter's casual suggestion that standards of rigorous (classical or bivalent) logic ought to be relaxed in the context of speech-act theory since the latter requires a more nuanced, flexible and context-sensitive approach.[97]

What Derrida finds so objectionable here – so downright 'shocking', especially when it comes from a self-appointed spokesman for the 'analytic' virtue of conceptual precision against the 'continental' vice of wilful obscurity – is that Searle fails to distinguish with anything like sufficient clarity between the various modes of speech-act usage or implicature as they occur in everyday language and those same modes as they figure in the discourse of speech-act theory. He seems to require that this easy-going recommendation extend to the domain of philosophical semantics or philosophy of language insofar as they treat the kinds and conditions of performative utterance, rather than restricting it to the first-order, natural-language domain where speech-acts can (supposedly) be known to function in a straightforward communicative way. With respect to this latter – 'ordinary language', as Austin dubbed it, whatever its more *extra*ordinary aspects when viewed close-up in Austin's (or Derrida's) manner – there are no doubt large allowances to be made for the fuzziness of certain distinctions or the difficulty (even impossibility) of holding such everyday talk to standards of clear-cut logico-semantic precision. However, as Derrida protests against Searle with more than a touch of ironic relish, there is no conceivable justification for counting philosophy – especially analytic philosophy of language – as subject to the same inherent limits on its scope for the precise articulation of its working concepts and categories. If he comes out strongly in defence of such standards – and in a way that is liable to disconcert those who take him to have 'deconstructed' them once and for all – his purpose is neither just to outflank Searle, nor to flummox his numerous detractors on the analytic side, nor again (though this is somewhat nearer the mark) to stake out his distance from both main parties in that pseudo-confrontation of 'analytic' rigour versus 'continental' license. Rather it is to situate his own work in precisely that region of logico-semantic-conceptual space where there exists the possibility of truths that surpass any presently available means of clear articulation yet whose failure to achieve such overt form may be signalled by the various tensions, non-sequiturs, dilemmas, aporias and other symptomatic blind-spots that Derrida is so adroit at bringing out.

This is why, in the above-cited passage, he specifies a strict regard for the standards of classical (bivalent) logic as a precondition for the validity of any claim that a deconstructive reading is able to 'transform and complicate' the protocols of that same classical logic. It must start out by observing those protocols and only at the point of maximal resistance – as they prove incapable of accounting for certain anomalous or recalcitrant features of the text in hand – be willing to suspend them and explore alternative (i.e. non-classical, non-bivalent or paraconsistent) logics. It is also what unites him with Badiou on the side of a basically realist approach to issues of truth and interpretation. That is, both thinkers maintain the possibility (indeed the conceptual necessity) that some statements, propositions or hypotheses be thought to possess a truth-value beyond whatever is capable of recognition on received or currently accepted terms. More than that, their truth-conditions must be somehow legible – 'there' to be discerned though not in any mode of direct, explicit or punctual presentation – through a critical analysis which thus brings about a changed understanding of how those terms should be construed. If truth-conditions are epistemically or evidentially unconstrained – if indeed (as the realist holds) they transcend the conditions for assertoric warrant or 'truth' to the best of our knowledge – then this need not be taken (as the anti-realist would have it) to show realism up as an unsustainable, self-contradictory or strictly nonsensical position. Rather it shows, in a manner analogous to Badiou's mathematically based arguments, that when truth exceeds knowledge or finds no place in the range of accredited truth-procedures, it may then assume a 'subtractive' dimension whereby its very absence generates tensions that can serve as pointers or symptomatic indices of that which eludes our present-best efforts of cognitive, intellectual or probative grasp.[98]

# VII

At this stage, it is worth noting that one major bone of contention between realists and anti-realists in philosophy of mathematics, logic and the formal sciences is the issue as to whether those disciplines have need of – or should properly find any place for – the classical axiom of double-negation-elimination. This is the principle commonly expressed as 'two negatives make a positive', or the jointly logical and grammatical rule that to insert two 'nots' or equivalent negating terms into any given sentence is to have them cancel out and thus restore the sentence to a straightforward assertion of whatever was originally stated or affirmed. It is the basis of arguments that work through *reductio ad absurdum*, that is, by means of a demonstrative (logical) sequence of reasoning to the effect that any denial or rejection of statement *x* has a plainly absurd or unacceptable consequence and hence (by double-negation-elimination) that *x* should be affirmed. Conversely it is maintained by those, like Dummett, who espouse an intuitionist or anti-realist approach to mathematics that the axiom need not and should not be upheld precisely on account of its conducing to a thesis which itself – in their view – goes against certain basic principles of right reason.[99] Chief among them, as we have seen, is the intuitionist/anti-realist precept that truth cannot intelligibly be supposed to transcend or exceed the bounds of whatever can be known, discovered, formally proved, empirically established or otherwise borne out by the best investigative methods or techniques to hand. On this account, the process of enquiry should not be envisaged as exploring regions of objective, pre-existent though hitherto unexplored conceptual or natural-scientific terrain but rather as opening up new paths of thought that in turn open up – indeed which create – new landscapes for the inventive designer-explorer. In which case there is clearly no need or room for the objectivist idea that thinking can find out truths beyond its present-best knowledge by following out certain logical implications that hold good despite and against our current state of ignorance concerning them.

It is here, I submit, that Derrida's work poses the greatest challenge to received ways of thinking in epistemology and philosophy of science. It is best seen as a form of highly detailed and sophisticated thought-experimental reasoning conducted in and through the encounter with texts which effectively constitute just such a challenge through their turning out to harbour unresolved problems, aporias or conceptual anomalies that act as a spur to otherwise strictly inconceivable advances in knowledge. Of course there has been much debate between those who affirm and those who deny that thought-experiments can deliver something more than purely analytic, that is, self-evident but wholly uninformative truths and can actually establish substantive theses with respect to various scientific and other regions of enquiry.[100] Starting out with Kant's arguments for the existence of synthetic *a priori* knowledge, this debate has typically swung back and forth between, on the one hand, assertions that such real-world applicable knowledge may indeed be achieved by means of speculative procedures run off-line in the 'laboratory of the mind' and, on the other, assertions that any results thus obtained cannot be more than disguised tautologies or the product of concealed definitions smuggled in under cover of some seemingly innocuous premise. What Derrida shows through close-readings of singular tenacity and also – *pace* Searle and other detractors – extreme conceptual precision is the possibility of finding out truths that cannot be expressed (i.e. which elude any overt, articulate and logically consistent presentation) in the text under analysis. Moreover, those truths are by no means confined to some purely linguistic or intra-discursive register of sense but must rather be seen as possessing a highly specific referential dimension and hence as pointing to genuine complexities or unresolved issues with respect to the given subject-domain. Beyond that – as emerges with increasing clarity in his later work – they articulate problems intrinsic to certain kinds of discourse on certain topics, those (such as justice, hospitality, forgiveness, friendship, democracy or cosmopolitanism) which analytic philosophers might recognize as belonging to the class of 'essentially contested concepts'.[101]

For Derrida, as likewise for many of the thinkers who have deployed this resonant phrase, such concepts are problematical not solely on account of their complex or elusive semantic content but in virtue of just that referential linkage with matters of real-world ethical, social, political, historical and not least (if one considers his writings on Rousseau and Lévi-Strauss) anthropological concern. It is for this reason chiefly that deconstruction can be characterized – *pace* Fish – as a negative theory but one with very real and potentially far-reaching consequences. (Whether or not it is properly described as 'anti-foundationalist' in anything like Fish's – or Rorty's – stock usage of that term is a complicated issue which need not detain us here.[102]) Nor should it be thought that his approaching these topics by way of texts from Plato to Husserl and Austin rather than by 'direct' engagement with them is itself a sure sign that Derrida is out to create extra problems of a purely exegetical or hyper-induced character. More specifically, it is often taken as evidence that he seeks to spin some ingenious web of multiple conflicting significations which then serves – in typically idealist fashion – to block any reference to topics or events 'outside' the all-encompassing (or all-consuming) realm of textuality. In his later writings, Derrida was at some pains to repudiate this misinterpretation of passages that seemed to espouse such an extreme anti-realist or ultra-constructivist view but which should properly be taken – so he now averred – to 'complicate' the nature and workings of referential language rather than deny that language could ever achieve anything more than an endlessly deferred simulacrum of reference.[103]

If such misapprehensions are perhaps understandable when the passages in question (as very often happens) are cited out of context, it is less so when the standard charges of idealism, solipsism, modish *linguisterie*, textualist mystification and so forth issue from readers laying claim to acquaintance with more than a handful of dubiously representative quotes. I have put the case here that Derrida's work does have significant implications for philosophy of language and logic, and that these result mainly – *contra* the dominant consensus among admirers and detractors alike – from its adopting what amounts to a critical-realist stance towards both the texts and the topic-domains with which those texts themselves engage. Deconstruction is very often assumed to belong squarely on the side of anti-realism, constructivism, cultural-linguistic relativism, irrationalism or a composite bugbear that incorporates all these and more. That in truth it belongs very firmly elsewhere is a point that finds plentiful evidence in Derrida's work but which again has been missed with curious tenacity by those ranged for and against it in various disciplinary quarters.

# Tractatus Mathematico-Politicus:
# Badiou's *Being and Event*

## I

In this chapter, I hope to persuade a certain group of readers – those with an interest in philosophy of mathematics, logic or the formal sciences and (no doubt a largely overlapping community) those of an analytic orientation – that they should make themselves better acquainted with Badiou's work. My purpose is two-fold: to offer those readers some further points of purchase on Badiou's extraordinarily far-reaching and ambitious project while also suggesting that this might signal a way forward from some of the more sterile or doldrum-prone regions of debate within mainstream analytic philosophy. It strikes me that those areas – among them the issue between realism and anti-realism as normally framed and the problem (or pseudo-problem) from Wittgenstein about what it means correctly to follow a rule – have been trodden into ruts over the past two decades and are unlikely to produce anything much in the way of philosophic insight.[1] More than that: their very nature or the manner of that framing – its conformity to certain (in my view highly cramping) presuppositions with regard to the proper aims and scope of philosophical enquiry – is such as to ensure that the debate will become increasingly narrow and self-occupied to the point where there sets in something like a law of sharply diminishing returns.

In these quarters, the received idea of what counts as a valid, constructive or philosophically reputable contribution to the field is one that has its source in the notion of all philosophy as aspiring to the condition of the analytic statement or the wholly self-evident (since purely tautological) proposition. As a result, philosophy of mathematics in that locally dominant tradition has tended to focus on conceptual issues which have less to do with the kinds of problems that typically attract the interest of working mathematicians than with the kinds of problems that mathematics is typically seen to pose for philosophers with their own distinctive agenda to pursue. Hence this near-obsessive concern with topics, like those mentioned above, that fall very much within its comfort zone, since they readily allow for that shift of focus from issues that have to be engaged mathematically, that is, through a distinctive, highly formalized but nonetheless creative or inventive mode of exploratory thought to issues that belong to the stock-in-trade of a certain philosophical discourse. Indeed one has only to consult any recent collection of essays on the subject to see how remarkably uniform they are – despite some otherwise sizeable differences of view – in their sense of where the discipline's centre of gravity lies and their assurance of raising the right sorts of question in the right (philosophically relevant) way.[2] So it is that the discussion comes to turn almost exclusively on matters epistemological or logico-semantic, that is, on topics that have been at the heart of philosophical enquiry throughout its history from Plato through Descartes to Kant and latterly (following the 'linguistic turn') from Frege and Wittgenstein down. To be sure, such concerns are by no means inherently alien to mathematicians and may occupy some part of any time that they might take off from the business of actually doing mathematics and choose to spend reflecting, in a general way, on the epistemic status or the assertoric warrant of their various doings and sayings. However, they are likely to regard such reflection as very much a sideline or a passing distraction from that other primary business, and not as in any way contributing to it through the kind of actively participant role – the *engagement with* mathematical problems rather than the curiously disengaged process of *thinking about* them – that would involve a very different kind of relationship between mathematics and philosophy.

What analytic philosophers most stand to gain from a reading of Badiou on the conceptual revolution (or the series of such revolutions) brought about by Cantor's discovery of the multiple orders of infinity and by kindred advances in post-Cantorian set theory is a heightened sense of just how creative and productive that relationship might yet become.[3] In part, this has to do with Badiou's regular practice of working through those stages of advance – for the benefit of less mathematically clued-up readers – with a care for detail and a power of vivid re-creative grasp that finds few rivals in the analytic literature. One way to characterize that difference is to say that his work holds out an answer to the problem so insistently posed by Derrida in his early writings on Husserlian transcendental phenomenology.[4] This is the question as to how we can conceive mathematical truths on the one hand (in realist, objectivist or Platonist terms) as absolute ideal objectivities – that is, as recognition-transcendent or 'epistemically unconstrained' – while on the other they are conceived as making themselves available (sometimes at any rate) to the ways and means of human investigative thought. Where Derrida treats this as an antinomy – a philosophically productive yet in the end irresolvable conflict of commitments or priorities – Badiou typically takes it as a starting point and constant source of motivating energy for the kind of advance that typifies certain breakthrough events in the history of mathematics, namely those that 'turn paradox into concept'. Moreover, he regards it as having close analogues in other, for example, natural-scientific, political and artistic modes of intellectual-creative endeavour. Indeed, what is required, if the reference to mathematics is to have any kind of formal validity or probative warrant, is something far more exacting and precise than a mere analogy between those other subject areas and certain well-established mathematical procedures, namely (for Badiou) the possibility of reckoning with the multiple orders of infinity that were opened up to investigation in the wake of Cantor's inaugural discovery.[5] Rather it is a question of structural homologies that provide for a rigorous thinking-through of issues in the topic areas concerned, that is to say, issues of their constitution – ontologically speaking – as domains for further exploratory treatment or investigative thought. Yet this also provides for a heightened grasp of those utterly singular events, in mathematics as likewise in politics and the arts, which can be seen to have marked a decisive break with the kinds of ontological commitment embodied in received or orthodox ways of thinking.

This distinction is very much at the heart of Badiou's project and may rightfully be said to mark his own book *Being and Event* as an occurrence of just that ontologically ground-breaking order.[6] Hence the other main aspect of his work that issues a powerful challenge to the normative values and assumptions of much analytic philosophy. This has to do with the relationship between knowledge and truth or the scope and limits of thought at any given stage in its development and the standard by which it would (counterfactually) be judged or to which it might (conceivably) be held accountable in the absence of just those limits. Badiou's major claim, in short, is that philosophy of mathematics has sold mathematics grievously short by focusing on questions like: What is mathematical knowledge? How can we be certain that we have it? What can or must be the nature of mathematical entities such as numbers, sets or classes if indeed we can have knowledge of them? It has thus been prevented from raising questions with regard to the primary (ontological as opposed to epistemological) issue of truth as that which might always surpass – and perhaps, in consequence of some future advance, eventually be known to have surpassed – a given, temporally indexed state of knowledge or present-best belief concerning it. Moreover, as follows directly from this, even if mathematics never achieved such a breakthrough advance in respect of some particular problem, dilemma or so-far unproven theorem, nevertheless its procedures would be under the necessity of working towards a truth that at present eluded its utmost epistemic grasp.

Thus Badiou takes a robustly objectivist view in maintaining that truth is epistemically unconstrained or – what amounts to the same thing – that it is verification-transcendent in the sense of always potentially exceeding what we are able to prove, demonstrate or even plausibly conjecture regarding it. Such is the character of mathematics as a formal yet always exploratory, rigorous yet incomplete and open-ended process of discovery that enables truth – more precisely: the existence of currently unknown or unknowable truths – to exert a steady pressure for conceptual innovation on account of precisely that existing shortfall in the scope of mathematical knowledge. According to Badiou's strongly realist conception, any genuine 'event' or signal advance towards making good such a deficit will involve both a sense of having newly discovered (rather than created or invented) some hitherto unknown or unproven mathematical truth and also, by no means incompatible with that, a sense of the limits placed upon knowledge by the plain incapacity of human reason to encompass the strictly inexhaustible range of such truths. Although this has been the case ever since the first stirrings of mathematical curiosity, it is brought home with particular vividness by the advent of post-Cantorian set theory. What resulted was the double realization first that thought is indeed capable – as against the previous orthodox view – of working with a concept of positive or actual as distinct from merely virtual or potential infinity and second (yet more counter-intuitive until one gets used to the idea) that there must exist infinite different 'sizes' or orders of infinity beyond that entry-level order equated with the infinite sequence of natural numbers.

## II

Hence Badiou's response to the question of the one and many, or the issue of priority between them, that preoccupied many of the Pre-Socratics, led on to some tortuous or aporetic reasoning in Plato's later dialogues, and thereafter – from Aristotle down – played a prominent role in numerous later philosophical disputes.[7] Quite simply, the multiple is that which both precedes and intrinsically exceeds any order placed upon it by the 'count-as-one', that is to say, any ordering procedure that seeks to contain the multiplicity of being within certain prescribed or stipulative limits. The same principle holds for the relation between 'inconsistent' and 'consistent' multiplicity, the former preceding and exceeding the latter insofar as it can only stand as the result of a procedure for likewise subsuming any discrepant, excessive or unruly multiples under a numeric-conceptual regime that operates according to the count-as-one. All this Badiou takes as a matter of strict axiomatic-deductive reasoning from the basic premises of set theory as developed, refined and extended by a series of thinkers – from Dedekind, Cantor and Gödel to Paul Cohen – who can be seen to have explored their implications not only through stages of ever-increasing logical and conceptual power but also, crucially for his own argumentative purposes, through a process of deepening ontological scope and grasp. Moreover, the implications reach out far beyond the domain of pure mathematics to connect with real-world instances such as the condition of those in a country like present-day France – chief among them the mainly North African *sans-papiers*, or undocumented 'economic migrants'/'illegal immigrants' – who find no place within the count-as-one that effectively decides who shall qualify for treatment as a citizen-subject in good civic–political–social–cultural standing.[8]

　　Here Badiou introduces a number of closely related distinctions – 'inclusion' as opposed to 'belonging', 'parts' as opposed to 'members', the 'state' as distinct from the 'state of the situation' – all of which serve to point up that central, set-theoretically derived contrast between whatever (or whoever) 'counts' in terms of some given mathematical or socio-political order and whatever (or whoever) fails so to count on the same jointly inclusive/exclusionary terms. Along with these, he deploys a range of other concepts to articulate the nature of those radically disruptive 'events' whereby some existing consensus of knowledge in the formal or physical sciences finds itself subject to challenge or some regnant socio-political order finds its stability threatened. Among them are 'excrescence', 'evental site' and 'point of excess', all of which signify the sudden emergence – as it seems, entirely out of the blue and without any prior intimation – of consensus-busting truths or inconvenient facts about the nature of presently existing 'democratic' societies, which may then (if taken up and worked through by 'militants of truth') turn out to have a radically transformative effect on subsequent thought and action. Above all, what Badiou wishes to emphasize is the objective character of any such truth, or perhaps more aptly – since talk of 'objectivity' is always apt to summon up that old Cartesian–Kantian dualist paradigm, most likely in one or other of its present-day linguistified forms – the fact that truth-values are there to be discovered through a faithful or dedicated process of enquiry rather than (as anti-realists and constructivists would have it) brought into being through an act of inventive or creative thought.[9]

Thus in his view, philosophers misrepresent the issue when they take it that mathematical truths must *either* be objective, hence recognition-transcendent, and hence ultimately unknowable *or else* brought back within the scope and limits of human cognition and therefore treated as knowledge-relative or epistemically constrained. That dilemma is a chief talking point of philosophy of mathematics in the mainstream analytic tradition where it has become tied up with kindred debates – often having their proximate source in Wittgenstein – about rule-following and the problem (if so one consents to regard it) of how thought can possibly conceive the existence of truths beyond its present power to ascertain.[10] Here again the idea is that we are stuck with a strictly insoluble quandary since any realist (or typecast 'Platonist') claim to the effect that we can indeed achieve such a thing is inevitably subject to the sceptical rejoinder that it places truth forever beyond the reach of knowledge, or at least beyond the reach of any knowledge that would meet its own impossibly exacting requirements.[11] However, as Badiou does well to remind us, when Plato performed his set-piece demonstration in the *Meno* of how a slave boy could be coaxed to find out for himself the truth of Pythagoras' Theorem, his intention was to show not only the existence of that and other truths as a matter of absolute ideal objectivity but also to exemplify the mind's active power in pursuing them.[12] This he clearly took to involve a passage beyond its present range of conscious deliberative grasp or, as the issue is more often framed nowadays, beyond the epistemic limit-point of what communally counts as accredited knowledge. Thus Plato's aim in constructing this didactic *mise-en-scène* was to bring out the sheer necessity of supposing – *contra* both sides in the current realist/anti-realist stand-off – that mathematical truth can indeed be objective (hence always *potentially* verification-transcendent) and yet lie partially within the compass of human cognitive grasp insofar as mathematicians have discovered some demonstrable means of finding it out or some formally adequate proof-procedure.

Of course, if they have not yet arrived at that stage with respect to a given hypothesis, conjecture or so-far unproven theorem, then its truth or falsity will lie beyond the bounds of presently achieved (perhaps humanly achievable) knowledge. This much will surely be accepted by the realist as quite simply following from what it means to have an adequate grasp of the distinction between truth and knowledge or knowledge and various lower-rank candidates for knowledge such as best opinion, expert belief or consensual judgement among those deemed best qualified to know. However, this is not what the anti-realists and constructivists have in mind when they mount their case against (typecast) 'Platonism' on the grounds of its involving a nonsensical or self-contradictory pair of premises. What they want us to accept is the idea that realism or objectivism about mathematics involves the jointly self-refuting, since flatly, contradictory claims (1) that there are unknown mathematical truths and (2) that we can know this since they lie within our powers of demonstrative proof or scope of epistemic warrant.[13] But, as scarcely needs saying, the realist is committed to no such ridiculous belief but rather to what he or she takes as the default position in mathematics and other branches of the formal as well as the physical sciences, namely that we know there are things we don't know even if – again as a matter of plain self-evidence – we don't and cannot presently know what they are or attach any definite truth-value to hypothetical statements concerning them. Although the anti-realist case would seem nothing more than a blatant confusion of these two quite distinct claims – the one downright absurd, the other straightforwardly acceptable – it is a line of thought that can be seen to undergird a whole range of kindred arguments from Dummettian intuitionism in philosophy of mathematics to the wilder forms of postmodernist or Rortian 'strong-descriptivist' thinking.[14]

However, there is absolutely no reason to accept the pseudo-dilemma thus forced upon a realist or objectivist outlook which in truth involves no such absurdity. One way of making the point is simply to lay out the anti-realist case, as I have done just above, and then put the question as to whether it constitutes a genuine challenge to mathematical realism or whether that challenge should not be thought to rest on a mistaken – even sophistical – turn of argument. However, there is room for other, more formal demonstrations to similar effect conducted on the home ground of first-order mathematical procedure rather than in the hinterlands (mathematically speaking) of epistemology or philosophy of mind. It is here that Badiou provides an object-lesson in the use of certain procedures drawn from the repertoire of post-Cantorian set theory so as to refute the sorts of anti-realist doctrine maintained by those philosophers of mathematics – along with similarly minded thinkers in other branches of philosophy – whose predisposed strength of doctrinal adherence tends to dictate their approach to issues in that primary domain. More specifically, he shows by a close and detailed working-through of certain major set-theoretical developments how it is possible for truth to surpass the limits of presently attainable knowledge and yet, by its very absence from the range of existing conceptual resources, serve to indicate those unresolved problems or symptomatic points of strain where a future breakthrough has its place marked out in advance.[15] Chief among these are the concepts of 'forcing' and 'the generic' devised by Paul Cohen as a means to give formal expression to precisely this power of mathematical thinking to reach out beyond its present-best state of achieved (or achievable) knowledge and gain an intimation of truths which can as yet figure only as inducements to a further exercise of reason in its jointly speculative and axiomatic-deductive modes.[16] Those concepts between them define the condition of possibility for that otherwise strictly inconceivable procedure whereby thought is able to envisage not merely the vague or shapeless possibility of some such future advance but the locus of a presently existing shortfall in knowledge to which it will come as the sole adequate solution.[17]

Badiou sees this procedure as finding its most cogent and powerful since formally articulated instance in the case of mathematical thought and also as having a much wider application to issues in the physical sciences, politics and art. What it gives us to understand with regard to such (on the conventional estimate) less formal or rigorous fields of investigation is how knowledge can be brought up sharp against its current limits by the encounter with that which surpasses its utmost epistemic-cognitive grasp yet which nonetheless exerts a pressure on thought to conceive the possibility of passing decisively beyond those limits. Thus great (as distinct from 'great') political events are not always the events that have gone down as such in official or text-book history, that is, from a retrospective viewpoint in line with the received, politically or ideologically dominant conception of what does or should so count. Rather they are most often the kinds of events that may very well have been accounted failures in their own time and ever since – abortive revolutions, suppressed risings, stirrings of dissent put down in blood and fire – yet the effects of which can still be felt to echo on through their power to enlist an answering strength of commitment in those willing to follow through on their so far unredeemed promise or potential. For Badiou, the chief example here is the Paris Commune of 1871, an event that he asks us to understand in just such mathematically inflected terms insofar as its sudden emergence on the socio-political scene can be grasped only by a disciplined yet highly responsive exercise of counterfactual thought. Only through such a jointly conceptual and imaginative stretch of mind can we grasp both its signal character – its extant power to act as a source of revolutionary ferment – and the conditions that have worked to ensure its routine consignment to the category of might-have-been (or have-been) quasi-events.[18]

The analogy is precise despite what will no doubt strike analytically trained philosophers of mathematics as its wildly analogical character or its dependence on a merely metaphoric relation between the two domains in question. Thus, the way that certain politically salient past events flash up at subsequent times of crisis is treated by Badiou as finding an exact, formally specifiable equivalent in the way that certain mathematical problems – such as the paradox that Bertrand Russell famously discovered in the conceptual foundations of classical set theory – may likewise act as an index of some present shortfall in knowledge and hence a token of some future possible breakthrough.[19] In both cases, the anomaly occurs at a certain location (or 'evental site') marked out as the focal point of all those tensions, conflicts or unresolved dilemmas that signify the limits of a given conceptual or socio-political dispensation and also – and for just that reason – signal the prospect (or at least the possibility) of a thinking that would pass decisively beyond those limits. If Russell's highly unsettling discovery typifies the shape that such problems take in mathematics, logic and the formal sciences, then a typical (and Badiou's most oft-cited) instance in the socio-political domain is that of the *sans-papiers*, or the large numbers of immigrant, mainly North African workers who exist on the outermost fringes of French society and lack any recognized communal, legal or civic-electoral status.[20] While excluded and, for all official purposes, deemed non-existent by the currently operative 'count-as-one', these marginal groups can make their presence felt and even constitute a standing threat to the politico-juridical order that has decreed their all-but socially invisible character. This they do by creating a suppressed yet active, that is, subliminal sense of just that glaring discrepancy between the way things actually stand with those disenfranchised minorities and the 'official', state-sponsored claim – so basic to the rhetoric of liberal democracy – that all sections of the community and all individual members have an equal right to 'count' in matters of communal concern.

Thus, the question what constitutes a genuine as distinct from a specious or ideologically constructed 'event' is one that can be answered only in light of that subsequent history – that aftermath of unforeseeable yet nonetheless rigorously consequent workings-through – which defines it in retrospect as having possessed such a character. This applies just as much to mathematical theorems or conjectures in the formal and physical sciences as it does to those instances (like the *sans-papiers*) that might seem to stretch the mathematical analogy to breaking-point and beyond. Yet here also it is a matter of some standing socio-political anomaly that may – or may not – eventually arrive at the critical point of transition from a state wherein it was concealed, suppressed or passed over through the effect of a prejudicial count-as-one to a subsequent state wherein that anomaly is shown up for what it was, that is, as the result of an ideologically determined failure or refusal to reckon with the multiple in question. Hence Badiou's resolute insistence – as against a large company of philosophers from Plato and Aristotle to the late nineteenth century – that thinking is under a strict obligation to deal with the infinite, that this infinite is real rather than merely virtual, and moreover that it leads straight on (as Cantor showed) to the idea that there must exist an endless succession of 'larger' infinities beyond that defined by the sequence of integers or natural (counting) numbers. Most strongly suggestive in this regard is the concept of the power set or the set that comprises all those subsets that are members (and whose members are members) of some given set. For the numerical excess of the power set over its parent set is one that increases exponentially with the size of the latter and which thus places maximal strain on the capacities of rational-calculative thought where the set in question is an infinite set of whatever 'size' or cardinality.

## III

So it is that Badiou can state it as axiomatic – against the weight of received philosophical doctrine from Plato down – that thinking must start out from an axiom according to which inconsistent multiplicity should be taken by very definition to exceed any instance of consistent ('properly' ordered or countable) multiplicity.[21] And so it is likewise that he can argue on a rigorous rather than vaguely analogical basis that, in the socio-political as well as the formal-scientific sphere, the count-as-one should be seen as imposing a conceptual or juridical limit on the otherwise open multiplicity of candidate multiples.

That limit is precisely what holds back the power of mathematical thought – or of presently existing social-democratic ideologies – to arrive at a fully inclusive conception of the criteria for membership of some given set, class, group, collective, community, electorate or civil society. As things stand with any current state of knowledge or socio-political *sensus communis*, those membership conditions are determined as a matter of 'belonging' in a more-or-less restrictive or exclusionary sense of the term, that is to say, as a matter of meeting the requirements laid down by certain received ideas of conceptual or socio-political acceptability. If thinking about politics is ever to accomplish a break with those ruling conceptions, then it will need to take a lesson from mathematics – more specifically, from modern set theory and its achievement of 'turning paradox into concept' – and thereby develop an equivalent capacity for passing through and beyond the limits of some given (ideational or ideological) state of accredited knowledge. And this despite the deep-laid prejudice that would seek to maintain a strict demarcation between the formal sciences (mathematics and logic) and on the other hand any mode of thought that cannot or should not aspire to that degree of conceptual precision since its interests lie in a subject domain where such standards are simply not applicable. On the contrary, he argues: there is absolutely no reason, prejudice aside, to suppose that the striving for social justice or political advance should be confined to a realm of more or less persuasive beliefs or merely approximative truth-values.

Nor is it the case that there must be something absurd about any attempt, like Badiou's, to import the conceptual rigour of mathematical discourse into the kind of loose-knit reasoning and constant veering between factual and evaluative language that typifies the discourse of politics. This is merely to take on trust the authority of a philosophic dogma (the fact/value dichotomy) which is then deployed in blanket fashion to enforce just such a sharp and socio-politically as well as philosophically damaging division of labour across the whole gamut of human intellectual, cultural and practical activities. So, it is that Badiou can cite two exemplary cases of moral heroism – Jean Cavaillès and Albert Lautmann, both of them eminent mathematicians who were shot by the occupying German forces as a result of actions undertaken for the French resistance – and argue that those actions were exemplary chiefly as instances of a rigorously logical determination to follow through on certain basic ethical precepts and commitments.[22] However, this should not be taken as suggesting any tendency on Badiou's part towards a Kantian-deontological conception of moral duty, obligation or responsibility. Indeed, it is an aspect of his vehemently anti-Kantian approach to ethical issues, an approach that very often involves a rejection of 'ethics' insofar as such talk overtly or implicitly subscribes to an idea of the thinking, judging and willing human subject as the locus of any moral agency meriting the name.[23] For Badiou, this betrays a conception of acts and events that is philosophically bankrupt since mortgaged in advance to an obsolete and ideologically compromised notion of individual autonomy and personhood. The latter turns out, on closer inspection, to involve a curiously self-contradictory or self-abnegating 'logic' whereby *subjectivity* thus conceived is also – and by the same token – shown up as a mode of *subjection* to rules, dictates, imperatives or maxims whose source is altogether outside and elsewhere.

If Kantian 'autonomy' is thereby revealed as a mode of heteronomous compulsion that dare not speak its name, then the way would seem open for Badiou – like Lacan and Foucault before him – to denounce that entire quasi-autonomist, quasi-enlightened, quasi-liberal discourse as merely another subterfuge adopted by the will-to-power masquerading as the will-to-truth, or by 'power-knowledge' as a strictly indissociable conjunction of truth-constitutive forces.[24] This is indeed one prominent feature of his thinking, at least to the extent that Badiou shares those thinkers' suspicion of humanist concepts and categories. However, where they arrived at it for the most part through a locally predominant post-structuralist version of the ubiquitous 'linguistic turn', Badiou has absolutely no time for the idea that language should figure as that which places an ineluctable limit on our scope of perceptual, cognitive and intellectual grasp.[25] Indeed, he loses no opportunity to anathematize this currently widespread notion in its various derivative or surrogate forms such as those that appeal to 'discourses' (Foucault), 'language-games' (Wittgenstein and Lyotard), 'signifying practices' (post-structuralism), *die Sprache* (Heidegger), 'strong description' (Rorty) and even that otherwise congenial strain within analytic philosophy that insists on the virtues of logical clarity and rigour but then spoils its case – so Badiou maintains – by taking language, properly a second-order interest, as its primary topic-domain.[26] However, this aversion goes along with a deeper, though closely related, commitment, namely his adherence to a view of truth according to which subjectivity is no longer conceived as a realm of inward, reflective experience or as finding its formal expression in a Kantian system of faculties individually specialized for this or that purpose. Rather he treats it as the adjunct or concomitant of certain imperative truth-procedures that bring the subject into being through the virtue of fidelity to that which hitherto existed only as a matter of so far unrealized potential.

At any rate, Badiou sees absolutely no reason to regard the linguistic turn as a major advance on account of its having thrown off all those old metaphysical burdens and embraced an alternative conception that avoids the giddy heights (or the murky depths) of the Kantian 'transcendental' subject. For if one thing is clear from the way that philosophical discussion has gone among language-first thinkers in the various lines of descent from Frege, Wittgenstein (early and late), Russell, Austin and Ryle – along with Heidegger, Gadamer, Foucault, Rorty and others – it is the fact that this 'turn' was indeed a revolution although more in the original (etymological) sense of that term, that is, a coming-around once again of that which had previously shown up in a superficially different but in fact deeply kindred form. Thus it is still very much a matter of the realism *versus* anti-realism debate – or the issue of truth as objective/ recognition-transcendent *versus* truth as epistemically constrained – that first emerged clearly to view with Kant's doctrine of the faculties and which now rumbles on, albeit minus a part of its erstwhile metaphysical baggage, in the kinds of argument typically engaged by present-day disputants. All that has changed is the way that these arguments are currently couched in logico-semantic terms, rather than in the idiom of 'subjective' as opposed to 'objective' idealism that took hold among thinkers like Fichte and Schelling in the immediate Kantian aftermath and found its dialectical come-uppance in the grand synthesis attempted by Hegel.[27] Nor is there anything more to be hoped for from naturalistically inclined variants of the linguistic turn, like that proposed by John McDowell, which pin their faith to a (supposedly) non-dualist reinterpretation of Kant grounded on his (again supposedly) non-dualist ideas of 'spontaneity' and 'receptivity', rather than the standard problem-inducing since categorically fissiparous pair of 'concept' and 'intuition'.[28]

As I have shown elsewhere, this latest edition of Neo-Kantianism succeeds no better than its precursor movements in overcoming what patently remains a deep-laid dualism and one that cannot be conjured away by any amount of verbal or conceptual legerdemain.[29] Worse still, as Badiou sees it, the linguistic turn works to obscure any idea of how truth might emerge through the kinds of procedure – most aptly figured in the sequence of major set-theoretical discoveries since Cantor – that cannot possibly be explained or understood by reference to pre-existing modes of thought or articulate expression. That is, they require neither an exertion of the Kantian 'faculties' somehow united despite their multiplex differences of scope nor again (least of all) a reduction to the compass of this or that pre-existing language/discourse/paradigm/framework. Rather they demand, on the contrary, a single-minded dedication to that which trans-cends the limits of our present-best cognitive, epistemic or discursive grasp. This is why Badiou is so fiercely opposed to that whole contemporary *doxa*, whether in its 'analytic' or its 'continental' form, which elects to treat language as the enabling as well as the limiting condition of any thought that can intelligibly count as such, and which thereby condemns itself – or so he would claim – to a state of passive and uncritical acquiescence in the currency of in-place or taken-for-granted belief. Beyond that, one can see how Badiou's deep aversion to this strain of anti-realism goes along with his even more pronounced antipathy to any form of self-advertised liberal or social-democratic thinking which likewise involves the passage through a certain conception of the human faculties – or their linguistic-expressive analogues – as establishing the scope of that which lies within our powers of humanly attainable grasp.

Such is the burden of his charge against Kant, Hannah Arendt, and other apologists for a cognitive as well as an ethical–social–political order that seeks to place limits on the power of thought to envisage certain as-yet unattainable states – whether states of knowledge, understanding or political justice – the possibility of which may nonetheless leave its mark on the present through a sense of indigence or shortfall that is rendered yet more acute through its failure to achieve fully articulate or conceptually adequate form.[30] For, there is a close and mutually reinforcing tie between the kind of thinking about mathematics and the formal sciences that tailors truth to the scope and limits of human knowledge and the kind of thinking that tailors justice to the scope and limits of what counts as such according to present-best conceptions of the socio-political good. Common to both is the idea that quite simply it cannot make sense – must constitute a nonsense or a self-refuting thesis in the strictest logical terms – to suppose that we could ever formulate a statement whose truth-value would be recognition-transcendent, that is to say, objectively true or false even though we had no means of finding it out or settling the issue either way.[31] To Badiou, this argument for ensuring that truth always falls within the compass of humanly attainable knowledge is also an argument for guaranteeing in advance that thought will never stray beyond the limits established by a due regard for currently prevailing notions of good, that is, communally sanctioned intellectual, epistemic, conceptual, procedural, ethical or socio-political conduct.

Hence his insistence that any truth-accountable conception of the knowing or willing subject – any conception that can block this slide into an ultimately communitarian or paradigm-relativist notion of 'truth' – must define the subject solely and strictly in relation to some specifiable truth-procedure in some specific discipline or field of thought. On the one hand, it involves a thorough-going critique of that entire doctrine of the faculties that took rise from Descartes' bare, ultra-rationalist *cogito* and found its high point of complexity in Kant's baroque variations on the theme. This way of thinking continues nowadays, as I have said, in the various scaled-down revisionist attempts by legatees of the linguistic turn to explain how an appeal to language as the bottom-line of philosophical enquiry is able to keep the relevant distinctions in play while disowning any such inherently dilemma-prone Kantian metaphysical commitments.[32] On the other hand, Badiou just as strenuously takes issue with liberal-reformist or social-democratic ideas of political justice which likewise point back to the Kantian tribunal of reason where criticism of existing beliefs, values and institutions is tempered by a constant moderating appeal to the *sensus communis* of shared opinion among those deemed fittest to judge. Indeed, it is his chief objection to this whole epistemologically oriented mode of enquiry from Descartes, through Kant to Husserl that it *cannot but* lead to a communitarian (or cultural-relativist) upshot since the focus on mental goings-on at whatever presumptive *a priori* or transcendental level must always founder on some version of the argument against 'private language'.[33] At which point – witness the path taken by analytic philosophy over the past six decades – this failed project will at length give way to a saving idea of language (aka 'discourse' or 'culture') as the sole means of rescuing the subject from its state of self-imposed epistemic solitude.

So it is hardly surprising that Kant and Wittgenstein figure as the two most conspicuous *bêtes noirs* in Badiou's very overtly partisan survey of those various thinkers throughout the history of Western post-Hellenic philosophy who have either advanced or set back the kind of intellectual progress that he finds best exemplified in the case of mathematical developments after Cantor. Basically they are held to a common standard which has to do with their effectiveness (or lack of it) in aiding the process of emancipation from false ideas of the limits placed upon thought by its subjection to existing habits of belief. In its modern guise, this has involved first the confinement of truth to *knowledge* as conceived in Kantian (finitist) terms and then its subjection to *language* conceived, after Wittgenstein, as the end-point of all enquiry. These doctrines are anathema to Badiou since they not only fail to explain how thinking has at times pressed decisively beyond any such presently existing horizon but also turn that failure into a full-scale doctrine based on the steadfast refusal to conceive how advances of that sort might possibly occur. Such is the programme of Dummettian anti-realism or intuitionism in philosophy of mathematics, and such – with various detailed tweaks or reservations – is the motivating interest of a good many kindred projects in recent epistemology and philosophy of science. Where they err, on Badiou's submission, is precisely in failing or refusing to see how knowledge can always fall short of truth, just as present-best belief or optimal judgement can always fall short of knowledge where knowledge is thought of not (in Wittgensteinian fashion) as a matter of communal warrant but rather as a matter of conformity to truth objectively or non-epistemically conceived. Anything less – he maintains – is a dereliction of the standards laid down by previous episodes of signal advance in the formal, physical and even certain branches of the social and human sciences.

This outlook is closely related, in political and ethical terms, to Badiou's deep suspicion of the liberal or social-democratic rhetoric that tends to go along with a basically Kantian conception of the knowing, thinking and willing subject as locus of autonomous agency and choice. That conception is not so much wrong in itself – since choice and activist commitment are absolutely central to his own idea of the subject as 'militant' of truth – but wrong insofar as it goes by way of an appeal to imputed aspects or dimensions of the subject that deny knowledge any access to truth except on condition of its making the passage either through some version of Kant's highly elaborate doctrine of the faculties or else through one or other of its scaled-down 'linguistified' latter-day variants. Hence Badiou's distinctly jaundiced view of ethics, or at any rate 'ethics' in the sense of that term that has figured most prominently down through the history of post-Kantian philosophic thought, including some recent chapters in that history whose protagonists would most likely count themselves well outside the Kantian fold.[34] What he puts in its place is a formal ethics but not, as with Kant, one that seeks to combine formal (deontological) rigour with a bid to conserve the subject as that which somehow – 'transcendentally' – exerts a power of jointly cognitive, reflective and volitional control over anything that falls within its epistemic or agentive purview. Rather, as in the case of those two *resistants*-mathematicians Cavaillès and Lautman, the rigour in question is a matter of following through with the utmost formal precision or logical consistency on certain basic commitments (major premises of guiding principle and minor premises of fact, circumstance, and probable outcome) which between them constitute an ethically decisive since rationally arrived-at conclusion. Moreover, Badiou finds additional grounds for his implacable hostility to Kantian ethics and epistemology in the fact that they have lately – since the advent of the 'linguistic turn' in its multiform guises – given way to a strain of anti-realist, conventionalist, constructivist, communitarian or cultural-relativist thinking which sets itself up in flat opposition to any idea of truth as objective, that is, as epistemically unconstrained or recognition-transcendent.

# IV

I must now offer some detailed commentary on the more technical aspects of his argument since otherwise these claims – in particular, my talk of conceptual and logical rigour – will most likely conjure suspicions of charitable license or special pleading. It is best, therefore, if I concentrate on a fairly short section of one major text where the relevant issues emerge with particular clarity and force. Meditations 28 to 30 of *Being and Event* are largely concerned with extending and clarifying Badiou's critique of those currently influential movements of thought in philosophy of mathematics and the formal sciences that seek to evade such a powerful challenge to their preconceived notions of rational accountability.[35] That is, they typically choose to take the path of least epistemic resistance by adapting their notions of validity or truth to some prevailing conception of present-best or future-best-attainable knowledge.

On Badiou's submission, this amounts to a vote of no confidence in the capacity of speculative reason to surpass or transcend any such current horizon through an anticipatory grasp of those singular, anomalous or so far unrecognized (since strictly 'supernumerary') events that will mark the occurrence of a decisive advance in the history of thought. What typifies those constructivist, anti-realist or intuitionist approaches is a failure or (sometimes) a dogmatic refusal to envisage that possibility, along with a likewise entrenched supposition that truth cannot intelligibly be thought to outrun the conceptual resources of this or that paradigm, 'ontological scheme', discourse, language or expert community of knowledge. 'In its essence, constructivist thought is a logical grammar', one whose self-appointed role it is to 'ensure that language prevails as the norm for what may be acceptably recognized as a one-multiple among representations' (*Being and Event*, p. 287). This it does by restricting such recognition to just those elements that are normally, routinely or 'properly' taken as belonging to the authorized count-as-one, or those parts that legitimately qualify as such just in virtue of their pre-assigned, pre-acknowledged status in that regard. '*Constructivist thought will only recognize as "part" a grouping of presented multiples which have a property in common, or which all maintain a defined relationship to terms of the situation which are themselves univocally named*' (p. 287; Badiou's italics). So it is – through a stipulative rule imposed by means of a conceptual-linguistic policing of ontological bounds – that such thinking effectively pre-empts or contains any truly consensus-threatening challenge from that which exceeds its utmost allowance for the advent of new and unlooked-for discoveries.

Thus constructivism in mathematics, logic and the formal sciences is another version of that same turn towards language – on whatever specific, more or less technical understanding of the term 'language' – that has characterized so much present-day thought in philosophy and other disciplines. What this brings about with respect to set theory, its status *vis-à-vis* other modes of knowledge and its wider bearing on issues of ontology is a drastic restriction of its scope for engagement with issues that lie outside or beyond the agenda of current debate. It regulates the terms of that debate so as to ensure that there doesn't emerge too conspicuous a gulf between belonging and inclusion, presentation and representation, members and parts or (again with political as well as mathematical pertinence) the situation and the state of the situation.[36] Hence, for instance, Leibniz's idea of a 'well-made' language, a 'universal characteristic' that would substitute symbolic or algebraic for natural-linguistic signs and thereby provide a perfectly adequate, clear and unambiguous means of conveyance for well-formed mathematical and scientific concepts or propositions. This would have as its governing aim and rationale the need to '[keep] as tight a rein as possible on the errancy of parts by means of the ordered codification of their expressible link to the situation whose parts they are' (p. 288; on Leibniz see also Meditation Thirty, pp. 315–23).

Such is the formal, logically regimented conception of 'language' – of what constitutes a language truly fit for purpose in philosophico-logico-mathematical terms – that has come down from Leibniz to Frege, Russell and others in the mainstream analytic tradition. However, Badiou's strictures apply just as much to that (in some respects) squarely opposed way of thinking that treats natural language, or what's expressible therein, as its final court of appeal. Here also, he maintains, there is 'always a perceptible bond between a part and terms which are recognizable within the situation', such that 'this proximity that language builds between presentation and representation . . . grounds the conviction that the state does not exceed the situation by *too* much, or that it remains commensurable' (p. 288). Beyond that, the linguistic turn may be remarked in forms as various and seemingly ill-assorted as the ancient Greek sophists, the logical empiricists with their drive for a sense-datum-based (phenomenalist) language of pure observation-statements, and Foucault with his relentlessly nominalist 'archaeologies' and 'genealogies' of knowledge. What these would all have in common, on Badiou's account, is their commitment to a negative thesis ('the indiscernible is not') and hence to its positive although in mathematical, scientific and political terms highly retrograde counterpart, that is, the thesis that everything is discernible since nothing can conceivably exist except insofar as it figures in the tally of objects, properties or relations picked out by some given language or conceptual-ontological scheme. Such is 'the thesis with which nominalism constructs its fortification, and by means of which it can restrict, at its leisure, any pretension to unfold excess in the world of indifferences' (p. 289).

It is for this reason also that constructivist thinking leaves no room for the event, if by this we understand – like Badiou – the kind of rupture with established theoretical, conceptual or procedural norms that would constitute a paradigm-change in something more than the notionally radical sense of that phrase taken up from Thomas Kuhn by his cultural-relativist apostles.[37] Constructivism doesn't, and by its own lights cannot, allow for such strictly exorbitant events since its motivating interest is chiefly in preserving a *modus operandi* for the formal and (in different ways but to similar effect) the natural and social sciences. Thus it seeks to deflect any frontal or genuinely testing encounter with anomalies – like the paradoxes of self-reference or the various sorts of 'excrescence', singularity or evental 'ultra-one' – that would otherwise constitute a sizable threat to its claims of consistency and logical-conceptual grasp. In Badiou's words: '[c]onstructivism has no need to *decide* upon the non-being of the event, because it does not have to know anything of the latter's undecidability' (p. 289). That is to say, it avoids setting out upon that other, more rigorous set-theoretical path whereby thinking is inevitably led to a moment of logical under-determination requiring that its project be staked on the existence of certain as-yet formally unproven truths that nonetheless decide the course of its present and future investigations. For the mark of a realist as opposed to a constructivist outlook is just this willingness to view the current state of knowledge as always falling short of certain truths that lie beyond its present-best powers of epistemic grasp. These are truths that thought is sometimes (exceptionally) able to glimpse through a sharpened sense of those anomalies, stress-points, unresolved dilemmas or symptoms of conceptual strain that indicate both the limits imposed by its current, historically defined stage of advancement and also – what distinguishes Badiou's thinking from any form of cultural relativism – the possibility of passing beyond those limits through a process of self-interrogation or immanent critique.

Hence his chief objection to constructivist thought: that it is 'in no way disturbed by having to declare that a situation does not change', or rather, 'that what is called "change" in a situation is nothing more than the constructive deployment of its parts' (p. 290). No doubt there is some kind of 'infinity' involved here, but not – most emphatically – the kind envisaged by Cantor and those who followed his (albeit wavering) example and took it to possess an ontological dimension beyond anything that might be captured in purely linguistic, discursive or representational terms.[38] On this latter conception, 'the *thought* of the situation evolves, [but only] because the exploration of the effects of the state brings to light previously unnoticed but linguistically controllable new connections' (p. 290). Thus any notion of 'infinity' here is one that in the end reduces to that of an infinite multiplicity of languages, discourses or modes of representation. These in turn must be construed as drawing their operative sense or content from the range of procedures or practices (e.g. those of mathematics and the formal sciences) presently in place among some given community of recognized exponents. Such conservatism doesn't altogether exclude the possibility of sometimes quite radical changes to the currency of received (i.e. scientifically accredited or communally sanctioned) belief. What it does rule out – in accordance with the mandate that such changes respect the scope and limits of present intelligibility – is any prospect that thought might achieve some decisive advance through a grasp of possibilities *latent in* but *inexpressible by means of* the language or conceptual register currently to hand. In constructivist (or nominalist) terms, '[a] new nomination takes the role of a new multiple, but such novelty is relative, since the multiple validated in this manner is always constructible on the basis of those that have been recognized' (p. 290).

It is here that Badiou is able to pinpoint most precisely the nexus between constructivist approaches to issues in the set-theoretical domain and that wider turn towards a notion of language as the ultimate horizon of enquiry that has characterized so much recent (especially Wittgenstein-influenced) philosophic thought. Thus '[t]he heterogeneity of language games is at the foundation of a diversity of situations', since insofar as 'being is deployed multiply', this must always be strictly on condition that 'its deployment is solely presented within the multiplicity of languages' (p. 291). In which case – to repeat – there is just no way that thinking might achieve a truly critical distance (a 'view from nowhere', in Thomas Nagel's far from dismissive phrase) on its in-place practices or currently favoured modes of reasoning.[39] Nor is this reliance on established procedures – this pull towards familiar, well-tried methods of proof or verification – by any means confined to mathematics, logic and the formal sciences. On the contrary, its implications extend well beyond that relatively specialized sphere to the entire range of natural-scientific, social-scientific and even humanities disciplines where the appellation 'human science' is liable to raise eyebrows, if not hackles. These are regions of enquiry where there is always some question of truth involved but where the operative notion of 'truth' turns out to be deployed in such diverse and often mutually exclusive ways – correspondence-based, coherence-based, pragmatist, hermeneutic, depth-ontological, framework-relative or socially/culturally/ linguistically constructed – as to render it more like a piece of fortuitous wordplay than a staking-out of significant common ground. For Badiou, this seeming diversity of truth-concepts should rather be seen as just a product of the nowadays dominant dualist or separatist conception which drives a pitiless wedge between understanding and knowledge, interpretation and analysis, intuition and concept, feeling and thought or the arts and the sciences. Moreover, the need to overcome these disabling dichotomies – to perceive them more clearly as ideologically motivated artefacts – is one that impinges with maximal force in all of those abovementioned 'discourses' or regions of enquiry, politics most emphatically included.

Thus '[t]he non-place of the event calms thought, and the fact that the event is unthinkable relaxes action . . . [so that] the constructivist orientation underpins *neoclassicist* norms in art, *positivist* epistemologies, and *programmatic* politics' (p. 291). In each case what results is a falling back upon uncritical habits of thought or routinely conventional modes of creative (or pseudo-creative) activity which thereby betray their own failure to grasp the crucial distinction – as Badiou sees it – between knowledge and truth. Here it is well to recall that he is not using 'knowledge' in the strictly factive sense that is most often deployed by analytic philosophers, that is, the sense in which genuine or veridical knowledge is by very definition (or at very least, since there are famously problems with showing this definition to be adequate) a matter of justified true belief.[40] Rather Badiou treats knowledge as belonging to the 'encyclopedia' of currently accepted (whether expert or everyday common sense) lore and hence as always potentially in error when set against the realist or objectivist standard of verification-transcendent truth. As regards neo-classicism, this amounts to a reactive trend which 'considers the "modern" figures of art as promotions of chaos and the indistinct', a viewpoint that is justified – or at any rate understandable – insofar as 'within the evental and interventional *passes* in art (let's say non-figurative painting, atonal music etc.) there is necessarily a period of apparent barbarism, of intrinsic valorization of the complexities of disorder' (p. 291). All the same, this reaction merely betrays a failure to grasp what such artistic developments reveal or portend, that is, a transformation that goes beyond matters of style or technique and which involves an altogether more radical break with past modes of expression. To confuse these two quite distinct orders of significance is, Badiou thinks, the mark of a decadent condition wherein *art* has very largely given way to *culture* as the term under which such issues are typically raised.

It is the same with those other primary spheres of human activity – science and politics – which he sees as subject to a kindred falling-away from the kinds of intellectual and creative ferment that characterize their practice during periods of revolutionary advance. Thus, so far as science and philosophy of science are concerned, 'under the injunction of constructivist thought, positivism devotes itself to the ill-rewarded but useful tasks of the systematic marking of presented multiples, and the measurable fine-tuning of language'. In short, '[t]he positivist is a professional in the maintenance of apparatuses of discernment' (p. 292). And when it comes to politics – to what nowadays passes for political involvement, activity or participation among the great majority of those inhabiting the present-day liberal democracies – there is a similar process of decline to be witnessed, one which has as its programmatic goal the reduction of all significant issues or debates to a dead level of expertly controlled 'management' where nothing is allowed to deflect or disturb the interests of corporate and military–industrial power.[41] Here also, it is crucially a question of language, this time a language that has been worked over to the point where it perfectly describes, represents, expresses or articulates all and only those conjunctures, situations or states of affairs that are recognized – or count as legitimate – according to those same dominant interests. 'A programme is precisely a procedure for the construction of parts: political parties endeavor to show how such a procedure is compatible with the admitted rules of the language they share (the language of parliament for example)' (pp. 292–3). Again this amounts to a version of the basic constructivist precept – one with its home-ground, formally speaking, in a knowledge-based rather than truth-based conception of mathematics – according to which politics is indeed the art of the possible, though only so long as 'the possible' is here defined as that which works for all present, practical or sheerly pragmatic (i.e. vote-winning, power-maintaining) purposes. In other words, it requires that thought renounce any lingering attachment to other, more strenuous or principled modes of political activity such as might open a visible rift between the presently existent state of things and things as they could and should be according to the interests of political justice.

Thus it is once more a question of discerning multiples but only multiples that 'properly' belong, that figure in the prevalent count-as-one, and which thereby serve to distract attention from those symptomatic stress-points – induced by the irruption of other, uncounted or 'illegal' multiples – which mark the emergence of a crisis in the system and hence the location of a likely evental site. These are the points where thinking is most forcibly brought up against the excess of inconsistent over consistent multiplicity or the numerical surplus always left out by any calculative method adopted in accordance with the dominant count-as-one. They are also, conversely, the points at which normality is most strongly reinforced by those 'rules of the language' that assign or withhold the status of proper, legitimate membership – or adjust the relevant descriptive/evaluative criteria – so as best to conceal that otherwise glaring lack of measure. 'This is in perfect conformity with the orientation of constructivist thought, which renders its discourse statist in order to better grasp the commensurability between state and situation' (p. 293). As in mathematics, so likewise in politics, the chief effect of constructivist thinking is to entertain seriously only such reformist projects and commitments that involve no threat to disrupt or destabilize the existing epistemic or socio-political order of things. To this extent '[t]he programme – a concentrate of the political proposition – is clearly a formula of the language which proposes a new configuration defined by strict links to the situation's parameters (budgetary, statistical, etc.), and which declares the latter *constructively* realizable – that is, recognizable – within the meta-structural field of the State' (p. 293). Thus, a 'programmatic' conception of politics (at the furthest remove from a radical-democratic or revolutionary conception) has this much in common with constructivist approaches to mathematics, logic and the formal sciences as well as conservative, for example, neo-classicist movements in the modern arts: that it offers a refuge from the prospect of anything that might stretch its conceptual, ethical or creative resources beyond the limits laid down by acculturated habits of thought.

If this applies in a fairly obvious way to the case of neo-classicist art – where the retreat to pre-existent styles, idioms or languages is a matter of overt choice – then it is just as relevant in the scientific context where positivism demands a 'unique and definitive "well-made" language', one that 'has to name the procedures of construction, as far as possible, in every domain of experience' (p. 292). Hence Badiou's relentless opposition to any form of constructivist thinking in mathematics or philosophy of mathematics, that is, any approach along intuitionist or anti-realist lines which rejects as strictly unintelligible the claim that there can and must exist objective (mind-independent, recognition-transcendent, or epistemically unconstrained) truths. Not that he dismisses such arguments out of hand as merely the result of philosophical confusion or failure to grasp what is truly at stake in these debates. On the contrary, he goes so far as to concede that constructivism in mathematics and elsewhere is 'a strong position', and indeed that 'no-one can avoid it' (p. 294). However, what Badiou plainly means by this is not that all thought is ultimately fated to embrace a constructivist outcome, strive as it may to avoid any such melancholy conclusion but rather that thinking has to go by way of an encounter or critical engagement with constructivism so as to take full measure of its challenge and thereby advance more decisively beyond the kinds of obstacle it puts up. Above all, this serves as a means of focusing attention on the single most vexing issue between realists (or objectivists) and anti-realists (or constructivists), namely the issue as to whether truth can possibly exceed or transcend the scope of our best knowledge, investigative methods, proof-procedures and so forth. It is precisely the difficulty (for some) of conceiving this to be the case – of seeing how on earth it could make rational sense to assert the existence of truths which lie beyond our utmost powers of cognitive or epistemic grasp – that lends constructivist approaches their strong *prima facie* philosophical appeal.[42]

Thus '[k]knowledge, with its moderated rule, its policed immanence to situations and its transmissibility, is the ordinary regime of the relation to being under circumstances in which it is not time for a new temporal foundation, and in which the diagonals of fidelity have somewhat deteriorated for lack of complete belief in the event they prophesize' (p. 294). Those 'diagonals' have to do with Cantor's celebrated proof of the existence of multiple infinities and also – crucially for Badiou's project – the capacity of thought to seize upon truths that exceed the compass of present-best knowledge or intuitive grasp.[43] What their mention signifies here – by way of very pointed contrast – is the extent to which thinking may lose any sense of its own capacity for just such a process of diagonalization, that is, for conceiving the existence of truths (whether mathematical, political or artistic) that require an allowance for whatever lies beyond its utmost conceptual range. This is the main reason for Badiou's turn to mathematics – and, by the same token, his turn against the current siren call of cultural-linguistic relativism – as a means to promote the interests of socio-political emancipation as well as those of intellectual freedom and the prospects of advancement in the formal, physical, social and human sciences. The trouble with constructivism, strategically considered, is that it is not so much 'a distinct and aggressive agenda' – one that could always be confronted, so to speak, across the barricades – but rather 'the latent philosophy of all human sedimentation, the cumulative strata into which the forgetting of being is poured to the profit of language and the consensus of recognition it supports' (p. 294). Such is the subterranean continuity of numerous, otherwise diverse, schools of thought, from Kant to his two main lines of modern philosophical descent – 'analytic' and 'continental' – wherein language has indeed very often become synonymous with knowledge, and knowledge in turn with that 'consensus of recognition' that depends upon language (or the communal norms embodied in some given language) for its stabilization and maintenance. Thus, '[k]knowledge calms the passion of being: measure taken of excess, it tames the state, and unfolds the infinity of the situation within the horizon of a constructive procedure shored up on the already-known' (p. 294).

# V

Badiou is quite ready to concede that, in mathematical-scientific as well as in political or psychological terms, there is a definite place for this constructivist idea of knowledge as the limit or horizon of truth, even though – especially when joined to some version of the linguistic turn – it must always constitute an obstacle to any major advance. It offers not only a, sometimes welcome, respite from that other, more strenuous or implacably demanding truth-based realist conception but also – through this very contrast – a keener sense of just how much is required by way of intellectual strength, commitment and courage in order to achieve any such advance by breaking with the currency of accredited 'knowledge' or consensually warranted belief. Hence Badiou's nicely judged ironic coda to Meditation 28: that '[e]ven for those who wander on the borders of evental sites, staking their lives upon the occurrence and the swiftness of intervention, it is, after all, appropriate to be knowledgeable' (p. 294).

All the same he makes it clear that significant progress in mathematics and elsewhere can come about only by adopting that other conception which stakes its claim on the standing possibility – indeed, the strong likelihood with regard to really challenging, creative or cutting-edge work – that truth will turn out to exceed the limits of presently achievable proof or ascertainment. Thus he goes straight on in Meditation 29 ('The Folding of Being and the Sovereignty of Language') to elaborate the contrast between Cantor's long-drawn, mentally exhausting, often baffled or self-divided wrestling with issues in set theory and the kind of inertly consensual or placidly conformist ethos that would result if constructivism were pushed to its logical or methodological conclusion. The particular problem that so preoccupied Cantor was the famous 'Continuum Hypothesis' according to which it could eventually be shown that 'the quantity of a set of parts is the cardinal which comes directly after that of the set itself, its successor', or again (more specifically) that 'the parts of denumerable infinity (thus, all the subsets constituted from whole numbers), had to be equal in quantity to $\omega_1$, the first cardinal which measures an infinite quantity superior to the denumerable' (p. 295). In other words, it was a question of whether or not there could be proven *not* to exist any 'size' or order of infinity that would come between $\omega$ and $\omega_1$, or the infinity of natural (counting) numbers and its power-set, this latter consisting of $\omega$ and all its constituent subsets.

That Cantor spent many sleepless nights on this 'terminal obsession' – that at times his efforts seem aimed towards falsifying rather than proving the hypothesis – would be merely a matter of anecdotal interest except that it conveys both the sheer intractability of the problem and also (crucially for Badiou's case) the way that creative thinking typically proceeds in such situations. What drove Cantor to dedicate the best efforts of his final years to resolving a perhaps, so far as he knew, insoluble problem was his conviction that this was a well-formed or truth-apt hypothesis and therefore that it must possess an objective truth-value regardless of whether or not that value lay within his own or anyone else's power of ascertainment. In this respect – if not in others – the process of thought whereby mathematical advances are achieved is analogous to the process whereby political revolutions come about through a sense of currently blocked possibility, or whereby the waning resources of some culturally dominant artistic genre, style or technique point forward to a radical transformation of those same, henceforth historically dated and, at least for creative purposes, obsolete modes of expression. What is involved in each case is that same aptitude for thinking beyond the limits laid down by present-best knowledge or practice and allowing that truth may often be glimpsed – or its conditions of discovery obliquely prefigured – through the anomalies, aporias, unresolved paradoxes or suchlike obstacles that stand in the way of its punctual achievement. And in each case also what prevents thought from attaining this sense of as-yet unrealized truth is the resort to some version of the anti-realist, intuitionist or constructivist doctrine which rejects the idea that there might indeed be truth-apt (objectively true or false) statements or hypotheses whose truth-value we are unable to prove or ascertain.

Such is the doctrine advanced by philosophers like Dummett, and such – as we have seen – the outlook on issues of truth, knowledge and belief that Badiou regards as nothing short of a downright affront to what serious thinkers should take as their primary vocation. Thus, in constructivist terms, '[w]hen you write "there exists α", this means "there exists a constructible α", and so on' (p. 301). From which it follows (by the logic of constructivism or anti-realism, though of course only if one takes their premises as valid) that truth cannot possibly – conceivably or intelligibly – transcend the limits of attainable knowledge. That is to say, 'it is impossible to demonstrate the existence of a non-constructible set, because the relativization of this demonstration would more or less amount to maintaining that a constructible non-constructible set exists' (p. 301). Or, differently phrased: realism cannot be coherently upheld since it entails the existence of verification-transcendent truths which *ex hypothesi* might always exceed our utmost powers of epistemic grasp and thereby place an insuperable gulf between truth (in this merely notional sense) and attainable knowledge. Yet, if one seizes the constructivist horn of this seeming dilemma – if one deems 'truth' to be verification-dependent or epistemically constrained – then, as Badiou says, 'the supposed coherence of ontology, which is to say the value of its operator of fidelity – deduction – would not survive' (p. 301). For it is precisely the always possible surpassing of knowledge by truth – or of known truths by those which as yet elude our best efforts of proof or ascertainment – that explains how deductive reasoning can do what would otherwise seem impossible, that is, offer the means to achieve positive advances in knowledge rather than serve purely to check the validity of pre-existent or already accomplished operations.

What brings this about despite the constructivist ban on any such crossing of the line supposedly fixed between attainable knowledge and objective truth is the way that thought will at times run up against conceptual obstacles which prompt a decisive advance beyond its foregone range of standing beliefs and commitments. According to Badiou, it is sheer dogma – or a bad case of begging the question – when anti-realists and constructivists routinely take it that truth must be conceived as proof-dependent or epistemically constrained. In short, '[t]he *hypothesis* that every set is constructible is thus a *theorem* of the constructible universe' (p. 303), rather than – as all hypotheses should be – a conjecture up for testing against the most rigorous proof procedures or methods of investigation. The effect is to render the constructivist 'theorem' immune to falsification or serious challenge, since it constitutes the very element (or 'universe') within which mathematical or other sorts of thinking are required to conduct their operations. Hence Badiou's question directed (as so often) at practising mathematicians: '[m]ust one have the wisdom to fold being to the requisites of formal language?' (p. 304). That some of them resist that demand even if they can't bring themselves to reject it outright is evident, he thinks, in the fact that for the most part these practitioners 'are reluctant to maintain the hypothesis of constructibility as an axiom in the same sense as the others' (p. 304). All the same what results from this qualified acceptance is a failure to conceive how mathematical truth might always exceed the compass of best-attainable knowledge or optimal epistemic grasp. To Badiou's way of thinking, on the contrary, it is clear enough from the history of mathematics and other disciplines that there can and do occur – no matter how rarely – transformative events, breakthrough discoveries or episodes of radical theory-change that go beyond anything remotely accountable in suchlike constructivist terms. These episodes cannot be explained except on the premise that truth may at times elude the powers of human cognitive grasp and yet – what the constructivist or anti-realist finds strictly inconceivable – offer a means of epistemic or investigative orientation precisely through the various symptomatic tensions, aporias, logical conflicts, unproven theorems or unresolved issues that point the way beyond some given conceptual impasse.

This is a theme that Badiou will pursue most energetically in Part VII of *Being and Event* with reference to Cohen's set-theoretical concepts of 'forcing' and the 'generic'.[44] For now, what chiefly need stressing are the reasons for his coming out so strongly against constructivism in its sundry present-day guises. Thus he principally objects to 'the normalizing effects of this folding of being, of this sovereignty of language, such that they propose a flattened and correct universe in which excess is reduced to the strictest of measures, and in which situations persevere indefinitely in their regulated being' (p. 304). As against the powerfully restrictive influence, that is, the force of intellectual and socio-political conservatism exerted by this levelling regimen Badiou asserts the countervailing force of the event – the decisive intervention – as that which arrives to disrupt and reconfigure any given ontological scheme or prior conception of the pertinent object-domain. Moreover, in so doing, 'it *refutes* . . . the very coherency of the constructible universe' since 'between the hypothesis of constructibility and the event a choice has to be made' (p. 304). If that choice is such as to acknowledge the event – its impact or transformative effect – rather than accept the binding power of in-place beliefs, precepts, methods, assumptions or doxastic norms, then this must entail rejecting any version of the argument that truth is epistemically constrained. Indeed, as Badiou notes, 'the discordance is maintained in the very sense of the word "choice": the hypothesis of constructability takes no more account of intervention than it does of the event' (p. 305).

Hence his emphasis on the set-theoretical axiom of choice as that which opens up a path of elective commitment on the part of those ('militants of truth') who adopt and carry forward some particular procedure.[45] This axiom holds that, for any given set whose members don't include the empty set, it is possible to construct another set such that it will select one element from each member of the original set without any further requirement or condition as to what qualifies that element for being so treated. The great value for mathematicians of adopting this axiom is that it allows the real numbers to be constructed as a well-ordered sequence through an iterative process that selects first one, then another, then another number from the infinite set that remains at every stage. That is to say, it offers a means for axiomatically generating the real-number sequence – and hence a working basis for the whole range of dependent mathematical procedures – in the absence of any determinate rule or prior specification that would place limits on its future-possible scope of exploration and discovery. So, when Badiou speaks of the 'infinite liberty' that is opened up by the axiom of choice, it is not at all in the sense of some ultimate freedom to construct or invent mathematical 'truths', like that proclaimed by an intuitionist such as Dummett for whom anti-realism is the only escape-route from the dilemmas that supposedly afflict any form of objectivist or Platonist thinking. Rather it is the liberty to go on discovering (not creating) truths which are nonetheless objective or recognition-transcendent for their having been arrived at by way of this procedure.

Thus, as Badiou conceives it, the axiom of choice is a chief resource in exposing the fallacious character of two dilemmas, or pseudo-dilemmas, that he regards as having hobbled a great deal of mainstream (analytic) philosophy of mathematics. On the one hand, it shows anti-realism to rest on the mistaken idea – rife across many present-day schools of epistemology and philosophy of science – that objectivity is quite simply not to be had except by placing truth inherently beyond human epistemic reach. On the other, it shows up the kindred confusion, this time with its main source in late Wittgenstein, which supposes the issue of truth or validity in rule-following to constitute another likewise insoluble dilemma unless by adopting some version of the Kripkean/Wittgensteinian 'sceptical solution', that is, the appeal to a shared understanding or communal agreement-in-judgement.[46] In both cases, the result, as he sees it, is to disarm thought and block any prospect of radical advances such as those that occurred when thinkers like Dedekind and Cantor saw fit to stake their projects on a truth that surpassed any presently existing conceptual resources or capacities of formal proof. And in both cases also there is a strong analogy – more than that, a precise structural homology – between mathematics thus conceived and political justice as a matter of programmatically discounting any preconceived idea or any prior specification (e.g. ethnic, class-based or religious) of those who should properly, legitimately count as members of this or that social community. This is why Badiou lays such emphasis on the precept that sets, members and elements be defined always in strictly extensional rather than intensional terms, that is to say, as partaking in an order of pure multiplicity where each has its membership conditions laid down solely as a function of its operative role within that order and not through any distinguishing mark or property that would set it apart from other constituents.[47] Although we are here dealing primarily with an issue in mathematics and philosophy of mathematics, there is no reason, disciplinary prejudice aside, to deny the possibility of its having a genuine and even a decisive import when applied to issues in the socio-political domain.

By this time I would hope to have allayed the suspicion – especially among analytically minded philosophers – that such ideas can amount to no more than an instance of abusive extrapolation, or that Badiou's use of phrases like 'axiom of choice' involves a grossly mistaken understanding of their technical sense as defined in set-theoretical terms. If he takes them to bear upon issues beyond that relatively specialist sphere, then he is equally at pains to insist that they can do so only in consequence of certain strictly formal considerations – having to do, paradoxically enough, with the scope and limits of formal proof – which entail the need to decide between alternative (constructivist and objectivist) ways of proceeding. Thus, the 'choice' invoked here is, on the one hand, what marks a certain rigorously specified point at which mathematics requires a commitment beyond the furthest range of demonstrative proof and, on the other, what signals the point of contact between mathematics and those other subject areas that are normally regarded as laying no claim to formal rigour. Badiou confronts us with the need to rethink such deeply entrenched distinctions yet to do so without the least compromise to intellectual standards of fidelity, precision and truth. This is the single most challenging aspect of a project that undoubtedly makes large demands of the reader but which just as surely offers commensurate rewards.

# Of Supplementarity: Derrida on Truth, Language and Deviant Logic

## I

Jacques Derrida's extended reading of Rousseau in *Of Grammatology* puts forward some far-reaching claims about the relationship between language and logic that have so far not been examined with anything like an adequate regard for their rigour, subtlety and scope of application beyond the particular case in hand.[1] What I shall seek to do here is outline that reading – albeit in highly condensed and schematic form – and then discuss its wider implications for philosophy of language and logic.

I had better say first (so as to pre-empt one likely rejoinder) that Derrida's commentary is *not* (or not only) a piece of interpretative criticism, one that fastens on certain themes – like the term 'supplement' in its various contexts of occurrence – and then deploys them with a view to subverting other, more orthodox interpretations. To be sure, he does spend a great deal of time expounding particular passages in Rousseau's work which have to do with a large variety of topics, from the origin of language to the development of civil society, from the history of music to the genealogy of morals, or from educational psychology to the role of writing as a 'supplement' to speech which (supposedly) infects and corrupts the sources of authentic spoken discourse. What these all have in common – so Derrida maintains – is a sharply polarized conceptual structure whereby Rousseau equates everything that is good (spontaneous, genuine, passionate and sincere) with the approbative term *nature* and everything that is bad (artificial, civilized, decadent, corrupt, merely conventional and so on) with the derogatory term *culture*. The same goes for those cryptic passages in the *Confessions* where Rousseau obliquely acknowledges his 'solitary vice' and reflects on the perversity of supplementing nature (the good of heterosexual intercourse) with a practice that substitutes imaginary pleasures and the 'conjuring up of absent beauties'.[2] So to this extent, granted, the Derridean reading has to do with certain distinctive (not to say obsessional) *topoi* that can be seen to exercise a powerful hold on Rousseau's memory, intellect and imagination and which lend themselves to treatment in something like the traditional expository mode. Still, as I have said, it should not be construed by philosophers as evidence that Derrida is here practising a mode of thematic or literary commentary, one that plays with certain 'philosophical' themes – like the logic (or quasi-logic) of supplementarity – so as to disguise that fact. Rather, what chiefly interests Derrida in the reading of Rousseau's texts is '[the] difference between implication, nominal presence, and thematic application' (*OG*, p. 135). In other words, it is the kind of difference that emerges – unnoticed by most commentators – when one strives to read Rousseau in accordance with his own explicit intentions (his *vouloir-dire*) only to find that those intentions are 'inscribed' in a supplementary logic beyond his power fully to command or control.

No doubt Rousseau '*declares* what he *wishes to say*', namely that 'articulation and writing are a post-originary malady of language', introduced with the passage to a 'civilized' (= corrupt, artificial) state of society when language would have lost its first (natural) character of spontaneous, passionate utterance. Yet it is also the case – on a closer reading – that Rousseau 'says or *describes* what he *does not wish to say*: articulation and therefore the space of writing operates at the origin of language' (*OG*, p. 229). For as he well knows – and indeed on occasion quite explicitly states – there *can never have been* any language that lacked those various articulatory features (phonetic structures, semantic distinctions, grammatical parts of speech, etc.) which alone make it possible for language to function as a means of communicative utterance. Nevertheless, according to Rousseau, these must all be counted 'supplementary' (bad or corrupting) additions to an 'original' language – an authentic speech of the passions – that would surely have had no need for such artificial devices since its purpose was fully served in the face-to-face (or the heart-to-heart) of intimate mutual exchange. Even now, he remarks, there are certain languages – those of Italy and Southern Europe – which continue to manifest something of that natural character since they have remained close to the wellspring of passionate speech and have not (like the 'Northern' tongues) acquired all manner of progressively debilitating structural traits. Yet Rousseau is once again compelled to acknowledge that this can be only a matter of degree and, moreover, that everything which *ought* by right to be considered merely a 'supplement' to language in its first (natural) state must rather be thought of as integral and prerequisite to any language whatsoever.

Hence the ambiguity – more precisely, the double and contradictory logic – that Derrida discerns in Rousseau's usage of the term across an otherwise diverse range of argumentative contexts. On the one hand, 'supplement' may be taken to signify: that which is added *unnecessarily* – by way of gratuitous embellishment – to something that is (ought to be) complete as it stands and which does not (should not) require – even tolerate – any such otiose addition. In this sense, the entire development of language away from its passional origins and towards more complex, articulate or structured forms of expression must be counted a definite *perversion* of language, that is to say, a melancholy sign of the way that 'supplementary' features or devices can somehow (deplorably) come to *stand in* for the living presence of authentic speech. However, there is a second sense of the term that obtrudes itself – most often – against Rousseau's express intent and which constantly threatens to make him say just the opposite of what he means. On this alternative construal, 'supplement' signifies: that which is required in order to complete what must otherwise be thought of as lacking or deficient in some crucial regard. Thus, the 'original' language of Rousseau's conception would quite simply *not have been* a language – would have lacked some or all of those constitutive features that define what properly counts as such – if indeed (as he thinks) it belonged to a time when human beings managed to communicate through a kind of pre-articulate speech-song wholly devoid of phonetic, semantic or grammatical structures. Hence that curious 'logic of supplementarity' which complicates Rousseau's texts to the point where his explicit statements of authorial intent are called into question by other (less prominent but strictly unignorable) statements to contrary effect.

This example gives substance to Derrida's above-cited cryptic remark that what interests him chiefly in Rousseau's texts is '[the] difference between implication, nominal presence, and thematic exposition' (*OG*, p. 135). Moreover, it is a characteristic of his writing that emerges in so many different connections – or across such a range of thematic concerns – that it cannot be put down to just a blind spot in his thinking about this particular topic. Thus, culture is invariably conceived by Rousseau as a falling-away from that original state of nature wherein human beings would as yet have had no need for those various 'civilized' accoutrements like writing as a bad supplement to speech, harmony as a bad supplement to melody, or civic institutions, delegated powers and representative assemblies as a bad supplement to that which once transpired in the face-to-face of oral community. That this fall should ever have occurred – that nature should have taken this perverse, accidental, yet fateful swerve from its first state of natural innocence – is the chief sign or diagnostic mark of those various 'supplementary' evils that have come to exert their corrupting effect on individual and social mores. In each case, however, it is Derrida's claim that Rousseau's overt (intentional) meaning is contradicted by certain other, strikingly discrepant formulations whose logic runs athwart the manifest sense of his argument. Thus, on the one hand, there, to be read plainly enough, is what Rousseau *wants to say* – and does quite explicitly say – with respect to the intrinsic and self-evident superiority of nature over culture, speech over writing, melody over harmony, passion over reason, the law of the heart over laws of state, and small-scale 'organic' communities over large-scale, anomic and overly complex societal aggregates. Yet on the other hand, there, to be read in certain passages – often in parentheses or *obiter dicta* where their disruptive effect may be least felt – is a series of concessions, qualifying clauses and seeming non-sequiturs that exert a constant destabilizing pressure on Rousseau's more explicit avowals of intent. In reading Rousseau, it is not so much a matter of discounting or routinely disregarding his intentions but rather of aiming, in Derrida's carefully chosen words, at 'a certain relationship, unperceived by the writer, between what he commands and what he does not command of the patterns of the language that he uses' (*OG*, p. 158).

This point is worth emphasizing since hostile commentators, John Searle prominent among them, have often charged Derrida with showing no respect for authorial intentions and with riding roughshod (or slipshod) over statements which make it quite plain what the author wanted to say.[3] Thus when, as in the above-cited passage and others like it, he professes to respect authorial intention at least up to a point, we should not be too quick to follow his detractors in regarding all this as a pious pretence of regard for principles – those of traditional exegesis or commentary – that Derrida is perfectly willing to flout whenever it suits his convenience. For it is a claim that is fully borne out by the detailed reading of Rousseau which forms its immediate context and also by those other readings – of philosophers from Plato to Kant, Husserl and Austin – where Derrida likewise combines a due regard for the author's professed intent with a *principled* (not merely opportunist) allowance that authorial intention cannot have the last word.[4] After all, 'the writer writes *in* a language and *in* a logic whose proper system, laws, and life his discourse by definition cannot dominate absolutely' (*OG*, p. 158). And again: '[h]e uses them only by letting himself, after a fashion and up to a point, be governed by the system' (ibid.). None of this should be taken to suggest – let me emphasize again – that authorial intentions are wholly irrelevant or even subject to a large discount when it comes to the business of deconstructing this or that text. Rather, it is a question – in the more familiar analytic parlance – of distinguishing 'utterer's meaning' from 'linguistic meaning', or what a speaker intends to convey by some particular form of words in some particular context of utterance from those background norms (semantic, syntactic, pragmatic, etc.) which determine what their utterance standardly means according to shared linguistic criteria.[5] What is distinctive about Derrida's approach is the fact that he reverses the usual order of priority whereby it is assumed that the utterer's meaning can always trump linguistic meaning if the speaker must be taken to intend something different from the standard or default interpretation.[6] On the contrary, Derrida maintains that although it is always possible for speakers (or writers) to express more than that could ever be grasped on a purely 'linguistic' construal, still there is a need to remark those counter-instances where logic countermands any straightforward ascription of utterer's intent or where analysis reveals a certain non-coincidence of authorial meaning and linguistic (logico-semantic) sense.

Such is the case with Rousseau's usage of the term 'supplement', a usage that cannot be reduced to the order of univocal meaning or intent and which thus holds out against any attempt to close or to reconcile this conflict of interpretations. That is, it has to function *both* in a privative, derogatory sense ('supplement' = that which subtracts and corrupts under the guise of adding and improving) *and also* – despite Rousseau's intention – in the positive sense: 'supplement' = that which fills a lack or makes good an existing defect. And this is a matter, Derrida writes, 'of Rousseau's situation within the language and the logic that assures to this word or this concept sufficiently *surprising* resources so that the presumed subject of the sentence might always say, through using the "supplement", more, less, or something other than he *would mean* [*voudrait dire*]' (*OG*, p. 158). What is 'surprising' – in the root etymological sense – about this logic of supplementarity is the way that it *overtakes* authorial intentions and twists them around, so to speak, through a kind of involuntary reversal that leaves Rousseau strictly incapable of meaning what he says or saying what he means.

No doubt it is the case that 'Rousseau would like to separate originarity from supplementarity', and indeed that 'all the rights constituted by our logos are on his side', since surely 'it is unthinkable and intolerable that what has the name *origin* should be no more than a point situated within the system of supplementarity' (ibid.: 243). Yet this system (or logic) cannot be ignored if one is to take account of the objections that rise against Rousseau's thesis *by his own admission elsewhere* and which constitute a standing refutation of his claims with respect to the order of priorities between nature and culture, speech and writing, or origin and supplement. For in each case the latter term can be seen to 'wrench language from its condition of origin, from its conditional or its future of origin, from that which it must (ought to) have been and what it has never been; it could only have been born by suspending its relation to all origin' (ibid.: 243). Which is also to say – if one reads Rousseau with sufficient logical care – that '[i]ts history is that of the supplement of (from) origin: of the originary substitute and the substitute of the origin' (ibid.). And this is not just a kind of wilful paradox-mongering on Derrida's part but a conclusion arrived at (as I seek to show here) through textual exegesis and logical analysis of the highest, most rigorous order.

II

At any rate, Derrida's main thesis with regard to the conditions of possibility for language is one that would most likely be endorsed by many analytic philosophers. What it amounts to is a version of the argument advanced by (among others) Donald Davidson: that in order for anything to *count* as a 'language', it must possess certain minimal features that permit it to function in a strictly non-denumerable range of expressive-communicative roles.[7] Of course, there are significant differences between Derrida and Davidson when it comes to specifying just what those features are or just what constitutes the threshold point beyond which language – as opposed to some proto-'language' of the passions – may properly be said to exist. For Derrida, this issue is posed very much against the background of mainly French debates, from Rousseau to Saussure, about the relative priority of *langue* and *parole*, or language-as-system (the object of study for structuralist linguistics) and language as produced by individual speakers in particular contexts of utterance. This in turn gives rise to the paradox – or the chicken-and-egg conundrum – that language (*la langue*) must already have existed in order for those individual speech-acts to possess any proper, linguistically communicable sense even though it is hard to conceive how *langue* could ever have developed except through the gradual sedimentation and codification of individual speech-acts or items of *parole*. Thus, Derrida's interest is chiefly in the way that a thinker like Rousseau attempts to resolve the paradox in favour of a speech-based account even though this involves the projection of a mythic 'original language' which must *either* have been no language at all *or else* have been marked by those very same traits (articulation, structure, difference, hierarchy) which supposedly belong only to language in its 'civilized' (decadent) state. As a result, when Derrida specifies the minimal conditions for what counts as a language, he does so in broadly Saussurean terms which depict Rousseau as a kind of proto-structuralist *malgré lui*, one whose intermittent grasp of those conditions compelled him to question the very possibility that language might once have existed in any such natural, innocent or prelapsarian state. From which it follows – on Derrida's account – that the structures concerned are primarily those which form the basis of Saussurean linguistic theory, that is to say, structures having to do with the various systemic and contrastive relationships that constitute *la langue* at the phonetic and semantic level.

For Davidson, conversely, the prerequisite features of language are those various logico-syntactic attributes – negation, conjunction and disjunction along with the quantifiers and sentential connectives – which can plausibly be argued to provide a common basis for inter-lingual translation.[8] This reflects his primary concern to explain how such translation (or mutual understanding) can indeed take place, despite the arguments for radical incommensurability mounted by paradigm-relativists of sundry persuasion.[9] Where these thinkers go wrong – Davidson argues – is in being decidedly over-impressed by the evidence that different languages (or language communities) operate with different *semantic* fields and just as decidedly under-impressed by the extent of those shared *structural* features that languages must possess if they are to function effectively as a means of communication. This is why, as he puts it, syntax is so much more 'sociable' than semantics, namely through its offering grounds for the assurance that reliable translation *can* indeed occur despite and across those divergences of 'conceptual scheme' that would otherwise render it impossible. So it is natural enough – given this agenda – that Davidson should place maximum stress on the logical connectives and allied functions rather than the structural-semantic aspects of language that tend to predominate in Derrida's approach.

All the same – as I have said – their thinking has more in common than might appear from this face-value characterization. For, with Derrida also, the main point of interest is not so much the ambiguity (or semantic overdetermination) of a word like 'supplement' in isolated instances of usage but rather the *logic* of supplementarity as revealed through a mode of conceptual exegesis that scarcely conforms to accepted models of textual or thematic exegesis. Indeed, there is a somewhat comical footnote in *Of Grammatology* (p. 243n) where he cites Rousseau on the supposed fact that 'the Arabs have more than a thousand words for *camel* and more than a hundred for *sword*, etc.', just as the semantical case for paradigm relativism makes much of the fact that the language of certain nomadic farmers picks out manifold shades of 'green', or that the Inuit language has many different words for 'white'. All the same, as Davidson sensibly remarks, Whorf makes a pretty good job of describing *in English* what it is like to inhabit the conceptual scheme of cultures very different from ours, just as Kuhn makes a fair shot at describing the worldview of pre-Copernican astronomy or the thinking of physicists before Galileo and chemists before Lavoisier (Davidson 1984: 184). What enables them to do so – despite and against their sceptical-relativist principles – is the existence of certain basic regularities (like the logical constants) which must be at work in any such process of inter-lingual or inter-paradigm translation. So likewise, when Derrida talks of the 'logic proper to Rousseau's discourse' (*OG*, p. 215), he is not referring only to certain blind-spots of logical contradiction in Rousseau's text or to the kind of paradoxical pseudo-logic that literary critics often treat as a hallmark of poetic value.[10] Still less he is suggesting – as Nietzsche and some deconstructionists would have it – that the ground rules of classical logic (such as bivalence or excluded middle) are in truth nothing more than illusory constraints that can always be subverted by a reading that demonstrates their merely persuasive (i.e. rhetorical) character.[11] Rather, his point is that Rousseau's discourse exemplifies a form of deviant, 'classically' unthinkable, but nonetheless rigorous logic which cannot be grasped except on condition – as Derrida declares in his response to Searle – that one attempts *so far as possible* to read his texts in accordance with those strictly indispensable ground rules.

This is why Derrida, like Davidson, rejects any theory that would treat semantics as prior to logic, or issues of meaning as prior to issues concerning the various logical functions that enable speakers to communicate reliably across otherwise large differences of linguistic or cultural context. Of course, this goes against the dominant idea – among hostile and friendly commentators alike – that Derrida is out to deny the very possibility of reliable communication, or at least any prospect that it might be based on trans-contextual regularities and constants of the kind that early Davidson seeks to establish. I say 'early Davidson' in order to distinguish the truth-based, logically grounded approach that he once developed with a view to countering Quinean, Kuhnian and other versions of the conceptual-scheme-relativist argument from the strikingly different (indeed, flatly incompatible) line of thought pursued in his later essay 'A Nice Derangement of Epitaphs'.[12] Here, Davidson famously proposes that 'there is no such thing as a language', if by 'language' we mean something like the notional object of theoretical linguistics, philosophical semantics, transformational-generative grammar or any such attempt to describe or explain what underlies and makes possible our various kinds of linguistic-interpretive-communicative grasp. Thus, according to Davidson's 'minimalist' view, we most often get along in figuring out people's meanings and intentions through an ad hoc mixture of 'wit, luck and wisdom', that is to say, through a socially acquired knack for responding to various context-specific cues and clues, rather than by working on a 'prior theory' that would somehow provide an advance specification of what it takes to interpret them correctly. This goes along with a generalized version of the Davidsonian 'principle of charity' which requires nothing more than our predisposed willingness to 'bring them out right' – or interpret them as saying something relevant and meaningful – even where they mis-speak themselves, use the wrong expression or utter some piece of (apparent) nonsense. Since we do this all the time – and manifest a striking degree of tolerance for verbal aberrations of just that kind – then surely it must indicate something important about what goes on in the everyday business of understanding others and getting them to understand us.

Davidson's main example here is that of malapropism, as in the title of his essay which is taken from Sheridan's play 'The Rivals' and alludes to Mrs Malaprop's comical penchant for mixing up her words, for example, saying 'a nice derangement of epitaphs' when what she means – and what the audience knows she means – is 'a nice arrangement of epithets'. However, this optimizing strategy is by no means confined to such extreme (pathological) cases or to speech-acts, like hers, where there is simply no connection between utterer's meaning and the sense of their utterance as given by a dictionary or survey of standard lexico-grammatical usage. For – on Davidson's account – it is a strategy everywhere involved in our capacity to interpret novel utterances, fresh turns of phrase, metaphors, ironies, oblique implications and even the most familiar items of language when these occur (as they always do) in new or at any rate slightly unfamiliar contexts. So linguistic competence is much more a matter of pragmatic adjustment, intuitive guesswork and localized (context-sensitive) uptake than of applying a set of interpretative rules that would somehow – impossibly – determine *in advance* what should or should not be counted a meaningful, well-formed or relevant usage. Hence Davidson's idea that 'prior theories', though playing some minimal role in this process, are largely irrelevant when it comes to interpreting particular speech-acts in particular contexts of utterance. What we chiefly rely on here is the kind of 'passing theory' – or informed guess as to what the speaker most likely intends to convey – that works well enough for such one-off applications but which has to be revised (or abandoned altogether) as soon as we are faced with a different speaker or the same speaker in a different context.

Thus we don't get much help – if any at all – from our generalized competence as language users, at least if this 'competence' is taken to involve the interpreter's possession of a prior theory (an innate or acquired grasp of meanings, structures, grammatical rules and so forth) which by very definition fails to provide the relevant sorts of guidance. There are, according to Davidson, 'no rules for arriving at passing theories, no rules in any strict sense, as opposed to rough maxims'.[13] On his view, 'the asymptote of agreement and understanding is where passing theories coincide', and if we want to explain this in terms of two people 'having the same language', then we shall need to qualify the claim by saying 'that they tend to converge on passing theories'.[14] In which case it follows that 'degree or relative frequency of convergence [is] a measure of similarity of language' (ibid.). So in the end there is no difference – or none that really counts in philosophical or linguistic-theoretical terms – between 'knowing a language' and 'knowing our way around in the world generally'. Both come down to our practical savvy, our 'wit, luck and wisdom' in judging situations, and – what amounts to the same thing – our readiness to junk any prior theory that doesn't fit the case in hand. By the same token, linguists and philosophers are getting things back-to-front when they try to produce some generalized (non-context-specific) account of the rules, regularities, semantic structures, generative mechanisms, or whatever, that supposedly subtend and explain our powers of everyday linguistic-communicative grasp. Such theories miss the point when it comes to describing how people *actually* manage to do things with words just as those people would themselves miss the point – fail to get their meanings across or understand what was said to them – if indeed they were wholly or largely reliant on the kinds of linguistic competence the theories purport to describe. So any project of this sort must inevitably fail 'for the same reasons the more complete and specific prior theories fail: none of them satisfies the demand for a description of the ability that speaker and interpreter share and that is adequate to interpretation'.[15]

I have taken this rather lengthy detour through Davidson's 'A Nice Derangement' because it has struck some exegetes as adopting an approach to issues of language, meaning and interpretation which invites comparison with Derrida's work, in particular, his deconstructive reading of Austin in 'Signature Event Context'.[16] What these thinkers have in common, so the argument goes, is (1) an emphasis on the capacity of speech-acts to function across a vast (unpredictable and unspecifiable) range of communicative contexts; (2) the rejection of any theory that would claim to establish normative criteria for deciding in advance just which kinds of speech-acts are meaningful, valid or appropriate in just which kinds of contexts; and (3) – resulting from this – a 'minimalist-semantic' conception of meaning which strives so far as possible to avoid all dependence on prior theories of whatever type. Thus, according to one of these commentators,

> [i]f a sentence can be put to any use, and if its meaning does not restrict its use in any way, and it retains the same meaning in the context of those multiple uses; or if a sign can always be removed from its context and grafted into another context and its identity as a sign does not hamper its functioning as that sign in those new contexts; then we had better posit only the minimum required semantically to constitute that sentence or that sign as that unit of language.[17]

For Derrida, this involves the notion of 'iterability' as that which enables speech-acts, written marks or other such linguistic tokens to be cited ('grafted') from one context to the next while avoiding any more specific appeal to identity-conditions or criteria for deciding what shall count as an appropriate or relevantly similar context.[18] For Davidson, as we have seen, it takes the form of a basically pragmatist approach according to which 'passing theories' (or ad hoc adjustments) are the best that we can reasonably hope for since they alone offer any prospect of achieving some measure of convergence between utterer's intent and communicative uptake. Hence the idea that Davidson and Derrida are likewise converging – albeit from different angles – on a kind of interpretative theory to end all theories or a minimalist conception that finds no room for more substantive specifications of meaning or context.

It seems to me that this proposal gets Derrida wrong on certain crucial points and that his readings of Austin and Rousseau (among others) have more in common with the 'early' Davidson position than with that advanced in 'A Nice Derangement of Epitaphs'. That is to say, what Derrida shares with early Davidson is the belief that interpretation cannot even make a start except on the premise that linguistic understanding is primarily a matter of the logical resources that alone make it possible for speech-acts or texts to communicate across otherwise unbridgeable differences of language, culture, social context, background presupposition and so forth. Early Davidson sets out these conditions in the form of a Tarskian (truth-based) formal semantics which – as he argues – can then be extended to natural languages by way of those various logical constants in the absence of which they would fail to qualify as 'languages', properly speaking. In which case there is no making sense of the Quinean, Kuhnian or Whorfian claim that since 'conceptual schemes' (semantically construed) vary so widely across different languages or cultures, translation from one to another is strictly impossible, or at best a matter of approximate convergence for practical purposes. After all, as Davidson pointedly remarks, 'Whorf. wanting to demonstrate that Hopi incorporates a metaphysics so alien to ours that Hopi and English cannot, as he puts it "be calibrated", uses English to convey the contents of sample Hopi sentences'.[19] The same goes for Quine's across-the-board talk of 'ontological relativity' and Kuhn's idea that scientific revolutions bring about such a wholesale paradigm shift that there is simply no room for comparing different theories in point of truth, explanatory power or predictive warrant. Where the error comes in, so Davidson maintains, is through these thinkers' shared tendency to promote issues of semantics – the fact that various languages differ in their range of lexical or descriptive resources – over issues concerning the elements of logical structure that all languages must have in common in order to qualify as such. Thus, 'what forms the skeleton of what we call a language is the pattern of inference and structure created by the logical constants: the sentential connectives, quantifiers, and devices for cross-reference'.[20]

All of this seems to go pretty much by the board when the later Davidson advances his claim that 'there is no such thing as a language' and puts the case for regarding 'prior theories' – among them (presumably) truth-based logico-semantic theories of just this type – as more or less redundant when it comes to the business of figuring out what speakers mean in particular contexts of utterance. One way of bringing this lesson home – he suggests – 'is to reflect on the fact that an interpreter must be expected to have different prior theories for different speakers – not as different, usually, as his passing theories; but these are matters that depend on how well the interpreter knows his speaker'.[21] In which case clearly the role of prior theories must be thought of as 'vanishingly small' or as subject to revision – or outright abandonment – whenever we encounter some speech-act that fails to make sense (or which yields an aberrant interpretation) on our currently accepted prior theory. What this amounts to is a massive extension of the early-Davidson 'principle of charity' which now requires not that we maximize the truth content of sample utterances by construing their sense in accordance with shared (presumptively rational) standards of accountability but rather that we simply ignore or discount the linguistic meaning of any utterance that doesn't make sense by our best interpretative lights. For if indeed there is 'no word or construction that cannot be converted to a new use by an ingenious or ignorant speaker' (*vide* Mrs. Malapop), and if linguistic uptake can amount to no more than 'the ability to converge on a passing theory from time to time', then surely it follows that 'we have abandoned . . . the ordinary notion of a language'.[22] But this is no great loss, Davidson thinks, since we can get along perfectly well by applying the extended principle of charity in addition to those elements of 'wit, luck and wisdom' that always play a part in our everyday dealings with language and the world.

So one can see why some theorists (or anti-theorists) have perceived a striking resemblance between late Davidson's 'minimalist-semantic' approach and Derrida's idea of 'iterability' as the best – least semantically burdened – account of how speech-acts or textual inscriptions can function across an open-ended range of possible contexts while somehow retaining just sufficient in the way of identity criteria from one such context to the next. However, as I have said, this resemblance turns out to have sharp limits if one looks in more detail at Derrida's readings of Austin, Rousseau and others. It then becomes apparent that he, like early Davidson, places more emphasis on the logical components of linguistic understanding – the connectives, quantifiers, devices for cross-reference, etc. – as opposed to the kinds of primarily semantic consideration that led thinkers like Quine, Kuhn and Whorf to raise large problems about inter-lingual translation or cross-paradigm understanding. To be sure, Derrida's 'logic of supplementarity' is one that might itself be thought to raise similar problems for any attempt – like early Davidson's – to resist the force of such sceptical arguments. Thus it does, undeniably, complicate our sense of the relationship between what Rousseau expressly intended to say and what – on a closer, more critical reading – turns out to be the counter-logic at work in various passages of his text. Yet this is *not* to say *either* that Rousseau's intentions must henceforth be counted irrelevant for the purposes of any such reading *or* that the 'logic of supplementarity' precludes our ability to grasp the operative concepts that organize Rousseau's discourse. Rather, it is to say that we can best understand what Rousseau gives us to read through the kind of close-focused textual exegesis that registers precisely those logical tensions and moments of aporia which mark the presence of incompatible themes and motifs. And such a reading could not even make a start were it not for the imperative – as Derrida conceives it – of applying the ground rules of classical (bivalent) logic right up to the point where those principles encounter some obstacle or check to their consistent application.

# III

I must now give substance to these general claims by examining a number of extended passages from *Of Grammatology* where Derrida spells out exactly what is involved in this logic of supplementarity. One has to do with the origins, nature and historical development of music, a subject that greatly preoccupied Rousseau and which called forth some typically complex sequences of assertion and counter-assertion. What Rousseau explicitly *says* about music is very much what one might expect him to say, given his general view that the 'progress' of civilization has everywhere been marked by a falling away from the innocence of origins and a decadent resort to the kinds of 'supplementary' device that typify latter-day European culture and language. So the story that Rousseau chooses to tell is one in which music at first arose from a spontaneous expression of the feelings which as yet had no need for merely decorous conventions or for supplements – such as harmony or counterpoint – whose advent signalled a thenceforth inevitable process of long-term decline. 'If music awakens in song, if it is initially uttered, *vociferated*, it is because, like all speech, it is born in passion; that is to say, in the transgression of need by desire and the awakening of pity by imagination' (*OG*, p. 195).

Indeed, music and spoken language have their shared point of origin in a kind of pre-articulate speech-song that would have served to communicate all those genuine emotions – prototypically, that of 'pity' or compassion – which set human beings apart from the other animals and must therefore be taken to have marked the emergence of human society from a pre-social state of nature. Moreover, just as spoken language began to degenerate with the development of grammar, articulation and other such gratuitous 'supplements', so music acquired those disfiguring features that Rousseau identifies with the predominant French styles and conventions of his time. Here again, he makes a partial exception of the Italian and other Southern European musical cultures where melody has retained at least something of its primacy as an authentic language of the passions and where music has not yet gone so far down the path towards harmonic-contrapuntal decadence. But, in general, the process has been one of progressive corruption which reflects – for Rousseau – the wider predicament of a culture whose ever more complex forms of social and political organization are likewise to be seen as so many symptoms of the same chronic malaise. What is more, this unnatural degenerative process finds an analogue in the way that writing – or the graphic 'supplement' to speech – comes to exercise an altogether bad and corrupting influence on the development of language in general, and especially those languages that count themselves the most 'advanced' or 'civilized'. For, 'if supplementarity is a necessarily indefinite process', then,

> writing is the supplement par excellence since it marks the place where the supplement proposes itself as supplement of supplement, sign of sign, *taking the place of* a speech already significant; it displaces the *proper place* of the sentence, the unique time of the sentence pronounced *hic et nunc* by an irreplaceable subject, and in turn innervates the voice. It marks the place of the initial doubling. (Derrida 1976: 281)

Thus, writing takes on for Rousseau the full range of pejorative associations – artifice, conventionality, removal from the sphere of authentic (face-to-face) communication – which Derrida brings out in a great many texts of the Western logocentric tradition from Plato to Husserl, Saussure and Lévi-Strauss.[23]

The most straightforward link between harmony (or counterpoint) and writing is simply the fact that whereas melodies can be learnt – or got 'by heart' – without any need for graphic notation in the form of a musical score, this becomes more difficult – and finally impossible – as music acquires harmonic complications beyond the unaided mnemonic capacity of even the best-trained musicians. However, the connection goes deeper than that and involves all those above-mentioned negative attributes or predicates which mark the term 'writing' as it figures in Rousseau's discourse. Thus, according to Rousseau, it was once the case – and would still be the case had language and music not taken this 'disastrous' wrong turn – that the human passions were fully expressed in a kind of emotionally heightened speech-song that communicated straight from heart to heart and which had no need for such supplementary adjuncts as articulation, grammatical structure, writing, harmony, musical notation or the 'calculus of intervals'. These latter he thinks of as having somehow *befallen* language and music through an accident of 'progress' that need not – should not – have happened yet which also (by a certain perverse compulsion) marked their development from the outset. This is why, as Derrida shows, Rousseau's language is itself subject to extreme complexities of modal and temporal articulation whenever it broaches the issue of priority between nature and culture, speech and writing, melody and harmony, or origin and supplement. In each case, what should by all rights have been a self-sufficient entity requiring (or admitting) no such addition turns out – by the logic of Rousseau's argument – to have harboured a certain incompleteness *at source* which belies that claim and thus complicates his argument despite and against its manifest intent.

This complication first enters at the point where Rousseau attempts to define what it is about passional utterance – speech or song – in its earliest (i.e. most natural, spontaneous) character that nonetheless sets it decisively apart from the expression of animal need. 'Everything proceeds from this inaugural distinction: "It seems then that need dictated the first gestures, while the passions wrung forth the first words"' (*OG*, p. 195). By the same token, music could only have arisen when speech had advanced to the stage of expressing passions – distinctively human passions – as opposed to mere snarls of 'anger', grunts of 'contentment' or other such non-human animal noises. Thus '[t]here is no music before language. Music is born of voice and not of sound. No prelinguistic sonority can, according to Rousseau, open the time of music. In the beginning is song' (ibid.: 195). 'Song', that is, in a sense of the term that would include those instances of passional language (or emotionally heightened speech) which had not yet become 'music', properly so called, but would exclude – as Rousseau firmly declares – any animal sound (such as birdsong) which lacks the distinctively linguistic attributes of meaning and articulation. 'That is why there is no animal music', as Derrida writes, closely paraphrasing Rousseau. 'One speaks of animal music only by looseness of vocabulary and by anthropomorphic projection' (ibid.: 195–6). Yet in that case one is surely entitled to ask what has now become of Rousseau's claim that language and music both arose from a 'natural' expression of feelings, emotions or sentiments which would somehow have remained as yet untouched by the corrupting ('supplementary') effects of culture or civilized artifice. There is simply no way that Rousseau can put this case while maintaining the distinction – equally crucial to his argument – between that which belongs to the realm of merely animal pseudo- or proto-'expression' and that which belongs to the human realm of articulate and meaningful language. Thus, if the stage of transition from 'sounds' or 'noises' to language in the proper usage of that term is the point at which culture supervenes upon nature – or the point at which intersubjective feeling takes over from the dictates of animal need – then clearly, *by the logic of Rousseau's argument*, one has to conclude that language could never have existed in any such 'natural' (pre-linguistic) state. And if song is indeed, as Rousseau declares, 'a kind of modification of the human voice', then just as clearly 'it is difficult to assign it an absolutely characteristic (*propre*) modality' (ibid.: 196). For it is just those defining or 'characteristic' features – of melody, cadence, emotional expressiveness, empathetic power – which Rousseau takes to distinguish song (authentically *human* song) from the kinds of song-like animal 'expression' which possess no genuine claim to that title.

The same complication emerges when Rousseau attempts to make good his argument for the 'natural' priority of melody over harmony or the straightforward expression of human sentiments through an unadorned singing line over the various false and artificial embellishments introduced by later composers, among them – preeminently – Rameau and the fashionable French figures of his day. (That Rousseau's own compositions in a more 'natural' Italianate style enjoyed no comparable measure of success is doubtless a fact of some psychological or socio-cultural significance but philosophically beside the point.) 'Melody being *forgotten*', Rousseau laments,

> and the attention of musicians being completely turned toward harmony, everything gradually came to be governed according to this *new object*. The genres, the modes, the scale, all received new faces. Harmonic successions came to dictate the sequence of parts. This sequence having *usurped the name* of melody, it was, in effect, impossible to recognize the *traits of its mother* in this new melody. And our musical system having thus *gradually* become purely harmonic, it is not surprising that its *oral tone* [*accent*] has *suffered*, and that our music has lost almost all its *energy*. Thus we see how singing *gradually* became an art entirely *separate* from speech, from which it takes its origin; how the harmonics of sounds resulted in the *forgetting* of vocal inflections; and finally, how music, restricted to purely physical concurrences of vibrations, found itself *deprived* of the moral power it had yielded when it was the *twofold voice of nature*. (cited by Derrida, 1976: 199–200 [italics Derrida's])

This passage brings out very clearly the logical strains that emerge within Rousseau's discourse when he attempts to theorize the origins of music and the causes of its subsequent decline. For how can it be thought – consistently maintained – that the fateful swerve from melody to harmony (or nature to culture) was something that befell music only by an accident of cultural change and not through its inherent propensity to develop and extend its resources in just that way? After all, on Rousseau's own submission, the earliest (most natural) stage of musical expression was one *already marked* by certain characteristics – 'the genres, the modes, the scale' – which could only have belonged to that post-originary (decadent) phase when melody had acquired a range of conventional forms and devices, along with the 'supplementary' traits of harmony and counterpoint.

Thus, far from having wrongfully 'usurped the name' of melody, harmony must rather be conceived as an integral component and defining feature of all melodious utterance, even at the outset – the mythic point of origin – when by right it should have found absolutely no place in the authentic speech-song of passional language. For has not Rousseau quite explicitly acknowledged that song is in itself and by its very nature 'a kind of modification of the human voice'? In which case, the 'twofold voice of nature' – originary speech and song – would not so much have 'suffered' a gradual decline and a process of increasing 'separation' that deprived it of its 'moral power' but would rather have taken the course that it did through a *natural* development of harmonic resources that were *always already* present at the earliest stage of melodic expression. And again, how could it have been that 'the harmonics of sounds resulted in the *forgetting* of vocal inflections'? For, according to Rousseau, those inflections *originally* came about through a certain harmonic modification of the human voice that marked the transition from a realm of animal noises (such as birdsong) provoked by nothing more than physical need to a realm of humanly significant passional utterance. To the extent that 'music presupposes voice, it comes into being at the same time as human society. As speech, it requires that the other be present to me as other through compassion. Animals, whose pity is not awakened by the imagination, have no affinity with the other as such' (*OG*, p. 195). Such feelings should have characterized the earliest stage of musical development, a stage (more properly) when 'development' had not yet occurred and when there was – as yet – no room for the 'desolating' split between nature and culture (or melody and harmony) which wrenched music from its otherwise preordained natural path. Yet it is impossible to ignore the counter-logic that runs athwart Rousseau's professed statements of intent and compels him to acknowledge – not without 'embarrassment' – the fact that this split must *already* have occurred by the time that music was able to express even the most basic of human feelings and emotions.

Rousseau strives to avoid this self-contradictory upshot by specifying just how the accident occurred and by means of what alien, parasitic device harmony managed to substitute itself for the melody of living song. It is the musical *interval*, he thinks, that must be blamed for having thus opened the way to all manner of subsequent abuses. For, the interval brings with it an element of 'spacing', a *differential* relationship between tones which disrupts the otherwise self-sufficient character of melody by introducing an unwanted harmonic dimension that breaches the original (natural) unity of speech and song. Such is at any rate what Rousseau wishes to say: that the interval obtrudes as a bad supplement, an accidental perversion of music or a source of harmonic conflicts and tensions that should never have befallen the development of music had it only remained true to its original (purely melodic) vocation. And he does indeed say just that in a number of passages – cited by Derrida – where the emphasis falls on this unnatural, perverse and above all *accidental* character of harmony as that which can only have impinged upon melody as a threat from *outside* its original (proper) domain. Yet there are other, symptomatically revealing passages where Rousseau is constrained to say just the opposite, namely that harmony is and was *always* implicit in melody, since the interval – or the differential 'spacing' of tones – is something which enters into all conceivable forms of musical expression, even those (such as monody, folk-song or 'primitive' chant) that *on the face of it* haven't yet arrived at the stage of multivocal harmony or counterpoint. For in these cases also it is a fact of acoustics as well as a subjectively verifiable truth about the phenomenology of musical perception that we don't hear only the bare, unaccompanied melodic line. Rather, that line is perceived as carrying along with it an additional range of harmonic overtones and relationships in the absence of which we should simply not perceive it as possessing the distinctive melodic traits of contour, cadence, modal inflection, intervallic structure and so forth.

Hence – to repeat – that curious 'logic of supplementarity' which brings it about that what *should* have been original, self-sufficient and exempt from addition, turns out to harbour a certain lack that can only be supplied by conceding its dependence on some 'accident' of culture or history which should *never have occurred* in the natural course of things. However, this logic is none the less rigorous – and Derrida's reading likewise – for the fact that Rousseau is compelled to articulate some 'classically' unthinkable conjunctions of claim and counter-claim with regard to these strictly undecidable issues of priority between nature and culture, speech and writing, melody and harmony, etc. To be sure, when his commentary comes closest to a *paraphrase* of Rousseau's arguments, then this requires some highly complex – at times even tortuous – deviations from classical logic, deviations that typically involve the recourse to modal or tensed constructions which strain the limits of intelligibility and often lean over into downright paradox. Thus, for instance (to repeat), the 'supplementary' character of articulation is that which 'wrenches language from its condition of origin, from its conditional or future of origin, from that which it must (ought to) have been and what it has never been; it could only have been born by suspending its relation to all origin' (*OG*, p. 243). In such passages, Derrida is no doubt pressing beyond any order of statement that might be acceptable in terms of those various modal or tense-logics that philosophers have lately proposed by way of extending and refining the resources of the first-order propositional and predicate calculus.[24] However, it should also be clear that he does so precisely in order to reveal the kinds of paradoxes and *illogicalities* that result when Rousseau attempts to make good his case for there having once existed a proto-language devoid of those necessary (language-constitutive) features which *must* have been already in place for the transition to occur from the realm of pre-articulate (merely 'animal') sounds. Granted, Rousseau 'wants us to think of this movement as an accident' (*OG*, p. 242). Yet despite his intentions, Rousseau 'describes it ... in its originary necessity', that is to say, as a 'natural progress' which 'does not come unexpectedly' upon the origins of spontaneous, passionate speech-song but which *must be there* from the very first moment when language arrives on the scene.

I hope to have communicated something of the way in which Derrida's commentary pursues the twists and turns of Rousseau's argument by citing passages that directly contradict his thesis and thereby expose the 'supplementary' logic that structures his entire discourse on the origins of language and music. As direct quotation gives way to paraphrase and paraphrase, in turn, to a detailed analysis of Rousseau's discourse and its various complexities of tense and modal implication, so also Derrida's reasoning can be seen to maintain a clearly marked distance from the text in hand or from anything like a straightforward proposal that the exegete endorse this logic of supplementarity as a substitute for 'classical' concepts. Indeed, it can be seen that Derrida *necessarily* deploys those concepts by way of showing how Rousseau's discourse is compelled to undergo such 'supplementary' swerves from manifest or overt expressive intent in order to avoid more blatant instances of self-contradiction and thereby preserve at least some semblance of coherent sense. So commentators like Graham Priest are right to find something of interest here for theorists of deviant, many-valued or paraconsistent logic but they are wrong to suppose that Derrida's exposition of Rousseau should be taken as a straightforward recommendation that we adopt the logic of supplementarity as another such alternative to classical norms.[25] Rather, it is a mode of paradoxical pseudo-logic that is forced upon Rousseau by those false premises which cannot but generate aporias or contradictions once subject to a reading that calls them to account in rigorous (bivalent or classically consistent) terms. Thus, where Rousseau claims to measure the degree of 'deviation' that separates civilized (articulate) language and music from their presumed 'natural' origin, Derrida estimates the 'deviant' character of Rousseau's discourse precisely by its ultimate failure to redeem that claim and its need to adopt such exiguous logical (or quasi-logical) resources in the effort to sustain its *strictly unthinkable* thesis. At any rate, it is clear from a careful reading of the above passage that Derrida is applying standards of consistency and truth which place his commentary decidedly at odds with the manifest purport of Rousseau's argument and which construe that argument in deconstructive terms (i.e. critical-diagnostic) rather than purely exegetical terms.

# IV

Thus Derrida's approach to philosophy of logic is in this respect more conservative – or classical – than that of empirically minded logical revisionists like Quine or anti-realists, such as Michael Dummett, who would renounce bivalence or excluded middle whenever it is a question of statements that lack any determinate proof-procedure or means of verification.[26] In their case, the willingness to revise logic is more a matter of foregone philosophical commitment, even if Quine takes it as something that might be forced upon us by certain empirical discoveries in physics (such as quantum wave/particle dualism) and Dummett is led to suspend bivalence chiefly on account of his intuitionist, that is, non-classical and anti-realist approach to issues in the philosophy of mathematics. Still both thinkers may with justice be said to incline very strongly in this direction and to do so for reasons which – although different – involve a predisposed readiness to give up the principles of classical logic. For Derrida, those principles hold, as a matter of strict necessity, *right up to the point* where it can actually be shown – on the textual evidence to hand – that they encounter some obstacle which leaves no alternative except to 'transform' or 'complicate' the logic that assigns truth values to a given statement.

Here again, we can see how his thinking converges with Badiou's on the requirement – the formal imperative – that standards of logical consistency and truth take precedence over (be allowed to trump) either those of 'straightforward' expressive intent or those of hermeneutic warrant as applied by some mainstream interpretive community. For each of them, this is the precondition of any decisive or ground-breaking advance, whether with respect to textual understanding or in the powers of ratiocinative thought. Indeed, I would claim that Derrida's exposition of the 'logic of supplementarity' as it emerges through his reading of Rousseau is in this respect more rigorously argued and more responsive to the demonstrable need for such analysis than either Quine's somewhat speculative arguments based on just one possible interpretation of quantum phenomena or Dummett's highly contentious understanding of the scope and limits of mathematical knowledge. Thus it has to do not only with certain curious blind-spots or logical anomalies in Rousseau's text but also with the plain *impossibility* that things could ever have been as Rousseau describes them, for example, as concerns the absolute priority of melody over harmony in music or of a natural 'language of the passions' over all those mere 'supplementary' devices – articulation, grammar, structural traits of whatever kind – that supposedly signalled the onset of linguistic and cultural decline. For there is simply no conceiving that idyllic phase when speech would have lacked those same *language-constitutive* features yet would still have been a 'language' in the sense of that term which Rousseau elsewhere (in his more theoretical, even proto-structuralist moments) considers to mark the stage of transition from animal noise to human speech.

That this impossibility is found to emerge through a meticulously argued reading of Rousseau should lead us to conclude that the aporias in question are not so much the products of 'textualist' ingenuity on Derrida's part but rather have to do with certain empirically warranted and theoretically ascertainable truths about language. His approach falls square with an argument like 'early' Davidson's concerning the minimal range of necessary attributes – quantifiers, devices for negation, conjunction, disjunction, anaphora, cross-reference, etc. – that any language surely *must* possess if it is to function effectively *as* a language rather than a means of vaguely emotive pseudo-communication.[27] So the Derridean 'logic of supplementarity' has this much in common with other, more 'classical' modes of logic: that while laying claim to its own kind of formal rigour and validity conditions, it must also correspond to the way things stand with respect to some given subject domain or specific area of discourse. That is to say, when Derrida finds Rousseau obliquely conceding (despite his declarations elsewhere) that 'harmony is the originary supplement of melody' or that melody could never have existed in a state of pure pre-harmonic grace, this has implications not only for philosophy of logic but also for our thinking about music and the history of music. For indeed it is the case – empirically so, as a matter of acoustics and the overtone series, and phenomenologically speaking, as concerns the ubiquitous role of harmony in our perceptions of melodic contour – that what *ought* (for Rousseau) to figure as a mere 'supplement' turns out to be the very *condition of possibility* for music and musical experience in general.

There is a sense in which Rousseau acknowledges this – recognizes it to follow from the basic principles of acoustics and music theory – but also a sense in which he constantly endeavours to deny or repress that knowledge. For 'Rousseau never makes explicit the originarity of the lack that makes necessary the addition of the supplement – the quantity and the differences of quantity that always already shape melody. He does not make it explicit, or rather he says it without saying it, in an oblique and clandestine manner' (*OG*, p. 214). And again: 'Rousseau wishes to restore a natural degree of art within which chromatics, harmonics, and interval would be unknown. He wishes to efface what he had . . . already recognised, that there is harmony within melody, etc. But the *origin must (should) have been* (such is, here and elsewhere, the grammar and the lexicon of the relationship to origin) *pure* melody' (ibid.). That Rousseau is unable to sustain this thesis against certain powerful objections that arise from the logic of his own discourse is a fact that should interest logicians as much as musicologists and cultural historians. For it offers a striking example of the way that complications which develop in the course of arguing from (apparently) self-evident premises to (apparently) sound conclusions can introduce doubt as to whether those premises are indeed self-evident or whether those conclusions are warranted by anything more than the strength of doctrinal attachment. This is also, as we saw in Chapter 4, why Badiou comes out so strongly against those movements of thought in mathematics and logic – such as intuitionism, anti-realism or (more broadly) constructivism – that reject the axiom of double-negation elimination and, along with it, the conceptual resources required for arguments by *reductio ad absurdum*. That requirement emerges very clearly from Derrida's analysis of certain passages in Rousseau's writing on the theory of music where he (Rousseau) effectively concedes as much through a curious reversal of the very terms – or the order of priority between them – which bear the whole weight of his argument. Thus: 'harmony would be very difficult to distinguish from melody, unless one adds to the latter the ideas of rhythm and measure, without which, in effect, no melody can have a determined character; whereas harmony has its own character by itself, independent of every other quality' (cited by Derrida, *OG*, p. 210). But in that case – as Austin might have said – it is harmony that 'wears the trousers' with respect to this conceptual opposition and melody that lacks the self-sufficient expressive resources which would enable it to manage perfectly well without the 'supplement' of harmony.

This I take to be the single most distinctive feature of the 'logic of supplementarity' as Derrida expounds it through his reading of Rousseau. That is to say, it is an exception to the general rule which requires that we distinguish logical *validity* from argumentative *soundness*, or the question what counts as a case of formally valid inference from any question concerning the truth of premises or of conclusions drawn from them. In this respect, the logic of supplementarity has more in common with certain kinds of abductive reasoning – or inference to the best explanation – than with classical (e.g. deductive) schemas of truth-preservation.[28] Abduction is essentially a mode of inference that reasons backwards (so to speak) from whatever we possess in the way of empirical evidence to whatever best explains or accounts for that same evidence. In so doing, it allows for the standing possibility that premises may be confirmed, infirmed, strengthened or indeed *discovered* through just such well-tried methods of reasoning, especially in the physical sciences. It is, therefore, a process of rational conjecture which involves the application of standard principles – such as bivalence and excluded middle – but which deploys them in a non-standard way so as to extend the resources of logic beyond its classical limits.

Among other things, this provides an answer to the 'paradox of analysis' or the claim that since deductive logic comes down to a matter of purely definitional (analytic) truth, therefore its conclusions must always be contained in its premises and hence be incapable of making any new or substantive contribution to knowledge.[29] The paradox received its classic statement in the following passage from C.H. Langford's essay 'The Notion of Analysis in Moore's Philosophy':

> Let us call what is to be analyzed the analysandum, and let us call that which does the analysing the analysans. The analysis then states an appropriate relation of equivalence between the analysandum and the analysans. And the paradox of analysis is to the effect that, if the verbal expression representing the analysandum has the same meaning as the verbal expression representing the analysans, the analysis states a bare identity and is trivial; but if the two verbal expressions do not have the same meaning, the analysis is incorrect.[30]

The approach through inference to the best explanation gets around this seeming paradox by maintaining (1) that abductive logic *can* provide grounds for a non-tautological (ampliative) process of knowledge acquisition, and (2) that this process is nonetheless consistent with an application of classical precepts such as bivalence and excluded middle. That is to say, it rejects any Quinean empiricist recourse to across-the-board logical revisability – or any Dummett-type anti-realist proposal to suspend those classical precepts – while nonetheless extending the scope of valid inference well beyond the highly restrictive terms laid down by a hardline deductive-nomological conception of valid reasoning. It may well be objected that arguments of this sort have their place in philosophy of science and other empirically oriented disciplines but not – surely – in the business of textual interpretation where the only 'data' are words on the page and where these are subject to entirely different (by which is meant, less exacting or rigorous) standards of accountability. However, this objection misses the mark if applied to Derrida's commentary on Rousseau since the operative standards here – as I have argued – are simply not those of 'interpretation' in the usual (literary-critical) sense of that term. Rather, they have to do with the evidence of certain logical anomalies that *cannot be ignored* by a sufficiently attentive reading and which therefore require an abductive revision of various 'self-evident' premises – such as the absolute priority of nature over culture, speech over writing, or melody over harmony – whose claim is countermanded by the logic of Rousseau's discourse.

Thus on his account, there once was (must have been) a time when speech and song had not yet gone their separate ways and when '[a]ccents constituted singing, quantity constituted measure, and one spoke as much by sounds and rhythm as by articulations and words' (cited by Derrida, *OG*, p. 214). Yet here already – as Rousseau is constrained to acknowledge – there is simply no conceiving how 'accent' is produced (or how languages might be compared in point of their accentual features) unless with regard to differential structures like 'quantity', 'measure' and 'articulation'. That is to say, it is impossible for Rousseau to maintain his position concerning the natural priority of melody over harmony without *either* ignoring these various items of counter evidence *or* allowing them to twist the logic of his argument against its own avowed or manifest intent. The same applies to Rousseau's concept of *imitation*, referring as it does to that which defines the very nature of human sociality – whatever lifts music and language beyond the realm of mere animal need – yet also to that which supposedly inhabits a realm of spontaneous (natural) human passion as yet untouched by the disfiguring marks of cultural progress. 'Rousseau has need of imitation', Derrida writes:

> [H]e advances it as the possibility of song and the emergence out of animality, but he exalts it only as a reproduction adding itself to the represented though it *adds nothing*, simply supplements it. In that sense he praises art or *mimesis* as a supplement. But by the same token praise may instantly turn to criticism. Since the supplementary mimesis adds *nothing*, is it not useless? And if, nevertheless, adding itself to the represented, it is not nothing, is that imitative supplement not dangerous to the integrity of what is represented and to the original purity of nature? (Derrida 1976: 203)

Thus 'imitation', like 'supplement', is a term whose logical grammar – whose 'syncategorematic' status to adopt the analytic parlance – is such as to induce an unsettling effect in any context of argument where it purports to establish that certain concepts (like 'nature', 'speech' and 'melody') must take priority over certain others (like 'culture', 'writing' and 'harmony').

In Rousseau's case, what emerges is a sequence of contradictory propositions which cannot be reconciled on the terms laid down by a classical (bivalent) logic and which therefore require *either* that this logic be abandoned *or* that Rousseau abandon his cardinal premise with respect to that supposedly self-evident order of priority. As I read him, Derrida regards the first option as philosophically a non-starter since it would licence any number of revisionist proposals – like the suspension of bivalence or excluded middle – whose effect would be to render thinking altogether devoid of conceptual clarity and precision. Rather what is required, here as in discussions of speech-act theory, is a rigorous deployment of bivalent logic – 'a logic of "all or nothing" without which the distinction and the limits of a concept would have no chance' – but one that goes on to reason abductively from certain contradictions in Rousseau's discourse to the necessity of revising or abandoning Rousseau's premises.[31] Thus, the Derridean 'logic of supplementarity' differs from other revisionist programmes in its insistence that any change in our thinking can be warranted – logically justified – only when arrived at through a strict application of bivalent ('all or nothing') criteria. Otherwise, it could offer no adequate grounds for drawing the kinds of conclusion that Derrida draws, that is, that *as a matter of logical necessity as well as a matter of empirical fact*, there cannot be melody without harmony or a language of the passions that is not already marked by those differential features – of accent, tonality, 'laws of modulation', etc. – that belong to a given (however 'primitive') stage of cultural development. And this not merely as an odd, unlooked-for consequence of Rousseau's obsessional desire to prove just the opposite but rather as a matter of linguistic, historical and logical necessity.

# V

My point is that Derrida arrives at these claims through a reading of Rousseau that undoubtedly places considerable strain on the precepts of classical (bivalent) logic but which is nonetheless obliged to respect those precepts – to follow them so far as possible – since it would otherwise be able to establish nothing concerning the self-contradictory nature of Rousseau's thematic premises. Thus, when Derrida notes the emergence of a different, that is, non-classical or 'supplementary' logic in Rousseau's text, it is only on the basis – as the logical outcome – of applying the axioms of bivalence and excluded middle to certain problematical passages which must then be seen to cast doubt on the coherence of Rousseau's project. This is why Derrida's commentary goes out of its way to insist on the strictly unresolvable tensions and logical strains that characterize not only Rousseau's writings about language, music, history and social development but also its own best efforts to produce a consistent (non-contradictory) reading of Rousseau. These complications arise at precisely the stage where commentary is obliged – logically compelled – to register the presence of a deep-laid conflict between 'implication, nominal presence, and thematic exposition'. They typically take the form of an attempt, on Rousseau's part, to establish a clear-cut conceptual distinction which *should* be sufficient to resolve the problem but which then turns out to require yet another distinction and so on to the point where his argument displays that repeated pattern of substitutive swerves from origin which Derrida terms the 'logic of supplementarity'. However, once again, this case would lack any semblance of demonstrative force – of philosophical cogency and rigour – were it not for Derrida's applying the precepts of classical logic in his own exposition of Rousseau's text and also his holding that text accountable to standards which *cannot be other* than those of bivalence and excluded middle. It is crucial to his argument that any relaxation of those classical criteria will produce a merely 'approximative' logic and a blurring of conceptual distinctions the effect of which is to render thought incapable of reflecting critically on its own premises or presuppositions.

Let me take one further example from Derrida by way of bringing out this requirement that bivalence retain its place even – or especially – where it encounters obstacles such as those thrown up by Rousseau's discourse on the origins of language and culture. Thus, according to Rousseau, the first societies exhibited a state of natural, harmonious human coexistence that was as yet unmarked by those various differential structures – rank, class, social privilege, delegated power, representative assemblies and so forth – which only later came to exert their artificial and corrupting social effect. However, it is clear as a matter of conceptual necessity as well as of historical, anthropological or socio-cultural reflection that such structures – in some form or another – must be taken to constitute the *very precondition* of societal existence. This is why, as Derrida remarks, all attempts to draw a line between 'nature' and 'culture' while counting some cultures more 'natural' than others must at length give rise to the kinds of logical complication that characterize Rousseau's text. In short, 'language is born out of the process of its own degeneration' (*OG*, p. 242), a statement that may seem wilfully paradoxical but which captures both the curious double-logic of Rousseau's discourse and the straightforward (conceptually self-evident) truth that there cannot ever have been any language – or any state of social existence – that would meet the requirement of transparent communion in the face-to-face of unmediated mutual understanding. Just as language depends on a system of differential structures, contrasts and relationships, so also society depends on – cannot be conceived in the absence of – those structures which articulate social or cultural distinctions of various kinds. And this applies just as much to that Rousseauist conception of 'nature' – a nature supposedly untouched by the ravages of cultural decline – which is yet paradoxically required to do service as a description of how human beings once lived in a state of (what else?) social co-existence under certain distinctively *cultural* rules and constraints. 'All the contradictions of the discourse are *regulated*, rendered necessary yet unresolved, by this structure of the concept of nature. *Before all determinations of a natural law, there is, effectively constraining the discourse, a law of the concept of nature*' (Derrida 1976, p. 33; Derrida's italics).

Hence the difference that Derrida constantly remarks between that which Rousseau *expressly wishes to say* and that which he is nonetheless *compelled to describe* by a logic that resists, contradicts or countermands his avowed meaning. Thus, 'Rousseau's discourse lets itself be constrained by a complexity which always has the form of a supplement of or from the origin. His declared intention is not annulled by this but rather inscribed within a system which it no longer dominates' (*OG*, p. 243). Moreover, this demonstrable non-coincidence of meaning and intent has implications beyond what it tells us concerning Rousseau's problematic ideas about the origins of human society. Nor are those implications by any means exhausted when Derrida extends his analysis to other texts – notably by Saussure and Lévi-Strauss – where a range of kindred binary oppositions (nature/culture, speech/writing, authentic passion *versus* civilized artifice) are likewise subject to a deconstructive reading (*OG*, pp. 27–73 and 101–40.). Rather, his case is that Rousseau's predicament is one that will inevitably mark any discourse on these or related themes beyond a certain stage of conceptual or logico-semantic complexity. This particular form of deviant ('supplementary') logic is sure to emerge whenever it is a question of fixing – or attempting to fix – some notional point of origin for language or society that would *not yet* partake of the defining traits (articulation, difference, structure, hierarchical relationship, etc.) in the absence of which no language or society could possibly have come into being. Indeed, Derrida remarks,

> [t]he expression 'primitive times', and all the evidence which will be used to describe them, refer to no date, no event, no chronology. One can vary the facts without modifying the structural invariant. In every possible historical structure, there seemingly would be a prehistoric, presocial, and also prelinguistic stratum, that one ought always to be able to lay bare. (*OG*, p. 252)

However, it is precisely Derrida's point – borne out by meticulous analysis of passages in Rousseau's text – that there is simply no conceiving this zero-point of history, society and language. That is, it cannot be described or evoked without giving rise to that counter-logic, or logic of logical anomalies, which marks the emergence of supplementarity and hence the non-existence (or the unthinkability) of anything that would answer to Rousseau's wishful description.

So it is wrong – a very definite misreading of Derrida's work – to suggest that deconstruction is really nothing more than a geared-up version of that same hermeneutic technique which has long been the stock-in-trade of literary critics professionally skilled in finding out instances of paradox, ambiguity or multiple meaning.[32] Indeed, Derrida is at pains – in *Grammatology* and other texts – to insist that his readings are not so much concerned with localized examples of semantic overdetermination but rather with the logical syntax of terms (such as 'supplement', 'différance', 'pharmakon' and 'parergon') whose contradictory meanings cannot be contained by any such familiar model of literary interpretation.[33] To be sure, Derrida makes this case through a critical-expository reading of Rousseau which promotes textual fidelity to a high point of principle and which even insists – in one notorious passage – that 'there is nothing outside the text' (*il n'y a pas de hors-texte*; more accurately: 'no "outside" to the text') (*OG*, p. 158). However, this should *not* be taken to suggest that he is concerned only with the sacrosanct 'words on the page' or that he must subscribe to some kind of far-gone transcendental-idealist doctrine according to which textual inscriptions are the only items that should figure in this drastically pared-down ontology. What he is claiming, rather, is that textual close reading of this kind is able to bring out certain logical complications which also have much to tell us concerning the real (as distinct from the mythic or idealized) conditions of emergence for language and society.

This is why, as I have said, Derrida's reading of Rousseau has less to do with thematic commentary in the literary-critical mode than with issues in philosophy of logic and philosophical semantics. Chief among them are (1) the status of 'deviant' *vis-à-vis* classical logics and (2) the question – at the heart of much philosophical debate from Aristotle to Kant and beyond – as to how logic can be *both* a matter of formal (or transcendental) warrant *and* a mode of reasoning that, in some cases, permits the extension or refinement of our knowledge concerning matters of empirical fact. Given time, one could pursue these topics back to Derrida's early, in many ways, formative studies of Husserl and his detailed account of the latter's attempt to reconcile those seemingly discrepant claims.[34] One could also instance the numerous passages in *Of Grammatology* where Derrida takes up this theme from Husserl – the opposition between logical 'structure' and empirical 'genesis' – and finds it prefigured in the texts of Rousseau at just those points where Rousseau's argument manifests the kinds of conceptual strain imposed by his attempt to theorize the natural (pre-cultural) origins of culture. Thus, according to Rousseau, there *should* or by right *must have been* at one time a mode of social existence – a 'perpetual spring', a 'happy and durable epoch' – when humankind enjoyed all the benefits of society without its subsequent corrupting effects. 'The more we reflect on it', he writes, 'the more we shall find that this state was the least subject to revolutions, and altogether the very best man could experience; so that he can have departed from it only through some fatal accident, which, for the public good, should never have happened' (cited by Derrida, *OG*, p. 259). Yet this idea is called into question by the counter-logic that regularly surfaces to undermine Rousseau's wishful professions of belief and to demonstrate the sheer impossibility that any such state could once have existed, let alone have formed 'the most happy and *durable*' epoch of human history. In Derrida's words, '[t]he passage from the state of nature to the state of language and society, the advent of supplementarity, remains then outside the grasp of the simple alternative of genesis and structure, of fact and principle, of historical and philosophical reason' (*OG*, p. 259).

# VI

It seems to me that logicians – especially those with an interest in issues of modal and tense-logic – have much to learn from a reading of Derrida which accords his text the kind of detailed attention that he brings to the texts of Rousseau. For it is among the most striking features of his Rousseau commentary that Derrida engages in some highly complex – at times logically and grammatically tortuous – attempts to reconstruct the rationale of Rousseau's argument in a form that would respect the principles of bivalence and excluded middle. That he fails in this endeavour and demonstrates rather the sheer impossibility of carrying it through is a sign not so much of Derrida's fixed intention to subvert those principles as of his fixed determination to apply them right up to the point where they encounter unignorable resistance from Rousseau's text.

Let me cite another extended passage from *Of Grammatology* which exemplifies the kinds of logical complication – the extraordinary twists of tense-logic and modal or hypothetical-subjunctive reasoning – which characterize Rousseau's discourse on the origins of language, music and society. The passage in question has to do with his attempt to explain how the 'grammar' of music – its codified conventions and (above all) its structures of harmonic development – might somehow be thought of *both* as having their source in the wellspring of natural melody *and* as having come upon that source from outside through an accident of culture that need not – better not – have happened. Thus:

> instead of concluding from this simultaneity [i.e. their common point of origin] that the song broached itself in grammar, that difference had already begun to corrupt melody, to make both it and its laws possible at the same time, Rousseau prefers to believe that grammar *must (should) have* been comprised . . . within melody. There *must (should) have* been plenitude and not lack, presence without difference. From then on the dangerous supplement, scale or harmony, *adds itself from the outside as evil and lack* to happy and innocent plenitude. It would come from an outside which would be simply the outside. This conforms to the logic of identity and to the principle of classical ontology (the outside is outside, being is, etc.) but not to the logic of supplementarity, which would have it that the outside be inside, that the other and the lack come to add themselves as a plus that replaces a minus, that what adds itself to something takes the place of a default in the thing, that the default, as the outside of the inside, should be already within the inside, etc. What Rousseau in fact describes is that the lack, adding itself as a plus to a plus, cuts into an energy which *must (should) have* been and remain intact. (Derrida *OG*, p. 215)

There are two main points that I wish to make about this passage – and about Derrida's reading of Rousseau more generally – by way of bringing out its relevance to issues in philosophy of logic. One is that it shows the complex array of tensed and modal constructions ('had already', 'must [should] have been', 'would come from', 'would be simply', 'would have it that', 'should be already', etc.) to which Rousseau typically has recourse in order to maintain the natural – supposedly self-evident – priority of passion over reason, melody over harmony, or spontaneous utterance over grammar and articulation. What Rousseau undoubtedly 'prefers to believe' with regard to these and other, kindred topics is expressed clearly enough in various propositions (or individual statements) concerning those respective orders of priority. However, it is far from clear that Rousseau can maintain this position if one looks beyond the presumptive self-evidence of authorial intent to the logical grammar of a term like 'supplement'. For, it then turns out that he cannot get around the obstacles to any straightforward (empirically plausible and logically coherent) statement of his views without having recourse to some tortuous locutions which symptomatically betray the stress-points in his argument. Yet, of course, those stress-points could never emerge – or register as such – were it not for Derrida's applying the precepts of classical (two-valued) logic and his doing so, moreover, in keeping with the strictest requirements of Rousseau's text. That is to say, Rousseau could not possibly advance a single proposition concerning those topics except on the understanding that every such statement is subject to assessment in bivalent (true-or-false) terms. And this condition applies whatever the extent of those modal, counterfactual or tense-logical complexities that Derrida brings out in his reading of Rousseau.

Hence my second point: that the 'logic of supplementarity' is *not* proposed by Derrida as a substitute, replacement or alternative to 'classical' logic but rather as a measure of just how far Rousseau is forced to equivocate in the effort to maintain his express position with regard to these various *topoi*. Here again I should wish to make the point that if Derrida is indeed a logical 'revisionist', then this is not so much – as with Quine or Dummett – a distinctive philosophical *parti pris* but a matter of remarking certain logical aberrations that characterize the discourse of certain writers, chief among them Rousseau. That is to say, there is no question of renouncing those classical precepts (such as bivalence or excluded middle) which alone provide Derrida with the necessary means by which to analyse Rousseau's text and to bring out its various tensions, complications and aporias. On the other hand, this is not merely a matter of Rousseau's having fallen prey to conceptual confusions which he might have avoided with a bit more care in framing his proposals or clarity in thinking through their implications. For the logic of supplementarity is both indispensable to Rousseau's argument – the only form in which he is able to articulate its various propositions – and also (as Derrida shows) the main point of leverage for a reading that effectively subverts all its governing premises. This is why Derrida is at pains to insist that deconstruction is in no sense a 'psychoanalysis' of philosophy or a depth-hermeneutical technique whose chief aim – as might be supposed – is to uncover certain 'repressed' or 'sublimated' themes in Rousseau's discourse. Rather it is concerned with those blind-spots of logical contradiction where that discourse runs up against the impossibility of straightforwardly saying what it means or meaning what it says.

Nor should this position seem so far removed from a good deal of work in the mainstream analytic line of descent, that is, the Frege–Russell tradition of thinking about issues in philosophy of language and logic. After all, it is taken for granted there that analysis can quite legitimately challenge the presumed self-evidence of utterer's intent – or the normative authority of 'ordinary language' – and concern itself with logico-semantic structures that need not be thought of as playing any role in the consciousness of this or that speaker. Frege's canonical account of the relationship between 'sense' and 'reference' and Russell's broadly similar 'Theory of Descriptions' are, of course, the paradigm examples of this approach.[35] Thus, Derrida's 'revisionism' is more like that which separates thinkers in the Frege–Russell camp from thinkers (such as Wittgenstein and Austin) who take it that 'ordinary language' is our best source of guidance in these matters, and hence that any claim to go beyond the deliverance of unaided linguistic intuition – or, worse still, to correct for certain 'blind-spots' in our everyday habits of usage – is so much wasted effort.[36] That is to say, Derrida takes the view – upheld by analytic 'revisionists like Gilbert Ryle – that ordinary language can be systematically misleading and that in such cases we are entitled to press the claims of logical analysis beyond anything explicable in terms of straightforward (philosophically untutored) linguistic grasp.[37] It is also one reason for his downright refusal to accept Searle's idea that concepts (or logical distinctions) need only be as precise as required by this or that context of usage, so that – for instance – an 'all-or-nothing' logic has no valid application in the context of Austinian speech-act theory. For the point is, surely, that *even if* such a loosening of clear-cut logical criteria has its place in some items of everyday parlance, then *even so* it should not be thought to carry over – or to licence a similar laxity of conceptual grasp – in the philosophic treatment of those same items.

Whence, to repeat, Derrida's remark that 'the writer writes *in* a language and *in* a logic whose proper system, laws, and life his discourse by definition cannot dominate absolutely' (*OG*, p. 158). This comment has a double pertinence as applied to Rousseau since his discourse can be seen to exhibit all the signs of a thinking that is caught between two logics – that of classical (bivalent) truth/falsehood and the logic of supplementarity – whose conflicting claims it has somehow to negotiate from one sentence to the next. But it also applies to any speaker or writer whose language might always be logically constrained to mean something other than what they intend or have it in mind to say. 'This is why', as Derrida writes,

> travelling along the system of supplementarity with a blind infallibility, and the sure foot of the sleepwalker, Rousseau must at once denounce *mimesis* and art as supplements (supplements that are dangerous when they are not useless, superfluous when they are not disastrous, in truth both at the same time) and recognize in them man's good fortune, the expression of passion, the emergence from the inanimate. (*OG*, p. 205)

Commentators like Priest are right to suggest that the Derridean 'logic of supplementarity' merits recognition as one among the range of deviant, non-standard or paraconsistent logics that have lately received a good deal of philosophical attention.[38] However, it is also important to emphasize that Derrida is not for one moment proposing the overthrow, abandonment or supersession of classical (bivalent) concepts. The point about *any* such deviant logic – whether adopted in response to anomalous quantum-physical data or to textual aberrations like those of Rousseau – is that it must be taken to indicate some problem or unresolved dilemma with respect to the topic in hand.[39] Thus, it requires not so much an outlook of unqualified endorsement – such as commentators often ascribe to Derrida concerning the logic of supplementarity – but rather a process of diagnostic reasoning that questions the premises (the 'unthought axiomatics') which can be shown to have produced that dilemma.

At any rate, there is no justification for the idea that Derrida seeks to subvert the most basic principles of truth, logic and reason. How this idea took hold in so many quarters is perhaps more a question for sociologists and chroniclers of academic culture than for philosophers who might instead take the time actually to read Derrida's work rather than endorse the standard dismissive estimate. Then they will find, I suggest, that his Rousseau commentary makes a highly original contribution to philosophy of logic and language, not least for its being cast in the form – one more familiar to literary critics – of a critical exegesis finely responsive to verbal details and nuances. What distinguishes Derrida's work is the way that he raises such issues through a mode of analysis that combines textual analysis with the utmost precision of logico-semantic grasp. Beyond that, he draws out some extreme complexities of modal, subjunctive or counterfactual reasoning – like those cited above – whose gist can be paraphrased (albeit very often at tortuous length) and whose logical form can sometimes be captured in a suitably refined symbolic notation but which serve above all to indicate the aberrant (logically anomalous) character of Rousseau's discourse. Thus Derrida implicitly rejects any approach that would assign the 'logic of supplementarity' to its rightful (albeit 'deviant') place within the range of alternative, that is, non-classical logics which might always be invoked at the analyst's convenience so as to accommodate some awkward or recalcitrant case. Quite simply, bivalence is the *sine qua non* for a reasoned and philosophically accountable treatment of these topics that would not rest content with an 'approximative' logic and thereby forego any claim to conceptual rigour. At the same time, *contra* theorists like Searle, Derrida insists on the absolute impossibility that philosophy of language should somehow attain a methodological perspective outside and above the kinds of problematic instance that provide its most challenging material. Hence his attraction to Austin as a thinker who remained keenly aware of the problems thrown up for his own theory by cases which failed to fit in with some existing categorical scheme. Yet it is also very clearly the case that Derrida never goes so far as his post-structuralist disciples would wish in renouncing the distinction between object-language and metalanguage, that is, the necessity that reading should aim 'at a certain relationship, unperceived by the author, between what he commands and what he does not command of the language that he uses' (*OG*, p. 158). In keeping with these principles – as I have argued here – his work offers some of the best, most searching and perceptive commentary anywhere to be found in the recent literature on philosophical semantics and philosophy of logic.

6

# Summa Pro Mathematica: Further Perspectives on *Being and Event*

## I

It will be clear by now that I consider Badiou a remarkably original thinker whose arguments are none the less cogent and precise for their sheer scope of application to topics ranging from mathematics and philosophy of the formal sciences to ontology, epistemology, politics, ethics, aesthetics and psychoanalysis.[1] Moreover, his way of finding common ground between these areas of discourse is not through some vaguely analogical or syncretist fusion of horizons – Hegel's 'night in which all cows are black' – but rather through a highly specific working-out of structural and logical relations that exhibits a degree of conceptual rigour fully equal to its speculative reach. Perhaps the best hope for anyone, like me, seeking to gain a receptive readership for Badiou among those trained up in typically 'analytic', that is, mainstream post-1950 Anglo-American modes of thought is to focus on his work in philosophy of mathematics since this is very much the heart of his project and also a core area of interest in the analytic tradition descending from Frege and Russell. As we have seen, Badiou makes a case for the crucial importance of post-Cantorian set theory as an indispensable resource for any thinking that would move beyond the various deadlocks and dilemmas – especially those concerning the infinite and the issue of priority between the one and the many – that have hobbled Western philosophy from the pre-Socratics and Plato down.

Analytic philosophers may well be suspicious of Badiou's extrapolations from developments within this rather technical or specialized domain to other subject areas where, on the face of it, mathematics can have little or nothing of interest to contribute. Thus while its record of success in the post-Galilean natural sciences can scarcely be denied – whatever the well-known philosophical problems with explaining just *why* this should be the case – still it is far from evident that mathematics should be thought to have any useful bearing on topics such as ethics, politics, aesthetics or psychoanalysis. At most, so the sceptics will say, it might be a source of suggestive ideas or of useful metaphors such as those often drawn from chaos theory, from Gödel's undecidability theorem, or from non-linear systems and equations in order to evoke certain kinds of irreducible complexity that supposedly exceed the utmost resources of 'classical' (i.e. traditional logic-based and strictly consecutive) thought. Otherwise it can serve only as a means by which to contrast the kinds of numerically based or quantitative method that have worked so well when applied to the formal and physical sciences with the kinds of interpretative, agent-centred or broadly hermeneutic approach that are called for in their social- and human-science counterparts. Badiou very firmly rejects this distinction between the *Naturwissenschaften* and the *Geisteswissenschaften* in all its multiform, whether 'analytic' or 'continental' (post-Kantian mainland-European) guises. Along with that he rejects the (to his mind) equally false and damaging split between formal methodologies pertaining to abstract entities such as numbers, sets or classes and empirical or physically based methodologies that may be capable of formal treatment up to a point in certain specific disciplinary or investigative contexts but which resist the kind of full-scale formalization attainable in logic and mathematics. These latter require a mode of thinking that is no doubt *sui generis* as regards its own truth-procedures (its methods of proof, axiomatization, hypothesis-testing, etc.) but which all the same bears a close and specifiable relation to developments in the other aforementioned fields.

Of course, the case needs a lot more in the way of detailed supporting argument before that assertion can be made good. Sufficient to say, at this preliminary stage, that when Badiou stakes his claim for mathematics as the basis of ontology – or for set theory as the sole adequate means of resolving the various paradoxes confronted by other, less developed and resourceful modes of ontological thought – he means this claim to be taken literally or at full philosophical strength.[2] Thus he insists not only on the crucial 'relevance', for philosophers, of various set-theoretical developments from Cantor to the work of Paul Cohen but also on the need to think them through with a properly informed and genuine (i.e. active and participant rather than merely mechanical or second-hand) grasp of the logico-mathematical procedures involved. This is why a text like *Being and Event* – the grand summation of Badiou's thinking up to the late 1980s – contains such a large amount of detailed, complex and often highly demanding material concerned with foundational issues in set theory and with the stages of increasing formal power and refinement that have marked its progress to date.[3] It is also where his approach differs strikingly from much analytic work in this area, since the latter – especially where most influenced by Wittgenstein – tends to focus on a handful of set-piece topics (like the rule-following 'paradox' or the question whether truth in mathematics can be thought of as potentially surpassing or transcending the limits of human epistemic grasp) which are likelier to engage the interest of philosophers than that of working mathematicians.[4] Moreover, this difference is reflected in the sharp contrast between Badiou's choice of complex, challenging and often problematical cases for discussion and the analytic fondness for examples (such as that of elementary addition or continuing the sequence 'n + 2') which may be thought to throw up interesting issues about truth, knowledge and sceptical doubt but which hardly require any great stretch of mathematical intelligence or (even less) intellectual creativity. Indeed, one aspect of Badiou's work that has probably antagonized those few analytical philosophers willing to give it a glance is his somewhat disdainful attitude towards those 'minor', unadventurous, ontologically modest modes of thought which eschew the risks and also the rewards of engaging such issues at the limits of current mathematical or mathematico-philosophical grasp.

Thus a good deal of his attention in *Being and Event* is devoted to a lengthy and (be it said) a carefully conducted *analytic* exposition of the various crises – the successive encounters with contradiction, aporia, logical inconsistency and self-referential paradox – that have punctuated the history of set-theoretical thought yet also provided its chief spur to conceptual innovation and self-renewal. In contrast, he maintains, analytic philosophy of mathematics in the wake of Frege, Russell and Wittgenstein has been notable chiefly for its preoccupation with narrowly technical or agreed-upon topics of debate, and hence for its failure – or downright refusal – to address such far-reaching exploratory concerns. In this final chapter, I shall seek to locate more precisely the points of divergence between the way that these debates have typically shaped up within the analytic camp and the alternative, more mathematically engaged and challenging approach exemplified in Badiou's writings.

# II

To be a realist about mathematics is to take it that the truth-value of our various mathematical statements, theorems, conjectures, hypotheses and so forth is fixed by the way things stand with regard to a domain of mathematical objects and relations between them, these objects and relations being no less real – and those truth-values no less objective – for their abstract or formal character.[5] Moreover, it is to claim that the range of objectively true or false statements far exceeds the restricted though expanding range of those for which we have some adequate proof-procedure or means of formal verification. To be an anti-realist is to find this claim wrong-headed or strictly unintelligible on the grounds that it just cannot make sense to conceive of our somehow having knowledge of objects or of truth-values concerning them if those objects and values are taken to exist in a realm that by very definition transcends our utmost powers of perceptual, epistemic or cognitive grasp.[6] Moreover, it is to find something plainly absurd in the idea that truth can come apart from knowledge – or knowledge from truth – in such a way as to vindicate the realist (objectivist) conception of truth as always potentially surpassing or eluding our best powers of ascertainment. For what could possibly count as adequate warrant for asserting the existence of recognition-transcendent truths that *ex hypothesi* we cannot know or to which we cannot assign a determinate truth-value by any means at disposal? This is how the argument has mostly gone in recent philosophy of mathematics, at least within the mainstream analytic line of descent.

Hence the otherwise curious fact that, in this context, 'realism' and 'Platonism' are pretty much equivalent terms. Realism about mathematical entities – numbers, sets, classes, etc. – is perfectly compatible (indeed synonymous) with conceiving those entities to occupy a realm of absolute ideal objectivity that renders them immune from the fluctuations of empirical knowledge or evidence. Nevertheless, as anti-realists are quick to remark, mathematical realism of this sort has very often gone along with a notable failure to explain just how – by what kind of cognitive modality – we are able to gain epistemic access to objects of this highly fugitive sort. At which point realists (or Platonists) just as promptly respond that, whatever the philosophical problems involved, mathematical knowledge is the surest, most secure kind of knowledge we have, and this not despite but precisely on account of its objective, recognition-transcendent character.[7] Mathematical anti-realism – as propounded by philosophers like Michael Dummett – has its main and, for some, its irresistible source in the puzzlement (or downright bafflement) that tends to be induced by just this claim, that is, that we can have *both* objective truth *and* humanly attainable knowledge, whether in the formal or the physical sciences.[8] Realism takes heart from the opposite conviction, namely that if truth didn't sometimes (and always potentially) transcend our best powers of recognition yet also on occasion fall within our epistemic grasp then quite simply we could make no sense of basic notions like knowledge or the progress of knowledge.[9] Only thus can we explain how certain past errors have later been exposed and corrected while certain hypotheses, conjectures or theorems have either been proven or now achieved the highest degree of rational or probative warrant. And if certain others eventually turn out to be false or to lack such warrant then this can be established only by devising and deploying more rigorous truth-procedures.

Such is the usual realist answer to that mode of sceptical meta-induction that argues from the falsity of most erstwhile scientific 'knowledge' to the overwhelming likelihood that most of our present-day thinking is likewise erroneous in ways we are currently unable to envisage or conceive.[10] From here the argument is often pressed to the point of endorsing a wholesale anti-realist claim, that is, that we can never have rational warrant for supposing truth to exceed knowledge or knowledge to exceed the bounds of present-best belief. In this sense, Badiou is just as much a realist about mathematics as about those other areas of knowledge or disciplines of thought – notably the physical sciences but also history, politics and psychoanalysis – which he takes to involve discovery-procedures deeply akin to those that characterize the development of post-Cantorian set theory.[11] In these cases also, it is a matter of encountering certain kinds of obstacle, paradox, aporia, limiting condition or conceptual double-bind and grasping how they might point a way forward to some otherwise strictly inconceivable advance in the range of available problem-solving or situation-transforming resources. After all, it is the single most striking feature of the way that set theory has developed over the past 100 years – since Bertrand Russell first threw a spanner in the works by discovering the paradox of self-predication – that it has managed to turn setback to advantage by tackling such problems head-on and thereby discovering new possibilities of progress.[12] Of course, the anti-realist may say that what's involved here is not so much a process of discovery as one of invention or a process of creating ideas that don't so much explore hitherto unknown or uncharted territory as devise new ways of proceeding that create their own conceptual landscapes as they go along. Such would be Dummett's view of the matter and such would be the impression one might well receive from some of those passages in *Being and Event* where Badiou stresses the creative character of mathematical thought and thereby its kinship with other domains of responsibly exercised human freedom such as politics and ethics. However, it should also be clear that he thinks of such freedom as exercised always under certain well-defined formal or situational constraints and hence as involving the acceptance of certain likewise inescapable restrictions on the range of valid statements, hypotheses, proposals, courses of action and so forth.

This is why Badiou finds an object-lesson for ethical conduct or political commit-ment in the cases of the two mathematicians Jean Cavaillès and Albert Lautman who were both very active and courageous members of the French resistance and were both shot by the occupying German forces. As Badiou sees it – and without in the least detracting from their moral stature – their actions may be thought in a sense to have bypassed the tribunal of subjective moral conscience by rigorously following out the extreme and unconditional demands placed upon them by pressures of historical circumstance.[13] It is also why there is something distinctly askew about readings of Badiou as an anti-realist with respect to mathematics and the formal sciences, let alone those other more directly or obviously 'real-world'-oriented disciplines of thought and action where there can be no doubting his commitment to radical change through various forms of concerted political engagement and practical agency. To be sure, he makes a point of distinguishing clearly between set theory as the basis of a formal ontology with its source in pure mathematics and set theory as applied to those other subject-domains where its logic comes up against the element of chance or contingent (historically situated) being-in-the-world. However, he is just as keen to insist that if mathematics typically progresses through the encounter with emergent obstacles to thought which bring about some hitherto unthinkable advance in its powers of conceptual grasp, then the same applies to those other sorts of case – for instance, pre-revolutionary states of socio-political crisis or situations of decisive import in terms of some particular life-history – where thinking likewise comes up against a strictly unique and unprecedented problem.

Hence Badiou's special interest in the process by which set-theoretical paradoxes like that discovered by Russell have in turn become the springboard for crucial developments that would not have been possible – for which there would have been no problem-solving impetus or rational incentive – in the absence of that specific provocation. Hence also the analogy with politics which, as I have said, Badiou intends as something more than a mere analogy and which indeed he expounds with a high degree of conceptual and logical precision. This has to do with the marked disparity between, on the one hand, those egalitarian and participatory values promoted in the name of Western liberal democracy (not to mention its socialist, 'social-democratic', or other such variant forms) and, on the other, the distorted or highly selective application of those values that has characterized their 'actually existing' manifestations to date.[14] Above all, the discrepancy leaps to view when one measures the continuing record of prejudice, privilege and exclusionary practice against the standard liberal-democratic appeal to a strictly inclusive, non-discriminatory politics. It is here – in attempting to define more exactly how this situation comes about – that Badiou deploys the conceptual apparatus of set theory and its range of resources for theorizing such issues. That is to say, there emerges a precisely specifiable mismatch between existing, often extreme inequalities of social-political status and the principles endorsed by a specious rhetoric of equal rights, entitlements and obligations. Such claims are belied – shown up as mere legitimizing gambits – by the gap between *membership* and *inclusion* or between what counts as communal 'belonging' by some current range of accepted, for example, state-sponsored criteria and what qualifies citizens for full and active participant membership according to standards (such as those of natural justice or shared humanity) which transcend any such limiting conditions.

Where Badiou's work most notably breaks new ground – and signals its distance from every other present-day movement of philosophic thought – is in the claim that these political issues are capable of being more clearly and productively addressed through the working out of their structural logic in set-theoretical terms. He shows to convincing effect how this approach can sharpen our analytic tools when applied to particular, historically and politically emergent situations like those of pre-Revolutionary France in the mid-to-late eighteenth century or Russia in the years leading up to 1917. Or again, in less positive vein, it throws a revealing light on the various failed, abortive or betrayed revolutions – prototypically those of 1848, 1871 and May 1968 – which can likewise be seen as instancing a certain kind of practical as well as conceptual impasse. Such are the historically salient episodes of setback or defeat that find their most telling analogue in those false dilemmas or obstacles to thought thrown up in the course of mathematical enquiry.[15] Of course there is nothing original about the observation that pre-Revolutionary France and pre-Soviet Russia were societies wracked by just the kinds of deepening crisis, class conflict, abuses of power and widespread popular grievance that could scarcely have issued in anything less than a wholesale change of political regime. Nor is it by any means a claim exclusive to Marxist thinkers like Badiou that such epochal occurrences can be understood, partially at least, through a mode of analysis based on class-interests and the more-or-less mediated structural nexus between these and the underlying forces and relations of production. What does very clearly distinguish his account of such world-transformative events – as well as of the powers that conspire to hold them in check – is Badiou's insistence that they have to be grasped by means of a material and social ontology which in turn finds its sole adequate basis in the conceptual resources of set theory. Only thus, he maintains, can thinking come to terms with the way that such events most often transpire as a result of prior developments concerning which it would not have been possible at the time to predict their outcome with any assurance, yet which proved to have just that decisive effect in shaping the course of history.

Central to his argument here is the set-theoretical notion of 'forcing', developed by the mathematician Paul Cohen in order to explain how advances might occur through a future-conditional or speculative grasp of what *would* necessarily be the truth of certain propositions or theorems *should it turn out* that they were justified by precisely the advance in question.[16] That is to say, such truths are prospective in character, unproven at their time of first enunciation as truth-apt conjectures or hypotheses and yet – *contra* intuitionists, constructivists and anti-realists like Dummett – objectively valid even before any proof is produced. Cohen's term 'forcing', therefore, has to do with the capacity of thought subliminally to grasp and hence pass beyond the limiting range of its currently in place formal procedures or conceptual resources. This involves a Platonist (realist) conception of truth as always potentially recognition- or verification-transcendent. It allows for the standing possibility of advances in mathematics, logic and the formal sciences through the process that receives its most articulate formal rendition in Cohen's work. More informally, it is the same process whereby we are able to grasp that present knowledge falls short of truth in some as yet indeterminate respect, a deficit signalled by the emergence of various tensions, dilemmas, aporias or (at the limit) logical contradictions. So the pursuit of mathematical truth can be seen as a process of 'working-through' – of testing various theorems so as to determine their consistency or otherwise with the body of accepted mathematical knowledge – in something akin to (though also crucially distinct from) the psychoanalytic usage of that phrase.[17] There it is a matter of trying out various interpretative hunches or hypotheses so as to see whether or not they make adequate, convincing, and hence therapeutically effective sense of the subject's memories and relevant life-history. This process may indeed be retroactive – akin to Freudian *Nachträglichkeit* or backward 'causality' after the event – but with the crucial difference that here, in the mathematical context, it is a matter of objective truths (rather than more-or-less plausible narrative accounts) that perform this validating role.

So there are various kinds of analytic working-through that involve very different criteria of truth and methods of proof, ascertainment or verification. This applies not only to mathematics and psychoanalysis – such an outlandish coupling by standard analytic-philosophical lights – but also (for Badiou) to natural-scientific, political, historical and socio-cultural regions of enquiry where again it is always a question of truth even if that question has to be posed in different, specific and precisely formulated ways according to the area or discipline concerned. At any rate it will be clear to any attentive and unprejudiced reader of his work that Badiou maintains the strictest regard for those various kinds of truth-condition – whether formal, empirical, socio-political, ethical or psychoanalytic – that impose their standards as a matter of necessity even if we are not (or not yet) in a position to grasp or consistently apply them. Any confusion or slackening of standards with regard to the relevant area of discourse is prone to encourage just the kind of sophistical or far-gone cultural-relativist thinking that Badiou sees as having resulted from the currently widespread 'linguistic turn'.[18] Nowhere is this more apparent, he thinks, than in Wittgenstein's widely influential idea of correctness in the case of mathematical or logical reasoning as a matter of compliance with some shared or communal rule which can itself possess no ultimate warrant – no truth-conditions or validating standard – beyond the mere fact of its acceptance within the particular community concerned.[19]

It is in this context that Badiou tackles the problem (the pseudo-problem, as he thinks it) of how to hold the line against relativism while somehow avoiding the supposed impasse of an objectivist/realist conception of truth that *ipso facto* places it beyond the reach of human epistemic or cognitive attainment. Indeed, his reflections on the debate between Platonism and anti-Platonism in recent analytic philosophy of mathematics might seem to cast doubt on my characterization of Badiou as a full-fledged realist or objectivist in this regard. Thus, he roundly rejects the version of Platonism defined (if not endorsed) by most analytic philosophers, namely that which views mathematics as 'the *discovery* of truths about structures which exist independently of the activity or thought of mathematicians'.[20] This is to get things completely wrong, Badiou asserts, since it presupposes a categorical distinction between subject and object, internal and external or knower and known that is utterly foreign to Plato's conception of ontology in general and of mathematical ontology in particular. So far from accepting such a drastic bifurcation of being and thought, Plato starts out from the Parmenidean premise that 'it is the same to think and to be'.[21] Thus, when mathematicians engage in a process of reasoning or formal proof-construction, they are not (*per impossibile*) gaining access to items such as numbers, sets or classes that exist in some utterly transcendent, mind-independent realm of absolute ideal objectivity but rather pursuing lines of thought that are none the less rigorous and truth-oriented for the fact that they occur – where else? – in the mind of this or that mathematical reasoner. Such, after all, is Plato's doctrine of knowledge as resulting from an act of *anamnesis*, of 'un-forgetting' or primordial remembrance, as presented in the *Meno* through his set-piece account of how Socrates managed to elicit an understanding of Pythagoras' Theorem from a slave boy who (purportedly) lacked any previous mathematical knowledge and was given only a minimum of prompts to help him along.[22]

Here as so often it is Plato's 'fundamental concern', according to Badiou, 'to declare the immanent identity, the co-belonging, of the knowing mind and the known, their essential ontological compatibility'.[23] And again: '[w]hat the metaphor of anamnesis designates is precisely that thought is never confronted with "objectivities" from which it is supposedly separated. The Idea is always already there and would remain unthinkable were one not able to "activate" it in thought'.[24] This would seem to place Badiou very firmly on the side of those within the analytic camp who have reached the pyrrhic conclusion that, in the case of mathematics at least, we can either have truth or knowledge but surely not both unless on pain of manifest self-contradiction. That is to say, the choice falls out between a Platonist (objectivist) conception of truth that places it beyond the utmost powers of human cognitive grasp and a scaled-down (epistemic) conception that brings it safely back within the bounds of human cognition but gives up any claim to objectivity. For some this is an ultimate dilemma or strict *tertium non datur* which leads them to declare that, quite simply, 'nothing works' in philosophy of mathematics, if 'working' here means 'managing to explain how we could ever have knowledge of abstract, transcendent, mind-independent, and hence to us unknowable entities'.[25] Then again, there are those who regard it as a false dilemma and who seek to negotiate some viable midway course between the twin problematical extremes of a hardline objectivist realism and the recourse to various kinds of anti-realist, conventionalist, fictionalist or communitarian (e.g. Wittgensteinian) doctrine. Most prominent among them are those who advocate a response-dependent or response-dispositional approach that would derive standards of correctness or truth in mathematics from an appeal to the exercise of best judgement under optimal conditions by those deemed fittest or best qualified to pronounce in such matters.[26] However – as Badiou would be quick to remark – such 'solutions' are really nothing of the kind since they yield crucial ground to the sceptic or the anti-realist on precisely the issue as to whether or not mathematical knowledge is aimed towards truths that might always surpass its most advanced, refined or sophisticated powers of proof or ascertainment.[27]

It is in this sense that Badiou can rightly be described (and indeed very often describes himself) as a mathematical Platonist, rather than the sense in which that term is mostly used by analytic philosophers, that is, one that tends to provoke the reactive retreat either to an outlook of downright epistemological scepticism or else to some purported compromise 'solution' that in fact leaves the problem very firmly in place. Moreover, it is only on the basis of this assumption – that truths are discovered (not invented, constructed or created) through a process that strictly precludes any dualism of subject and object or knower and known – that Badiou can plausibly stake his claim for mathematics as fundamental ontology. Otherwise there could be no justification for his use of set-theoretical concepts, in particular Cohen's notion of 'forcing', as a means to make sense of signal advances not only within mathematics but also (allowing for the relevant differences) in other subject areas such as politics and art. That notion would itself make no sense were it not for the existence of objective, that is, verification-transcendent conditions that determine what can and what cannot truthfully be thought in response to some given situation, state of knowledge or conceptual predicament. This is why Badiou is so insistent that mathematical 'Platonism', properly understood, locates those conditions neither 'outside' the subject in a realm of utterly transcendent (hence strictly unknowable) forms or ideas nor 'inside' the subject where any constraints – any standards of validity or truth – would have to be thought of as self-imposed in accordance with whatever the subject takes them to be. For it is then a short distance to those various sceptical or anti-realist positions that despair of reconciling objectivity with knowledge, or again, to the sort of 'sceptical solution' that Kripke and others have derived from Wittgenstein, namely the idea that communal warrant or widespread 'agreement in judgement' is the most that we can hope for and (happily) all that we need.[28]

Badiou has no very high opinion of mainstream analytic philosophy of mathematics, regarding it as mostly preoccupied with issues – like those summarized above – that result from a basic failure to grasp both the nature of mathematical truth and the relationship between truth and knowledge in this and other disciplines. Above all, he rejects the kinds of debate about rule-following and how to stop the endless regress from first-order rules to second-order rules for the application of those first-order rules (and so forth) that have typified so much Wittgenstein-influenced discussion. On Badiou's account, this is merely the upshot of a trivialized conception that takes its cue from a narrowly logicist view of the relevant subject domain and thereby not only boxes itself into sceptical corners of its own contriving but also perversely closes its mind to the scope and power of genuine mathematical thought. It is just his point – repeatedly made against proponents of the 'language-first' approach – that such a scaled-down view of what mathematics (and philosophy of mathematics) might properly hope to achieve goes along with a likewise scaled-down view of the capacity of thought to transcend the limits of some given communal practice or widely shared state of belief.

Hence Badiou's strongly marked aversion to those varieties of pragmatist, hermeneutic, post-structuralist, postmodernist, Dummettian anti-realist or 'post-analytic' approach whose chief common feature – despite their otherwise large divergences of view – is the claim that language in some sense goes all the way down, in which case truth (so far as we can possibly know it) must be construed in language-dependent or language-relative terms. This is why he is fond of quoting Spinoza's peremptory rationalist dictum 'Enim ideam veram habemus' ('For we have a true idea'), representing as it does a well-nigh scandalous affront not only to these schools of thought but also to thinkers of just about every epistemological persuasion from Kant to the present.[29] It is Badiou's principled and passionately held conviction that truth can always exceed or transcend our present-best powers of knowledge and must therefore be thought to set the standard for whatever we can rightly (or intelligibly) say about it. In which case it follows – *contra* the Wittgensteinians, pragmatists, anti-realists, *et al* – that the criterion for what should count as an adequate, knowledge-conducive deployment of language is that it measure up to the requirement of truth, rather than the other way around. Like Spinoza, but unlike many philosophers nowadays, Badiou thinks of language – at any rate in certain disciplines such as philosophy – as properly aspiring to the highest degree of conceptual-semantic clarity and precision, and hence as subject to regulative norms that are not just those of customary practice or communal warrant. He is one of the few present-day commentators who take seriously Spinoza's attempt, in the *Ethics*, to lay out his arguments *more geometrico*, that is, in a Euclidean fashion that purports to arrive at its conclusions through a process of rigorous deductive reasoning along with the full logico-mathematical apparatus of definitions, axioms, propositions, corollaries and scholia.[30]

In this respect – as in others – he takes a view sharply opposed to that of his colleague and erstwhile intellectual sparring-partner Gilles Deleuze.[31] On Deleuze's account, all that creaky Spinozist scaffolding should best be ignored and the *Ethics* read not for its (pseudo-) demonstrative logical structure but rather for the moments of passional intensity and highly charged personal reflection that erupt at various points of the text, especially in the scholia. Not that Badiou is in the least inclined to ignore this 'other' Spinoza or to overlook the signs of a restless, unruly, desirous physical being that Deleuze places very much at centre stage. On the contrary, his reading makes much of those stress-points, anomalous passages and other such crucial (though often disregarded) junctures in the *Ethics* where the supposedly seamless progression from stage to stage in its sequence of argument is interrupted by moments of a strikingly different, that is, highly charged passional character. Thus Badiou, no less than Deleuze, rejects any reading that would focus on its logical (or quasi-geometrico-deductive) structure at the cost of downplaying – or ignoring – that other, intensely affective dimension of Spinoza's life and work. Indeed, it is crucial to his own thinking that Spinoza's resolutely monist ontology – his conception of mind and body or thought and matter as two 'attributes' of the self-same substance – should be subject to just such uncontrollable intrusions not only from the realm of passional experience but also from the world of contingent historical and socio-political events. After all, Badiou's entire philosophic project involves precisely this constant dialectic between, on the one hand, the order of being as revealed or discovered through enquiry into the set-theoretical foundations of ontology and, on the other, the order of events as that which inherently eludes any such account and which sets new standards – new fidelity-conditions – for the exercise of thought in its various spheres of engagement.

Spinoza famously broke off his work on the *Ethics* in order to write the *Tractatus Theologico-Politicus* and thereby intervene, to the best of his powers, in the crisis of conflicting religious as well as political allegiances which at that time threatened to overthrow the Dutch Free Republic.[32] Badiou's reading gains credence from this salient fact, along with the extent to which Spinoza's passions, both positive and negative, were so often evoked by his intense participation in this struggle to preserve the hard-won freedoms of thought and speech. On the other hand – against Deleuze – he holds that we shall underrate the ethical and political as well as the philosophic force of Spinoza's thought if we treat its geometrico-deductive mode of presentation as just a handy formal device or a means of achieving maximum rhetorical and argumentative effect. What Badiou finds so intriguing about Spinoza is precisely this unique combination of a mind fixed upon truths that are taken to subsist *sub specie aeternitatis*, or as always potentially transcending the compass of time-bound human cognition, with an intelligence keenly and deeply aware of its temporal (e.g. cultural-historical and socio-political) involvements.

Spinoza thus stands as a test-case and notable precursor for the two major theses that between them motivate Badiou's entire philosophical project. His thinking prefigures what Badiou has to say – with the advantage of set-theoretical, Marxist, psychoanalytic and other kinds of informative hindsight – concerning mathematics as the basis of all ontology and the event as that which redefines our intellectual and ethico-political responsibilities *vis-à-vis* some contingently entered upon but thereafter strictly binding (since truth-oriented) project. In this respect, he manages to straddle the two major camps of recent French Spinoza interpretation. On the one side were those – like Althusser and the early Balibar – who recruited him to the cause of a 'structuralist' or critical-rationalist Marxism conceived very much in the Spinozist manner as a quest for truth and knowledge ideally unclouded by the effects of false, deceptive, imaginary or ideological belief.[33] On the other were those, including Deleuze, who reacted strongly against this idea (as much with regard to issues in present-day politics as issues in Spinoza scholarship) and who swung right across to the opposite extreme of a reading that emphasized the philosophically exorbitant character of Spinoza's thought and its affinity with such notions as desiring-production, libidinal economy or 'deterritorialized' energy flows.[34]

As I have shown elsewhere, each of these drastically opposed readings is able to claim a good measure of exegetical warrant through the direct appeal to certain strongly supportive passages in Spinoza's text.[35] However, what is conspicuously missing from both interpretations – and what Badiou sets out to provide – is an adequate account of how the method of reasoning *more geometrico* relates to Spinoza's treatment of the passions (positive and negative) along with his response to the pressures and prospects of historical-political life. Thus, Spinoza is a central figure in Badiou's genealogy of modern thought since he, like Badiou, was above all concerned to understand the relations between truth and knowledge, theory and practice, reason as that which aspires to a timeless (prototypically mathematical) order of truth and reason as subject to practical constraints, that is, when required to adapt itself constantly to changing historical and socio-political conditions. However – and this is where Badiou parts company with Deleuze – we shall be in no position no appreciate the strength or intensity of Spinoza's political passions and convictions unless we are willing to measure them against the demonstrative force of his reasoning *more geometrico* and not treat the latter as a mere excrescence or a misconceived attempt to achieve scientific credibility for some otherwise highly questionable premises and conclusions. And again, we shall fail to grasp an important aspect of that reasoning – namely its role as both a critical check upon those passions and a motivating source for them – if we adopt an ultra-rationalist position, like Althusser's, that very largely ignores both the affective dimension and the circumstantial details of Spinoza's conjoint life-and-thought.

To be sure, there is a strong case to be made for viewing Spinoza as a thinker far ahead of his time and one who, moreover, managed to elaborate a proto-Marxist theory of truth, subjectivity and ideological misrecognition. This he achieved – so Althusser maintains – through his distinction between the 'first' and 'second' kinds of knowledge, or his account of how 'confused' or 'imaginary' ideas should properly give way to their 'adequate', that is, their clear and distinct (since rigorously theorized) counterparts.[36] Yet as Althusser's critics have been quick to point out, it is hard to extract any convincing account of political agency or motivation from his high-structuralist account of how subjects are passively interpellated by – or recruited for – this or that dominant ideological formation.[37] What is lacking in his general approach to these matters, as likewise in his reading of Spinoza, is what Badiou most importantly aims to provide: an account of how philosophy might reconcile the claims of conceptual rigour, clarity and precision with a readiness to make full allowance for the unpredictability of real-world events in whichever sphere of intellectual, political or creative endeavour.

Hence the strong sense of underlying affinity despite what would seem the outright conflict between Spinoza's radical monism and Badiou's commitment to an equally radical conception of the multiple as that which precedes, subtends and surpasses any unity imposed upon it by various operations of the 'count-as-one'. Hence also the lesson for those who might be tempted to dismiss Badiou's writing on set-theoretical themes as at best a somewhat fanciful diversion and at worst a display of pseudo-expertise in a discipline utterly remote from his genuine or home-ground interests, that is, politics, aesthetics and psychoanalysis. They would be wrong about this for a number of reasons, among them – as I have said – the high sophistication and conceptual range of Badiou's mathematical thought and the extent to which his ontological (i.e. set-theoretical) concerns intersect with his treatment of those other themes. For, it is just Badiou's point that they constitute the chief enabling 'conditions' for a project that would keep its sights firmly fixed on the standard of truth while nonetheless taking adequate account of those various kinds of events that can always intervene in such a way as to redefine what qualifies as thinking, acting or living one's life in accordance with that same standard. This is why he is so critical, even contemptuous, of much that passes for philosophy of mathematics in the recent analytic tradition, focused as it is on narrowly technical or hyper-inflated issues – such as the Kripkensteinian debate around rule-following – that (in his view) merely trivialize the subject and deflect thinking from other, philosophically as well as mathematically more challenging paths.[38] It is also why he rejects any version, no matter how qualified, of the Frege-Russell logicist programme that would seek to derive all the basic truths of mathematics from a handful of set-theoretical axioms and strictly deductive procedures of proof and demonstration.[39]

Not that Badiou is for one moment denying the absolute centrality of logic to all mathematical reasoning and, beyond that, to any exercise of thought in those above-mentioned 'conditioning' spheres where truth is still very much at issue even if subject to different (no less stringent but historically or temporally indexed) standards. Nor is he much impressed by arguments against the logicist approach that point to the paradoxes of self-predication – along with Russell's 'solution' in the form of a purely stipulative veto – as evidence that the programme cannot be carried through. After all, those paradoxes play a central role in his own account of how advances come about, in this and other realms of enquiry, through the encounter with problems or anomalies that may not be laid to rest once and for all but which serve as an indispensable spur to renewed efforts of investigative thought. However – and this is Badiou's main complaint with regard to logicism in its pure-bred form – such advances can occur only on condition that mathematics be conceived in more ambitious, ontologically expansive terms or in such a way to engage issues beyond the scope of a narrowly axiomatic-deductive approach. That is, they involve not only the realist (Platonist) presupposition that mathematical truths are objective and recognition-transcendent but also the realist (non-abstract, empirically contentful) claim that such truths nevertheless have decisive implications for our knowledge of and dealings with a physical world that is likewise (very largely) independent of our various beliefs concerning it. This may remind us of the physicist Eugene Wigner's famous puzzle about the 'unreasonable effectiveness' of mathematics in the natural sciences, by which he meant the extraordinary fact that a discourse so concerned with abstract entities could have so profound and far-reaching an involvement with our knowledge of the physical world.[40] Still it is a puzzle that must have some solution – *contra* the defeatists, paradox-mongers or downright mysterians – since there is just no ignoring the copious evidence from Galileo down that mathematics does have this remarkable degree of applied-scientific or technological purchase.

Yet there is clearly a sense in which Badiou stands apart from other philosophers of mathematics who have sensibly taken this much for granted and then set about to reconcile the two kinds of realism rather than raising the (apparent) conflict between them into a full-scale dilemma or the pyrrhic conclusion that, quite simply, 'nothing works' in philosophy of mathematics.[41] The most favoured line of argument among these thinkers is one that combines this powerful appeal to the sheer self-evidence of our knowledge of the growth of knowledge with a moderately naturalized epistemology according to which we can have all the objectivity we want or require while keeping it safely within the bounds of knowability or epistemic reach.[42] That is to say, mathematical knowledge can stand as a paradigm case of the need to preserve a due measure of mind-independence for the objects of our knowledge and the truth-value of statements concerning them along with a due allowance for their mind-accessible or even, in some sense, mind-involving character. Such approaches range from the 'strong' response-dispositional account (which realists will reject *tout court* as leaning too far in the opposite direction), through notions of 'humanized Platonism' that attempt (vainly, opponents will say) to resolve the dilemma by grasping both of its horns, to positions – like that of Philip Kitcher – that conserve the objectivity of truth in mathematics while seeking to explain both how we acquire mathematical knowledge and also how that knowledge may be thought of as connecting with the world of scientific discovery or everyday experience.[43] Kitcher suggests that we conceive mathematical truths as deriving from certain 'affordances' of nature – of the way things stand in physical reality – that possess sufficient objectivity to count as truth-makers on a realist view while nonetheless offering sufficient scope for the exercise of human intelligence or cognitive grasp involved in their discovery or uptake. Only thus, he suggests, can we hope to overcome those counsels of despair that exploit what they regard as the strictly non-negotiable divide between objective truth and humanly attainable knowledge. Or again, only thus can a solution be found to the otherwise interminable stand-off between realist (i.e. Platonist or Fregean) conceptions that steadfastly reject any recourse to empirical grounds of knowledge-acquisition and empiricist accounts – following J. S. Mill – which purport to be the sole means of explaining how and why mathematics has achieved such massive success in the physical sciences.[44] On this view even the furthest, most abstract or speculative branches of pure mathematics have their ultimate ground in such basic operations as counting, grouping or assembling into sets.

There might seem very little in common between Kitcher's patiently problem-solving or bridge-building approach and Badiou's (on the face of it) more venturesome forays into regions of thought where analytic philosophers would most likely hesitate to follow. However, I think there is a case to be made that something very much like Kitcher's idea of 'affordance' – of the way that reality lends itself to thought and thought to apprehending the nature and structure of reality – must at bottom be entailed by Badiou's conception of mathematics as the starting point and ultimate basis of any adequate ontology. That is, it presupposes the non-standard, 'analytically' heterodox but altogether more convincing version of Platonism that Badiou puts forward in response to the stock dilemma according to which we can either have (some limit-point notion of) objective truth or (some sensibly scaled down conception of) attainable knowledge but surely not both unless at the cost of manifest self-contradiction. As we have seen, Badiou regards this as a gross misreading of Plato and a failure to take his point – in the *Meno* and elsewhere – that mathematical truths must be conceived as ontologically objective or mind-independent and yet as cognizable by human intelligence just so long as it has attained an adequate, that is, truth-conducive or reliable means of finding them out.

Hence Badiou's emphasis, again following Plato, on the active character of mathematical thought and on the error of supposing that such truths could somehow stand apart from the activity through which they are discovered or from the process of reasoning that brings them to light. In this respect, he stands firmly opposed to those philosophers, among them Heidegger and Wittgenstein, who go so far as to deny that mathematics involves 'thinking' in any proper sense of the term, that is, any sense that would not confuse thinking with mere calculation, mechanical reasoning or rule-governed formal procedure.[45] Thus, *contra* Heidegger, Badiou rejects the depth-hermeneutical idea of language – or our well-attuned hearkening to language – as the source of primordial truths covered over by the fateful turn towards technology, science, mathematics and other such products of the Western drive for conceptual mastery over nature and humankind alike. To be sure, poetry (especially that of Mallarmé) has pride of place within Badiou's conception of art as one of those enabling 'conditions' that allow us to grasp the history of truth as progressively revealed through a sequence of world-transformative 'events' which set new terms for artistic, political, scientific or ethical fidelity.[46] On the other hand, he takes issue with the Heideggerian notion of poetic language as the sole or at any rate uniquely privileged locus of truth.[47] Insofar as that role is occupied by any one discipline, it is mathematics, rather than poetry, that Badiou conceives as pointing back to the ancient Greek 'inauguration' of a thinking that decisively breaks with the *doxa* of received opinion or common sense belief and thereby launches both its own and other truth-based projects of enquiry.

So likewise with Wittgenstein's thoroughgoing version of the modern 'linguistic turn', that is, his idea that various language-games or life forms constitute the ultimate horizon or condition of intelligibility from one cultural context to another. Badiou sees this as a latter-day form of sophistry which, like its ancient precursors, betrays the philosophical vocation by renouncing the quest for truth in favour of a passive acquiescence in opinion and the mind-bending force of persuasive or rhetorical language. His objection to this Wittgensteinian outlook goes along with his insistence that mathematics *thinks* in the strongest possible (creative or inventive but also truth-seeking and objectively oriented) sense of that term. Moreover, it connects with Badiou's claim that mathematics, thus conceived, is the royal road to truth not only in those disciplines or subject areas (such as the physical sciences) closest to its own domain but also – what will seem a scandalous assertion to most analytic philosophers – in the areas of politics, ethics, art and love. For it is just in virtue of its double involvement with a realm of objective, recognition-transcendent truths on the one hand and a realm of encounters, pairings, classes, groups, collectivities or state-imposed inclusions and exclusions on the other that set theory (according to Badiou) can overcome the various false dualisms endemic to most philosophy of mind and knowledge. Not least among these – he maintains – is the mistaken view of mathematical Platonism that has exerted such a hold on recent analytic discourse and that would, if valid, leave no other choice than to redefine 'truth' as epistemically constrained (i.e. as synonymous with best-attainable knowledge) or to place it altogether beyond the reach of human thought and cognition.

That neither is a viable option and that the choice amounts to nothing more than a false *tertium non datur* is Badiou's chief claim in advancing his alternative, non-dilemmatic and (above all) realism-compatible version of the Platonist approach. Realism, that is, *both* in the objectivist (ontological) sense, which allows that truth may sometimes surpass the limits of proof or ascertainment, *and* in the range of senses more relevant to epistemological enquiry, that is, those having to do with the scope and limits (as well as the specific methods and procedures) of human knowledge-acquisition. It is here that Badiou's thinking is at its most original and also – as I have said – that it has most to offer in the context of present-day analytic philosophy. For we should, I think, give serious credence to his claim that this alternative understanding of Platonism by way of developments in set theory has implications outside and beyond the purely mathematical, logical or formal-scientific domains. Thus, it offers a means to comprehend how truth might be construed as always in principle recognition- or verification-transcendent yet also as setting the standard for knowledge in various particular and strongly 'conditioning' (truth-apt) contexts of discovery. Each of these – as Badiou understands it – can be seen to involve a distinctive relation between its range of pre-given structural resources as defined most perspicuously in set-theoretical terms and its openness to just those kinds of disruptive and inaugural events that place new demands on the fidelity of anyone aiming to redeem their as yet unrealized promise. In each case, there is a definite and specifiable condition for what properly counts as an event in that particular domain and also for what counts as truth or fidelity with respect to any such genuine, that is, knowledge-, world-, or life-transformative event.

If this seems a wildly improbable claim by most standards – if it appears to sink ontological differences (like that between the formal and the physical sciences or, more flagrantly, that between scientific knowledge in general and the realm of subjectivity or lived experience) with a reckless or wilful disregard – then the charge is one that finds a powerful rejoinder in Badiou's *Being and Event*. That is to say, it is amply refuted by his various detailed demonstrations of the way that veridical events (discoveries or new beginnings) in such diverse areas of knowledge and experience can be shown to relate, in however indirect or mediated a fashion, to those procedures whereby mathematical truths are derived on the basis of axiomatic-deductive reasoning. The event, as Badiou defines it, is that which radically resists assimilation to the order of being (or the discourse of ontology), since it emerges with unforeseeable disruptive force from a set of enabling conditions which only later – in the philosophic wisdom of hindsight – assume that explanatory role. Yet those conditions cannot be understood, even retrospectively, except insofar as they are grasped through their function of having made possible certain events – discoveries in the widest (though nonetheless rigorously specified) sense of that term – which would otherwise surely have remained beyond the scope of human cognizance. This is what Badiou has chiefly in mind when he speaks of mathematics as fundamental ontology and devotes some of the most densely argued pages of *Being and Event* to an account of how these two dimensions have to be conceived as radically distinct (since the event always comes to disrupt or subvert any prior ontological scheme) yet thinkable only in relation to each other (since what counts as a genuine event can be defined only in terms of that same distinction). These occurrences leave their mark on history at the point where some contingent yet truth-conducive event intervenes in such a way as to create new conditions – new criteria of scientific knowledge, political progress, creativity in the arts or fidelity in matters of personal commitment – which henceforth set the operative standards for that particular domain.

It is here that Badiou's thinking comes closest to Spinoza even though he rejects the Spinozist idea of a single, undifferentiated order of being (interchangeably 'God' or 'nature') manifest to us epistemically restricted human knowers only in the guise of those various 'modes' that constitute the objects of phenomenal experience.[48] So likewise with the two 'attributes' of mind and body which Spinoza conceives – in company with some present-day physicalist or central-state-materialist philosophers of mind – as a false dualism brought about by our humanly limited powers of apprehension. (Indeed, Spinoza thought that there might well exist any number of other such 'attributes' that were unknown and probably unknowable to us on account of those same endemic restrictions on our range of perceptual, cognitive or intellectual grasp.) So it is not surprising that Badiou – whose ontology starts out from the notion of infinitely multiple infinities constrained by the stipulative count-as-one in its various forms – should make a point of staking his distance from Spinoza as the philosopher most committed to a radically monistic or anti-dualist, that is, anti-Cartesian metaphysics of mind and world. After all, it was Badiou who caused considerable upset among the followers of Gilles Deleuze by claiming that the latter – especially in his thinking about issues in mathematics – betrayed all the symptoms of covert attachment to a radically monist or Parmenidean metaphysics and ontology despite his overt celebration of difference, heterogeneity, or multiple and endlessly proliferating 'lines of flight'.[49]

I shall not here attempt to adjudicate the issue between Badiou and Deleuze except to say that it reflects their very different views with respect to crucial topics in the history of philosophy from Plato down and – most crucial of all – the relationship between mathematics, philosophy and the various 'conditions' that constitute philosophy's means of access to truth. Very likely they can be brought out in partial agreement, at least as regards the strict impossibility of thinking the multiple without reference to the count-as-one as that which seeks (albeit vainly) to comprehend the multiple and thereby enables thought to get a purchase on what would otherwise by very definition exceed its capacities of rational grasp. Again one can see how deep and far back are the sources of Badiou's thinking, in this case (again) having their origin in the ancient dialectic of the one and the many bequeathed by Parmenides to Plato, Aristotle and numerous subsequent thinkers. However, the main point I wish to make is that Badiou's thinking never loses touch with 'real-world' (i.e. political, social and practical-ethical) concerns despite this engagement with issues in the realms of metaphysics and fundamental ontology that might well appear highly abstract or rarefied. Indeed, he makes it clear that there is nothing in the least other-worldly about his kind of mathematical Platonism, that is, a conception according to which the objectivity of truth or its recognition-transcendent character is perfectly compatible with a realist outlook as concerns our knowledge of the growth of knowledge and the prospects for further advancement in that regard. In other words, it is a conception that rejects the pseudo-dilemma erected by some analytic thinkers – those, like Paul Benacerraf, who conclude that quite simply 'nothing works' in philosophy of mathematics – and instead takes a robustly realist line in both (i.e. objectivist and cognitivist) senses of the term. Moreover, it holds out the promise of resolving that other great puzzle of recent analytic philosophy, namely (in Wigner's plangent phrase) the 'unreasonable effectiveness' of mathematics when applied to the physical sciences.

What lies at the root of such worrisome but misconceived problems is precisely the failure to follow-through on that ancient Greek insight that gave mathematics absolute pride of place as the starting point of all ontological enquiry and the basis for any philosophically adequate epistemology or theory of knowledge-acquisition. Hence Badiou's claim – so remote from the currency of analytic discourse as to seem well-nigh unintelligible – that set theory provides not only the best means to conceptualize developments in mathematics, logic and the formal sciences but also a privileged point of entry to the four 'conditioning' (extra-philosophical yet philosophically pertinent) spheres of science, politics, art and love. Hence also those passages of highly speculative yet nonetheless rigorous argument where Badiou sets out the different kinds of truth-procedure specific to each of these domains through a point-by-point analogy with set-theoretical developments from Cantor to Cohen. What most needs stressing in this regard is Badiou's insistence that each be thought of as autonomous, that is, as exerting a proper claim to treatment on its own distinctive terms while nonetheless displaying certain formal features – certain typical patterns of genesis, structure, internal development, external relationship, conflict resolution, crisis management and so forth – which define its logical conditions of being and hence its range of potential or conceivable manifestations. For there is no doubting Badiou's adherence to the basic rationalist precept: that whatever can be thought consistently with the principles of logic and also in accord with certain axioms that themselves are either self-evident to reason or known not to contradict any such self-evident truth must itself *ipso facto* be taken as a true belief and hence as entailing the existence (or reality) of just those objects, attributes or properties that make up its content. Such, after all, is the necessary (i.e. the sole adequate) basis for his claim that mathematics *just is* fundamental ontology, rather than a highly effective means of bringing out certain salient structures that characterize this or that ontological domain.

Hence Badiou's emphatic declaration that 'mathematics thinks' as against those who would maintain – on Heideggerian, Wittgensteinian, conventionalist or constructivist grounds – that it amounts to no more than 'correctly' following a rule where what counts as 'correct' is itself just a matter of applying some purely formal procedure or complying with communal norms. On the contrary, he argues: from Plato down every genuine break with the currency of common-sense, intuitive, received or philosophically entrenched belief has come about through a more-or-less overt turn to mathematics as a means of rethinking the most basic issues of ontology and epistemology. Thus, despite his rejection of Spinoza's monist ontology, Badiou can subscribe unreservedly to the Spinozist dictum 'For we have a true idea', and moreover to the Spinozist claim – on the face of it one with radically monist implications – that 'the order of things' and the 'order of ideas' are in fact one and the same order under different descriptions or aspects.[50] This follows from his acceptance of mathematical Platonism construed (as we have seen) in a non-standard way according to which – *contra* the sceptics, anti-realists and conventionalists – there is simply no distinguishing the object-domain of mathematical entities and truths from the various procedures or acts of thought whereby they are brought within range of discovery or formal-demonstrative proof.

What saves this conception from the much-touted Platonist 'dilemma' of objective truth *versus* humanly attainable knowledge is Badiou's refusal (with good Platonist warrant) to allow any such gap to open up in the first place, along with his equally firm insistence on the way that mathematics – as our paradigm case of truth-oriented thought – typically achieves its most signal advances through a constant dialectic of problem-creating and problem-resolving initiatives. It is in the restless movement between these poles that mathematics exhibits both its own capacity for creative self-renewal and the ways in which its various formal procedures bear upon other fields of human experience, knowledge and enquiry. This is why Badiou takes his cue in matters ontological from those passages in Plato's *Sophist* and *Parmenides* where Socrates most directly confronts the aporias of the one and the many, and where thinking sets out on the long and tortuous path that will eventually lead to the paradoxes of classical set theory and the various attempts (by Russell and others) to resolve or at any rate defuse those paradoxes. Like Derrida's deconstructive commentaries on Plato, Rousseau, Husserl, Austin and others, Badiou's is essentially a diagnostic reading which aims to draw out those symptomatic moments of recalcitrant, resistant or non-assimilable sense that signal the presence of a counter-logic at odds with the thinker's overt professions of intent.[51]

It is precisely through coming up against the paradoxes of time, change, motion, multiplicity and the infinite or infinitesimal that certain components of Plato's 'official' doctrine – including the theory of forms – encounter their most radical challenge. Moreover, the challenge acquires its special force from the fact that it is intrinsic or self-generated, that is, that it emerges by the strictest order of logical necessity from just those *echt*-Platonist premises (chief among them the ideal unity and intelligibility of being) that are placed in doubt once the question arises as to how they could possibly be sustained against the rival claim of inconsistent multiplicity or whatever precedes the count-as-one. All of which might seem to shrink the distance between Badiou's idea of inconsistent multiplicity as that which can never be subsumed or conceptualized without remainder by any such procedure and Deleuze's stress on those various kinds of irreducibly plural, non-self-identical, 'molecular' *versus* 'molar' or 'intensive' *versus* 'extensive' multiplicities that are likewise conceived as holding out against any form of systematic or top-down, hierarchical ordering.[52] However, the main difference between them – as Badiou makes clear in his study of Deleuze – is with regard to the precise role of mathematics as a means of pointing up this constant disruptive pressure exerted by inconsistent multiplicity, especially when raised to its highest power through reflection on the set-theoretical paradoxes and the limits of self-assured conceptual grasp brought about by reckonings with the multiple infinite.

Deleuze takes his mathematical bearings from *topoi*, like that of the infinitesimal calculus, which lend themselves directly to his purpose insofar as they have to do with techniques for assigning values, specifying functions or deriving equations in the case of continuous or non-discrete phenomena whose nature it is to elude such treatment except through a mode of gradual approximation. This is also why geometry, rather than arithmetic, is the branch of mathematics most favoured by Deleuze for its capacity to show up the limits of a purely calculative, rational, logic-based or axiomatic-deductive mode of thought and thereby reveal whatever slips through the grid of established concepts and categories. That is to say, it focuses on just those qualitative rather than quantitative aspects – intensity, open multiplicity, rhyzomatics, 'desiring-production', the 'body without organs', energy-flows, endlessly divergent (or 'deterritorialized') lines of flight, etc. – that Deleuze equates with a power to resist all the structures of ideological or socio-political control.[53] For Badiou, conversely, any genuine resistance will have to go by way of a critical engagement with those same structures which in turn requires that they be understood – like certain obstacles to thought in mathematics or logic – through a rigorous procedure that takes full account of their conceptual genesis and logical form.

Hence Badiou's claim for set theory as the paradigm instance of mathematical reasoning, especially in its handling of problems concerned with the existence of multiple orders of infinity and the various disparities between belonging and inclusion, consistent and inconsistent multiplicities, or the count-as-one and whatever is thereby excluded or debarred from membership. Its greatest virtue – on his account – is that a grasp of set-theoretical developments from Cantor to Cohen demonstrates the need for formal rigour and conceptual precision even where the upshot is to generate problems or paradoxes which call for ever more complex or technical solutions. Hence also his reservations with regard to the Deleuzean as well as the wider postmodernist emphasis on all those branches of current mathematics and science – from the differential calculus to fractals, chaos-theory, quantum mechanics (on one interpretation), and so forth – which might be seen as bearing out Deleuze's claim for a new mode of thought that breaks altogether with that classical framework. Such would be a thinking that pitched the continuous against the discrete, intensive against extensive multiplicity, force against form and the realm of purely qualitative difference against that of quantity, numerical identity or calculable function.

According to Badiou, this approach offers only the appearance of a radical break since it lacks the requisite degree of conceptual or logico-mathematical rigour to think its way beyond the classical antinomies first exposed by Plato through Socrates' somewhat baffled encounter with the Parmenidean aporias of the one and the many.[54] It is on these grounds chiefly that he offers the verdict so hotly disputed by Deleuze loyalists, namely that the whole Deleuzean project is compromised – deprived of its radical force – by the failure (or refusal) to press those antinomies through and beyond their point of maximal resistance.[55] What then transpires is just the kind of ironic reversal familiar from many episodes of intellectual history, that is, a reflex movement of thought whereby the celebration of one set of values (Deleuzean immanence, intensity, qualitative difference, etc.) cannot but evoke the opposite set – of unity, identity, discrete numerical existence – and thereby reveal its conceptual dependence on them. If thinking is to achieve genuine critical force, then it must do so through procedures that yield absolutely nothing in rigour or precision to more conservative modes of discourse (e.g. that of mainstream analytic philosophy) that would otherwise – in the absence of any such challenge – claim a rightful monopoly in matters of just this sort.

This is why it is important to stress that when Badiou introduces set-theoretical concepts, it is always in a highly specific context of argument and with due care to specify how they relate to various (on the face of it) wildly miscellaneous topics – from science to politics, ethics, art and psychoanalysis – that constitute his main fields of enquiry. Thus he seeks to specify the various orders of structural, logical or (ultimately) mathematical relationship that can be seen to emerge in each case with the passage from 'inconsistent multiplicity' to the 'count-as-one', that is to say, from the strictly non-denumerable range of possibilities that precedes every event to the occurrence of that particular event as the outcome of choices, decisions and pressures of circumstance which narrow those alternatives down to the point of seeming inevitability. It is just this sense of a willed, yet somehow, predestined commitment to certain specific modes of thought or action – a sense nicely captured in the ambiguity of the phrase *determined to* – that Badiou aims to render through his usage of the set-theoretical concept of 'forcing'. This involves the transference of Cohen's technical term to a context utterly remote from its original field of application but one in which it can nonetheless be seen to possess a real power of conceptual, philosophical and ethico-political clarification. What it shows to most striking effect is the way that certain contingent, that is, in some given situation or state of knowledge strictly unforeseeable events may yet possess a radically innovative, even world-transformative character which then sets the relevant conditions for any thinking that would truly lay claim to intellectual, political, artistic or personal fidelity.

Moreover, as emerges when Badiou discusses Leibniz in *Being and Event*, this is not just a matter of human ignorance *vis-à-vis* the total chain of concatenated causes and effects or a product of our limited powers of rational grasp *vis-à-vis* those of an omniscient knower for whom *ex hypothesi* nothing would be contingent since everything would occupy its rightful place in the necessary order of things.[56] Rather, *contra* Leibniz, it is a question of necessities that come into being only as a consequence of certain events – certain epochal changes or discoveries – whose extraordinary character is precisely a matter of their having been prepared for or their advent guaranteed by no such providential scheme. After all, Badiou's entire project rests on the distinction between mathematics as fundamental ontology (and hence as pertaining to an order of truths strictly unaffected by changes in our state of knowledge concerning them) and those various kinds of historically located thought, knowledge and experience that provide the essential enabling 'conditions' for philosophy. Where they come into contact is not through some Leibnizian God's-eye perspective wherein that distinction would fall away and the idea of contingent matters of fact – as opposed to necessary truths of reason – at last be revealed as merely a product of our time-bound perceptual, intellectual or other such creaturely cognitive limits. On the contrary, according to Badiou: it is through the always unfolding and strictly open-ended dialectic between those two dimensions that philosophy discovers its true vocation as a creative as well as a rigorous and disciplined mode of enquiry.

Hence – to repeat – his highly unusual set-theoretically based approach to a range of subject areas that are nonetheless treated with a due regard for their distinctive characters, truth-conditions, criteria of knowledge or progress and (not least) their various demands upon philosophy insofar as it claims to articulate and clarify these differential features. Hence also his constant fascination with thinkers like Plato, Pascal, Spinoza and the mathematician-philosophers from Cantor to Cohen who can all be seen as engaged in the process of exploring the paradoxes of infinity and extending or refining the conceptual resources whereby to harness – in the literal sense of a doubtless overworked phrase – their thought-provoking capacity. It is precisely in this space opened up between the realm of 'inconsistent multiplicity' and the various domains of the 'count-as-one' – extending as they do from the formal and natural to the social and human sciences – that Badiou locates the potential for a thinking that would constantly test those resources to and beyond their existing limit. No present-day philosopher comes close to Badiou for the ambitiousness, scope and speculative reach of his thinking, allied to a power of conceptual grasp as applied to logic and mathematics that far exceeds anything commonly exhibited by philosophers in the mainstream analytic line of descent. If the latter have steadfastly ignored his work up to now, then most likely it is for just these reasons, that is to say, because it ranges across and beyond all the customary bounds imposed by the standard analytic division of labour. Badiou's approach could not be further from the sorts of philosophically vexatious but mathematically uninteresting problem – like the sceptical 'paradox' about rule-following derived by Kripke from Wittgenstein – that have typified so much recent work in that tradition.[57] What sets it so decisively apart is the strength of his commitment to the claim for mathematics as the sole adequate basis for ontology in general and, beyond that, for those particular or regional ontologies that form the subject-matter of the various sciences. It is also his remarkable ability to think in a way that unites the maximum degree of conceptual precision with the kind of creativity – or courage to venture into new and philosophically uncharted seas of thought – that tends to be regarded by analytic types as leading in an opposite, imprecise and (some would say) philosophically disreputable direction. That Badiou presents so powerful a challenge to this still fairly commonplace set of assumptions is yet further reason to count him among the most significant thinkers of our time.

# Notes

## Chapter 1

1 Alain Badiou, *Pocket Pantheon: Figures of Postwar Philosophy*, trans. David Macey (London: Verso, 2009).

2 Jacques Derrida, *Spectres of Marx: The State of the Debt, the Work of Mourning, and the New International*, trans. Peggy Kamuf (London: Routledge, 1994).

3 Michel Foucault, 'My Body, This Paper, This Fire', *Oxford Literary Review*, IV(1) (1979), pp. 9–28.

4 See for instance Harold Bloom, *The Anxiety of Influence: A Theory of Poetry* (New York: Oxford University Press, 1973).

5 Badiou, *Being and Event*, trans. Oliver Feltham (London: Continuum, 2006).

6 See Badiou, *Being and Event* (op. cit.); also *Number and Numbers*, trans. Robin Mackay (London: Polity Press, 2008).

7 See especially Michael Sprinker (ed.), *Ghostlier Demarcations: A Symposium on Jacques Derrida's* Spectres of Marx (London: Verso, 1999).

8 For his most forceful statement of this view, see Badiou, *Manifesto for Philosophy*, trans. Norman Madarasz (Albany, NY: State University of New York Press, 1999).

9 For further discussion of these and allied developments, see Christopher Norris, *The Truth About Postmodernism* (Oxford: Blackwell, 1993) and *On Truth and Meaning: Language, Logic and the Grounds of Belief* (London: Continuum, 2006).

10 Badiou, *Pocket Pantheon* (op. cit.), p. 138.

11 On this and associated themes, see especially Badiou, *Metapolitics*, trans. Jason Barker (London: Verso, 2005); *Polemics*, trans. Steve Corcoran (London: Verso, 2007); *The Century*, trans. Alberto Toscano (London: Polity Press, 2007).

12 Badiou, *Being and Event* (op. cit.); also *Infinite Thought: Truth and the Return to Philosophy*, trans. Oliver Feltham and Justin Clemens (London: Continuum, 2003); *Theoretical Writings*, ed. and trans. Ray Brassier and Alberto Toscano (London: Continuum, 2004).

13 See Derrida, 'Différance', in *Margins of Philosophy*, trans. Alan Bass (Chicago, IL: University of Chicago Press, 1982), pp. 3–27.

14 For his full-scale philosophical treatment of this theme, see Badiou, *Logics of Worlds*, trans. Alberto Toscano (London: Continuum, 2009).

15 For some classic examples, see Derrida, *'Speech and Phenomena' and Other Essays on Husserl's Theory of Signs*, trans. David B. Allison (Evanston, IL: Northwestern University Press, 1973); *Of Grammatology*, trans. Gayatri. C. Spivak (Baltimore, MD: Johns Hopkins University Press, 1974); *Writing and Difference*, trans. Alan Bass (London: Routledge & Kegan Paul, 1978); *Dissemination*, trans. Barbara Johnson (London: Athlone Press, 1981); *Margins of Philosophy*, trans. Alan Bass (Chicago, IL: University of Chicago Press, 1982).

16  See especially Theodor W. Adorno, *Negative Dialectics*, trans. E. B. Ashton (New York: Seabury Press, 1973).

17  Badiou, *Pocket Pantheon* (op. cit.), p. 136.

18  See especially Derrida, *Of Grammatology* (op. cit.), pp. 157–8.

19  Badiou, *Pocket Pantheon* (op. cit.), p. 138.

20  Badiou, *Logics of Worlds* (Note 14, above).

21  Badiou, *Pocket Pantheon* (op. cit.), pp. 137–8.

22  For further discussion, see Norris, *Minding the Gap: Epistemology and Philosophy of Science in the Two Traditions* (Amherst, MA: University of Massachusetts Press, 2000).

23  See Note 8, above.

24  Badiou, *Being and Event* (op. cit.), pp. 112–20.

25  Badiou, *Being and Event*; also entries for Derrida under Note 15, above.

26  See Graham Priest, 'Derrida and Self-Reference', *Australasian Journal of Philosophy*, 72 (1994), pp. 103–11 and *Beyond the Limits of Thought* (Cambridge: Cambridge University Press, 1995); also Norris, 'Derrida on Rousseau: deconstruction as philosophy of logic', in *Language, Logic and Epistemology: A Modal-Realist Approach* (London: Palgrave-Macmillan, 2004), pp. 16–65.

27  Badiou, 'Being: Multiple and Void. Plato/Cantor', in *Being and Event* (op. cit.), pp. 21–77; also 'The Subtraction of Truth', in *Theoretical Writings* (op. cit.), pp. 95–160.

28  Plato, *Parmenides*, trans. Mary L. Gill and Paul Ryan (Indianapolis, IN: Hackett, 1966).

29  On the often heated debate around Cantor's claims concerning the multiple 'sizes' of infinity and Hilbert's enthusiastic endorsement, see especially Marcus Giaquinto, *The Search for Certainty: A Philosophical Account of the Foundations of Mathematics* (Oxford: Oxford University Press, 2002).

30  Badiou, *Being and Event* (op. cit.), p. 33.

31  Ibid., p. 33.

32  See Note 11, above.

33  Jean-Paul Sartre, *A Critique of Dialectical Reason*, Vol. 1, *Theory of Practical Ensembles*, trans. A. Sheridan-Smith (London: New Left Books, 1976) and Vol. 2, *The Intelligibility of History*, trans. Quintin Hoare (London: Verso, 2006); also Badiou, 'Jean-Paul Sartre (1905–80)', in *Pocket Pantheon* (op. cit.), pp. 14–35.

34  Paul J. Cohen, *Set Theory and the Continuum Hypothesis* (New York: W. A. Benjamin, 1966). See also Michael Potter, *Set Theory and Its Philosophy: A Critical History* (Oxford: Oxford University Press, 2004).

35  Sartre, *Being and Nothingness*, trans. Hazel Barnes (London: Routledge, 2003), p. 9.

36  See Note 26, above; also Paul Livingston, 'Derrida and Formal Logic: formalizing the undecidable', *Derrida Today*, 3(2) (2010), 221–39 and Norris, 'Deconstruction, Science and the Logic of Enquiry', ibid., pp. 178–200.

37  See entries under Note 15, above, and Derrida, 'The Parergon', in *The Truth in Painting*, trans. Geoff Bennington and Ian McLeod (Chicago, IL: University of Chicago Press), pp. 15–147; also – for the more obviously 'topical' turn in his later work – Derrida, *Of Hospitality*, trans. Rachel Bowlby (Stanford, CA: Stanford University Press, 2000); *On Cosmopolitanism and Forgiveness*, trans. Mark Dooley and Michael Hughes (London: Routledge, 2001); *Rogues: Two Essays on Reason*, trans. Pascale-Anne Brault and Michael Naas (Stanford U.P., 2005); *Beast and the Sovereign*, Vol. 1, Michel Lisse, Marie-Louise Mallet, and Ginette Michaud (eds), trans. G. Bennington (Chicago, IL: University of Chicago Press, 2009).

38  See Notes 2 and 37, above; also Cathy Caruth and Deborah Esch (eds), *Critical Encounters: Reference and Responsibility in Deconstructive Writing* (New Jersey: Rutgers University Press, 1995).

39  Roland Barthes, 'Myth Today', in *Mythologies*, trans. Annette Lavers (London: Granada, 1973), p. 112.

40  For further discussion (albeit from a decidedly idiosyncratic angle), see Paul de Man, *The Resistance to Theory* (Manchester: Manchester University Press, 1986); also Norris, *Paul de Man and the Critique of Aesthetic Ideology* (New York: Routledge, 1988).

41  Ludwig Wittgenstein, *Tractatus Logico-Philosophicus*, trans. David Pears and Brian McGuiness (London: Routledge, 1961) and *Philosophical Investigations*, trans. G. E. M. Anscombe (Oxford: Blackwell, 1954).

42  See entries under Note 9, above, for more extended analysis and critique of these various (as I see them) closely related developments.

43  Derrida, *Of Grammatology* (op. cit.), p. 158; also Note 38, above.

44  See Note 7, above.

45  Wittgenstein, *Philosophical Investigations* (op. cit.).

46  See Notes 27, 29 and 34 above.

47  For further discussion, see Norris, *Language, Logic and Epistemology* (op. cit.).

48  See especially W. V. Quine, *Ontological Relativity and Other Essays* (New York: Columbia University Press, 1969) and 'Two Dogmas of Empiricism', in *From a Logical Point of View*, 2nd edn. (Cambridge, MA: Harvard University Press, 1961), pp. 20–46.

49  Michael Dummett, *Frege and Other Philosophers* (Oxford: Oxford University Press, 1996).

50  Derrida, *Of Grammatology* (op, cit.), p. 158.

51  Ibid., p. 158.

52  Ibid., p. 158.

53  Derrida, 'Afterword: toward an ethic of conversation', in Gerald Graff (ed.), *Limited Inc* (Evanston, IL: Northwestern University Press, 1989), pp. 111–54; p. 123. For the background to this rejoinder, see also Derrida, 'Signature Event Context', *Glyph*, Vol. 1 (Baltimore, MD: Johns Hopkins University Press, 1975), pp. 172–97; John R. Searle, 'Reiterating the Differences', ibid., pp. 198–208; Derrida, 'Limited Inc abc', *Glyph*, 2 (1977), pp. 75–176.

54  See Note 36, above; also Derrida, 'The Double Session', in *Dissemination* (op. cit.), pp. 173–286.

55  Kurt Gödel, 'On Formally Undecidable Propositions of *Principia Mathematica* and Related Systems', trans. B. Meltzer (New York: Basic Books, 1962); see also Ernest Nagel and James Newman, *Gödel's Theorem* (London: Routledge & Kegan Paul, 1971) and S. G. Shanker (ed.), *Gödel's Theorem in Focus* (London: Routledge, 1987).

56  Badiou, *Pocket Pantheon* (op. cit.), p. 130.

57  Ibid., p. 128.

58  Derrida, *Spectres of Marx* (Note 2, above).

59  See Note 7, above.

60  Badiou, *Pocket Pantheon* (op. cit.), pp. 130–1.

61  See Notes 26 and 36, above.

62  For classic statements of the 'strong' logical-revisionist case, see Quine, 'Two Dogmas of Empiricism' (op. cit.) and Hilary Putnam, *Mathematics, Matter and Method* (Cambridge: Cambridge University Press, 1975); also Norris, *Hilary Putnam: Realism, Reason and the Uses of Uncertainty* (Manchester: Manchester University Press, 2002).

63   See for instance Mark C., Taylor, *Erring: A Postmodern A/Theology* (Chicago, IL: University of Chicago Press, 1984) and John D. Caputo, *Prayers and Tears of Jacques Derrida: Religion without Religion* (Bloomington, IN: Indiana University Press, 1997); also Arthur Bradley, 'Derrida's God: a genealogy of the theological turn', *Paragraph*, 29(3) (2006), pp. 21–42. For a powerful and timely antidote to such thinking, see Martin Hägglund, *Radical Atheism: Derrida and the Time of Life* (Stanford, CA: Stanford University Press, 2008).

64   See entries under Note 53, above.

65   See especially Michael Dummett, *Truth and Other Enigmas* (London: Duckworth, 1978) and *The Logical Basis of Metaphysics* (Duckworth, 1991); also Christopher Norris, *Truth Matters: Realism, Anti-Realism and Response-Dependence* (Edinburgh: Edinburgh University Press, 2002) and Neil Tennant, *The Taming of the True* (Oxford: Clarendon Press, 2002).

66   See Note 39, above.

# Chapter 2

1   See especially Alain Badiou, *Ethics: An Essay on the Understanding of evil*, trans. Peter Hallward (London: Verso, 2001).

2   See especially Badiou, *Metapolitics*, trans. Jason Barker (London: Verso, 2005); *Polemics*, trans. Steve Corcoran (London: Verso, 2006); *The Century*, trans. Alberto Toscano (Cambridge: Polity Press, 2007).

3   Badiou, *Manifesto for Philosophy*, trans. Norman Madarasz (Albany, NY: State University of New York Press, 1999); *Infinite Thought: Truth and the Return to Philosophy*, trans. Oliver Feltham and Justin Clemens (London: Continuum, 2003); *Theoretical Writings*, ed. and trans. Ray Brassier and Alberto Toscano (London: Continuum, 2004).

4   See for instance Immanuel Kant, *Political Writings*, Hans Reiss (ed.) (Cambridge: Cambridge University Press, 1991).

5   See especially Ludwig Wittgenstein, *Philosophical Investigations*, trans. G. E. M. Anscombe (Oxford: Blackwell, 1951).

6   Badiou, *Manifesto for Philosophy* (op. cit.).

7   For some highly relevant commentary, see Ronald Beiner and Jennifer Nedelski (eds), *Judgment, Imagination, and Politics: Themes from Kant and Arendt* (Lanham, MD: Rowman and Littlefield, 2001).

8   See for instance Avital Shimony and D. Weinstein (eds), *The New Liberalism: Reconciling Liberty and Community* (Cambridge: Cambridge University Press, 2001).

9   Badiou, *Being and Event*, trans. Oliver Feltham (London: Continuum, 2005); also Christopher Norris, *Alain Badiou's* Being and Event: *A Reader's Guide* (London: Continuum, 2009).

10   See especially Suzanne Barnard and Bruce Fink (eds), *Reading Seminar XX: Lacan's Major Work on Love, Knowledge, and Feminine Sexuality* (Albany, NY: State University of New York Press, 2002).

11   See Badiou, *Metapolitics* (op. cit.).

12   Badiou, 'Spinoza', in *Being and Event* (op. cit.), pp. 112–20 and 'Spinoza's Closed Ontology', in *Theoretical Writings* (op. cit.), pp. 81–93.

13  See Badiou, *Being and Event* and *Theoretical Writings*; also Michael Potter, *Set Theory and its Philosophy: A Critical Introduction* (Oxford: Oxford University Press, 2004).

14  For some highly illuminating discussion, see A. W. Moore, *The Infinite* (London: Routledge, 2001).

15  Bertrand Russell, *Introduction to Mathematical Philosophy* (London: Allen & Unwin, 1930).

16  See especially Badiou, *Polemics* (op. cit.).

17  Badiou, *The Century* (op. cit.).

18  See for instance Iris Marion Young, *Justice and the Politics of Difference* (Princeton, NJ: Princeton University Press, 1990); also Todd May, *The Moral Theory of Poststructuralism* (Philadelphia, PA: Pennsylvania State University Press, 1994) and – for a critique of such thinking – Christopher Norris, *The Truth About Postmodernism* (Oxford: Blackwell, 1993) and *Truth and the Ethics of Criticism* (Manchester: Manchester University Press, 1994).

19  Badiou, *Saint Paul: The Foundation of Universalism*, trans. Ray Brassier (Stanford, CA: Stanford University Press, 2003). For some illuminating cultural-historical background, see also Bruce W. Winter, *Philo and Paul among the Sophists* (Cambridge: Cambridge University Press, 1997).

20  Immanuel Kant, *Critique of Pure Reason*, trans. N. Kemp Smith (London: Macmillan, 1964).

21  Immanuel Kant, *Critique of Practical Reason*, trans. Werner Pluhar (Indianapolis, IN: Hackett, 2002).

22  See also Badiou, *Number and Numbers*, trans. Robin MacKay (London: Polity Press, 2008).

23  Badiou, *Number and Numbers* (op. cit.).

24  Plato, *Parmenides*, trans. Mary L. Gill and Paul Ryan (Indianapolis, IN: Hackett, 1996); also John A. Palmer, *Plato's Reception of Parmenides* (Oxford: Clarendon Press, 2002).

25  For an extended and sharply angled critical treatment of these themes, see Richard L. Harland, *Superstructuralism: The Philosophy of Structuralism and Post-Structuralism* (London: Methuen, 1987).

26  The sorts of approach that Badiou has in mind are fairly represented by the essays collected in Paul Benacerraf and Hilary Putnam (eds), *The Philosophy of Mathematics: Selected Essays*, 2nd edn. (Cambridge: Cambridge University Press, 1983) and W. D. Hart (ed.), *The Philosophy of Mathematics* (Oxford: Oxford University Press, 1996).

27  See Martin Heidegger, *Being and Time*, trans. John McQuarrie and Edward Robinson (Oxford: Blackwell, 1980) and W. V. Quine, *'Ontological Relativity' and Other Essays* (New York: Columbia University Press, 1969); also – for a full-scale critique of such thinking – Christopher Norris, *Resources of Realism: Prospects for 'Post-Analytic' Philosophy* (London: Macmillan, 1997) and *New Idols of the Cave: On the Limits of Anti-Realism* (Manchester: Manchester University Press, 1997).

28  See for instance Dale Jacquette, *Ontology* (Montreal, QC: Queen's University Press, 2002).

29  See especially Martin Heidegger, *Poetry, Language and Thought*, trans. Albert Hofstadter (New York: Harper & Row, 1971) and *Early Greek Thinking*, trans. David Krell and Frank Capuzzi (Harper & Row, 1976).

30  See entries under Note 26, above.

31  See Note 18, above; also Badiou, *Number and Numbers* (op. cit.) and *The Concept of Model: An Introduction to the Materialist Epistemology of Mathematics*, trans. Zachary Luke Fraser and Tzuchien Tho (Victoria: re-press, 2007).

32  See Michael Potter, *Set Theory and its Philosophy* (op. cit.).

33  See Note 26, above; also Hilary Putnam, *Mathematics, Matter and Method* (Cambridge: Cambridge University Press, 1975); Crispin Wright, *Wittgenstein on the Foundations of Mathematics* (Cambridge, MA: Harvard University Press, 1980), *Realism, Meaning and Truth* (Oxford: Blackwell, 1987) and *Truth and Objectivity* (Cambridge, MA: Harvard University Press, 1992).

34  For a detailed account, see Christopher Norris, *Minding the Gap: Epistemology and Philosophy of Science in the Two Traditions* (Amherst, MA: University of Massachusetts Press, 2000); also Leila Haaparanta (ed.), *Mind, Meaning, and Mathematics: Essays on the Philosophical Views of Husserl and Frege* (Dordrecht and Boston: Kluwer, 1994).

35  See for instance Jacques Derrida, '"Genesis and Structure" and Phenomenology', in *Writing and Difference*, trans. Alan Bass (London: Routledge & Kegan Paul, 1978), pp. 154–68; *Edmund Husserl's 'Origin of Geometry': An Introduction*, trans. John P. Leavey (Lincoln, Neb.: University of Nebraska Press, 1989); *The Problem of Genesis in Husserl's Philosophy*, trans. Marian Hobson (Chicago, IL: University of Chicago Press, 2003).

36  Paul J. Cohen, *Set Theory and the Continuum Hypothesis* (New York: W. A. Benjamin, 1966).

37  See especially Badiou, *Being and Event* (op. cit.), pp. 325–43.

38  Ibid., p. 327.

39  See especially Badiou, *Manifesto for Philosophy* (op. cit.).

40  See Note 10, above; also Jacques Lacan, *Ecrits: A Selection*, trans. A. Sheridan (London: Tavistock, 1977) and *The Language of the Self: The Function of Language in Psychoanalysis*, trans. Anthony Wilden (Baltimore, MD: Johns Hopkins University Press, 1968).

41  Badiou, *Being and Event*, pp. 391–435; also E. Cadava, P. Connor and J.-L. Nancy (eds), *Who Comes After the Subject?* (London: Routledge, 1991) and Paul Smith, *Discerning the Subject* (Minneapolis, MN: University of Minnesota Press, 1988).

42  René Descartes, *Selected Philosophical Writings*, J. Cottingham (ed.) (Cambridge: Cambridge University Press, 1988).

43  Jacques Lacan, 'The Insistence of the Letter in the Unconscious, or Reason Since Freud', trans. Jacques Ehrmann, *Yale French Studies*, 36/7 (1966), pp. 112–47.

44  Badiou, 'Ontology is Mathematics', in *Theoretical Writings* (op. cit.), pp. 3–93.

45  Joshua Gert, 'Toward an Epistemology of Certain Substantive *A Priori* Truths', *Metaphilosophy*, 40(2) (2009), pp. 214–36; p. 222.

46  See for instance the essays on this topic collected in Roberto Casati and Christine Tappolet (eds), *Response-Dependence* (*European Review of Philosophy*, Vol. 3 [1998]).

47  For further discussion, see Christopher Norris, *Truth Matters: Realism, Anti-realism, and Response-Dependence* (Edinburgh: Edinburgh University Press, 2002).

48  See for instance Mark Johnston, 'How to Speak of the Colours', *Philosophical Studies*, 68 (1992), pp. 221–63 and various contributions to J. Haldane and C. Wright (eds), *Reality, Representation and Projection* (Oxford: Oxford University Press, 1993).

49  Badiou, *Being and Event*, pp. 391 and 393.

50  See Note 41, above.

51  Jean-Paul Sartre, *Critique of Dialectical Reason*, Vol. 1, *Theory of Practical Ensembles*, trans. Alan Sheridan-Smith (London: New Left Books, 1976) and Vol. 2, *The Intelligibility of History*, trans. Quintin Hoare (London: Verso, 1994).

52  See Christopher Norris, *Minding the Gap* (op. cit.) for a detailed account of the relevant episodes in this critical-rationalist line of descent.

53  Badiou, *Being and Event*, p. 431.

54  See especially Badiou, *Infinite Thought* (op. cit.).

55  See Christopher Norris, *Truth and the Ethics of Criticism* (op. cit.); also *Uncritical Theory: Intellectuals, Postmodernism, and the Gulf War* (London: Lawrence & Wishart, 1992).

56  Badiou, 'The Paris Commune: a political declaration on politics', in *Polemics* (op. cit.), pp. 257–90.

57  Michael Dummett, *Elements of Intuitionism* (Oxford: Oxford University Press, 1977); also *Truth and Other Enigmas* (London: Duckworth, 1978) and *The Logical Basis of Metaphysics* (Duckworth, 1991). For a critique of Dummett's arguments, see Christopher Norris, *Truth Matters* (op. cit.) and *Philosophy of Language and the Challenge to Scientific Realism* (London: Routledge, 2003).

58  See Badiou, *Number and Numbers* (op. cit.) and 'Ontology is Mathematics', in *Theoretical Writings* (op. cit.), pp. 3–93.

59  Badiou, *Being and Event* (op. cit.), p. 248.

60  Michael Dummett, *Elements of Intuitionism* (op. cit.); also L. E. J. Brouwer, *Brouwer's Cambridge Lectures on Intuitionism*, D. van Dalen (ed.) (Cambridge: Cambridge University Press, 1981).

61  Badiou, *Being and Event* (op. cit.), p. 223.

62  See W. V. Quine, *'Ontological Relativity' and Other Essays* (op. cit.) and 'Two Dogmas of Empiricism', in *From a Logical Point of View*, 2nd edn. (Cambridge, MA: Harvard University Press, 1961), pp. 20–46.

63  Badiou, *Being and Event* (op. cit.), pp. 112–20.

64  Alfred Tarski, 'The Concept of Truth in Formalized Languages', in *Logic, Semantics and Metamathematics*, trans. J. H. Woodger (Oxford: Oxford University Press, 1956), pp. 152–278.

65  See for instance Michael Sandel, *Liberalism and the Limits of Justice* (Cambridge: Cambridge University Press, 1982) and Michael Walzer, *Spheres of Justice* (Oxford: Blackwell, 1983); also – for a more philosophically nuanced anti-Kantian but not purely communitarian approach – Bernard Williams, *Ethics and the Limits of Philosophy* (London: Fontana, 1985).

66  For an account of these complex, often tortuous passage of argument in Kant's writings on ethics, aesthetics and politics along with a critique of some of the uses to which they have been put by recent especially 'postmodernist' commentators, see Christopher Norris, 'Kant Disfigured', in *The Truth about Postmodernism* (Oxford: Blackwell, 1993), pp. 182–256.

67  Immanuel Kant, *Political Writings*, Hans Reiss (ed.) (Cambridge: Cambridge University Press, 1991).

68  See Badiou, *Manifesto for Philosophy* (op. cit.); also Christopher Norris, *The Truth About Postmodernism* (op. cit.), for further discussion of this lately emergent nexus of themes and ideas.

69  See especially Richard Rorty, *Philosophy and the Mirror of Nature* (Oxford: Blackwell, 1980); *Contingency, Irony, Solidarity* (Cambridge: Cambridge University Press, 1989); *Objectivity, Relativism, and Truth* (Cambridge U.P., 1991).

# Chapter 3

1 See for instance Christopher Norris, *Against Relativism: Philosophy of Science, Deconstruction and Critical Theory* (Oxford: Blackwell, 1997); *Language, Logic and Epistemology: A Modal-Realist Approach* (London: Macmillan, 2004); *Fiction, Philosophy and Literary Theory: Will the Real Saul Kripke Please Stand up?* (London: Continuum, 2007); *Re-Thinking the Cogito: naturalism, Reason and the Venture of Thought* (London: Continuum, 2010).

2 See especially Jacques Derrida, *'Speech and Phenomena' and Other Essays on Husserl's Theory of Signs*, trans. David B. Allison (Evanston, IL: Northwestern University Press, 1973); *Of Grammatology*, trans. Gayatri C. Spivak (Baltimore, MD: Johns Hopkins University Press, 1976); *Writing and Difference*, trans. Alan Bass (London: Routledge & Kegan Paul, 1978); *Edmund Husserl's 'Origin of Geometry': An Introduction*, trans. John P. Leavey (Pittsburgh, PA: Duquesne University Press, 1978); *Dissemination*, trans. Barbara Johnson (London: Athlone Press, 1981); 'The Parergon', in *The Truth in Painting*, trans. Geoff Bennington and Ian McLeod (Chicago, IL: University of Chicago Press), pp. 15–147.

3 John R. Searle, 'Reiterating the Differences: A Reply to Derrida', *Glyph*, Vol. I (Baltimore, MD: Johns Hopkins University Press, 1977), pp. 198–208.

4 See Derrida, 'Signature Event Context', *Glyph*, Vol. I (op. cit.), pp. 172–97 and 'Limited Inc. a b c', *Glyph*, Vol. II (Johns Hopkins U. P., 1977), pp. 162–254; 'Afterword: toward an ethic of conversation', in *Limited Inc*, Gerald Graff (ed.) (Evanston, IL: Northwestern University Press, 1979), pp. 111–60; *The Post Card: from Socrates to Freud and beyond*, trans. Alan Bass (Chicago, IL: University of Chicago Press, 1987).

5 J. L. Austin, *Philosophical Papers* (Oxford: Oxford University Press, 1961) and *How to Do Things With Words* (Oxford: Clarendon Press, 1963); also Gilbert Ryle, *Dilemmas* (Cambridge: Cambridge University Press, 1954).

6 See especially Derrida, 'Signature Event Context' and *The Post Card* (Notes 2 and 4, above).

7 For some witty variations on this theme, see Shoshana Felman, *The Literary Speech-Act: Don Juan with J. L. Austin, or Seduction in Two Languages*, trans. Catherine Porter (Ithaca, NY: Cornell University Press, 1983).

8 For further discussion, see Christopher Norris, *Re-Thinking the Cogito* (op. cit.) and 'Ethics, Normativity and Deconstruction', in *Fiction, Philosophy and Literary Theory* (op. cit.), pp. 35–76.

9 Austin, 'A Plea for Excuses', in *Philosophical Papers* (op. cit.), pp. 123–52; p. 130.

10 Ibid., p. 130.

11 Ryle, *The Concept of Mind* (London: Hutchinson, 1949).

12 Richard Rorty (ed.), *The Linguistic Turn: Essays in Philosophical Method* (Chicago, IL: University of Chicago Press, 1967).

13 See for instance Rorty, *Philosophy and the Mirror of Nature* (Oxford: Blackwell, 1980); *Contingency, Irony and Solidarity* (Cambridge: Cambridge: Cambridge University Press, 1989); *Objectivity, Relativism, and Truth* (Cambridge U.P., 1989).

14 Rorty, 'Philosophy as a Kind of Writing: an essay on Derrida', in *Consequences of Pragmatism* (Brighton: Harvester Press, 1982), pp. 89–109 and 'Is Derrida a Transcendental Philosopher?', in *Essays on Heidegger and Others* (Cambridge: Cambridge University Press, 1991), pp. 119–28; also Christopher Norris, 'Philosophy as *Not* Just a "Kind of Writing": Derrida and the claim of reason', in Reed Way

Dasenbrock (ed.), *Re-Drawing the Lines: Analytic Philosophy, Deconstruction, and Literary Theory* (Minneapolis, MN: University of Minnesota Press, 1989), pp. 189–203 and Richard Rorty, 'Two Versions of "Logocentrism": a reply to Norris', ibid., pp. 204–16.

15   See relevant entries under Note 2, above.

16   Paul de Man, 'Preface' to Carol Jacobs, *The Dissimulating Harmony: Images of Interpretation in Nietzsche, Rilke and Benjamin* (Baltimore, MD: John Hopkins University Press, 1978), p. xiii.

17   Ibid., p. xiii.

18   See Derrida, 'Limited Inc. a b c' and 'Afterword: toward an ethic of conversation' (Note 2, above).

19   de Man, *The Resistance to Theory* (Minneapolis, MN: University of Minnesota Press, 1986), p. 13.

20   Ibid., pp. 18–19.

21   See for instance Stanley Fish, *Is There a Text in This Class?: The Authority of Interpretive Communities* (Cambridge, MA: Harvard University Press, 1980).

22   See Note 14, above.

23   Derrida, 'Afterword' (op. cit.), pp. 122–3.

24   For a classic exposition of this view, see E. D. Hirsch, *Validity in Interpretation* (New Haven, CT: Yale University Press, 1967).

25   For further argument to similar effect, see Christopher Norris, *Deconstruction and the Unfinished Project of Modernity* (London: Athlone Press, 2000).

26   Jacques Derrida, *Of Grammatology* (op. cit.), pp. 157–8.

27   See especially Jacques Derrida, *Edmund Husserl's 'Origin of Geometry': An Introduction Speech and Phenomena, and Writing and Difference* (Note 2, above).

28   Jacques Derrida, ' "Genesis and Structure" and Phenomenology', in *Writing and Difference* (op. cit.), pp. 154–68; p. 160.

29   Immanuel Kant, *Critique of Pure Reason*, trans. N. Kemp Smith (London: Macmillan, 1964).

30   John McDowell, *Mind and World* (Cambridge, MA: Harvard University Press, 1994).

31   Christopher Norris, 'McDowell on Kant: redrawing the bounds of sense' and 'The Limits of Naturalism: further thoughts on McDowell's *Mind and World*', in *Minding the Gap* (Amherst, MA: University of Massachusetts Press, 2000), pp. 172–96 and 197–230.

32   For further discussion, see M. C. Dillon (ed.), *Ecart and Difference: Merleau-Ponty and Derrida on Seeing and Writing* (Atlantic Highlands, NJ: Humanities Press, 1997) and Jack Reynolds, *Merleau-Ponty and Derrida: Intertwining Embodiment and Alterity* (Ohio: Ohio University Press, 2004).

33   See for instance A. J. Ayer, 'Novelist-Philosophers V: Jean-Paul Sartre', *Horizon*, No. 12 (July 1945), pp. 12–26 and No. 13 (August 1945), pp. 101–10.

34   Ludwig Wittgenstein, *Philosophical Investigations*, trans. and ed. G. E. M. Anscombe (Oxford: Blackwell, 1958).

35   J. L. Austin, 'A Plea for Excuses' (op. cit.), p. 129; see also Robert L. Arrington, 'Can There Be a Linguistic Phenomenology?', *Philosophical Quarterly*, 25(101) (1975), pp. 289–304 and Jerry Gill, 'Linguistic Phenomenology', *International Philosophical Quarterly*, 13 (1975), pp. 535–50.

36   See especially Geoffrey Hartman, *Saving the Text: Literature/Derrida/Philosophy* (Baltimore, MD: Johns Hopkins University Press, 1981).

37  Jacques Derrida, 'This Strange Institution Called Literature: an interview with Jacques Derrida', in Derek Attridge (ed.), *Acts of Literature* (New York: Routledge, 1992), pp. 33–75; p. 52.

38  Ludwig Wittgenstein, *Philosophical Investigations* (op. cit.).

39  See Christopher Norris, 'Extraordinary Language: why Wittgenstein didn't like Shakespeare', in *Fiction, Philosophy and Literary Theory* (op. cit.), pp. 159–211 and 'Provoking Philosophy: Shakespeare, Johnson, Wittgenstein, Derrida', *Journal of Literary Criticism*, 12(1 and 2) (June/December 2008), pp. 51–107.

40  Jacques Derrida, 'This Strange Institution Called Literature' (op. cit.), pp. 69–70.

41  Jacques Derrida, 'White Mythology: Metaphor in the Text of Philosophy', in *Margins of Philosophy*, trans. Alan Bass (Chicago, IL: University of Chicago Press, 1982), pp. 207–71.

42  Jacques Derrida, 'The Supplement of Copula: Philosophy *Before* Linguistics', in *Margins of Philosophy* (op. cit.), pp. 175–205.

43  See Note 13, above; also Richard Rorty, *Essays on Heidegger and Others* (op. cit.).

44  Emile Benveniste, *Problems in General Linguistics*, trans. Mary E. Meek (Coral Gables, FL: University of Miami Press, 1971).

45  Donald Davidson, 'On the Very Idea of a Conceptual Scheme', in *Inquiries into Truth and Interpretation* (Oxford: Oxford University Press, 1984), pp. 183–98.

46  For a flat-out statement of the strong-revisionist case – albeit one that is markedly qualified elsewhere in his writings – see W. V. Quine, 'Two Dogmas of Empiricism', in *From a Logical Point of View*, 2nd edn. (Cambridge, MA: Harvard University Press, 1961), pp. 20–46. For further highly relevant discussion, see Graham Priest, 'Derrida and Self-Reference', *Australasian Journal of Philosophy*, 72 (1994), pp. 103–11 and *Beyond the Limits of Thought* (Cambridge: Cambridge University Press, 1995); also Susan Haack, *Deviant Logic: Some Philosophical Issues* (Cambridge: Cambridge University Press, 1974); Christopher Norris, 'Derrida on Rousseau: deconstruction as philosophy of logic', in *Language, Logic and Epistemology: A Modal-Logical Approach* (op. cit.), pp. 16–65; Nicolas Rescher, *Many-Valued Logic* (New York: McGraw-Hill, 1969).

47  W. V. Quine, 'Two Dogmas of Empiricism' (op. cit.) and *Ontological Relativity and Other Essays* (New York: Columbia University Press, 1969); Hilary Putnam, *Mathematics, Matter and Method* (Cambridge: Cambridge University Press, 1975); Christopher Norris, *Hilary Putnam: Realism, Reason and the Uses of Uncertainty* (Manchester: Manchester University Press, 2002).

48  W. V. Quine, 'Two Dogmas of Empiricism' (op. cit.).

49  For a range of views, see Sandra G. Harding (ed.), *Can Theories be Refuted?: Essays on the Duhem-Quine Thesis* (Dordrecht: D. Reidel, 1976).

50  Thomas S. Kuhn, *The Structure of Scientific Revolutions*, 2nd edn. (Chicago, IL: Chicago University Press, 1970); also Christopher Norris, *Resources of Realism: Prospects for 'Post-Analytic' Philosophy* (London: Macmillan, 1997); *New Idols of the Cave: On the Limits of Anti-Realism* (Manchester: Manchester University Press, 1997); *On Truth and Meaning: Language, Logic and the Grounds of Belief* (London: Continuum, 2006).

51  For a critical account of these developments, see Norris, *Against Relativism* (op. cit.).

52  See especially Gilles Deleuze, *The Logic of Sense*, trans. Mark Lester, Constantin Boundas (ed.) (London: Athlone Press, 1990) and *Difference and Repetition*, trans. Paul Patton (London: Athlone Press, 1994).

53  For further discussion, see Norris, *Fiction, Philosophy and Literary theory* (op. cit.).

54  See for instance J. Hillis Miller, *Fiction and Repetition: seven English novels* (Oxford: Blackwell, 1982); *The Linguistic Moment: from Wordsworth to Stevens* (Princeton, NJ: Princeton University Press, 1985); *The Ethics of Reading* (New York: Columbia University Press, 1987).

55  See also Norris, *Deconstruction and the Unfinished Project of Modernity* (op. cit.).

56  de Man, *The Resistance to Theory* (op. cit.). See also de Man, *Allegories of Reading: figural language in Rousseau, Nietzsche, Rilke, and Proust* (New Haven: Yale University Press, 1979); *The Rhetoric of Romanticism* (New York: Columbia University Press, 1984); *Aesthetic Ideology*, A. Warminski (ed.) (Minneapolis, MN: University of Minnesota Press, 1996); Norris, *Paul de Man: deconstruction and the Critique of Aesthetic Ideology* (New York: Routledge, 1988).

57  de Man, *The Resistance to Theory* (op. cit.), p. 14.

58  Ibid., p. 13.

59  Ibid., pp. 18–19.

60  de Man, *Allegories of Reading* (op. cit.), p. 131.

61  de Man, *The Resistance to Theory* (op. cit.), p. 19.

62  Stanley Fish, *Is There a Text in This Class?* (op. cit.); also *Doing What Comes Naturally: change, rhetoric and the practice of theory in literary and legal studies* (Oxford: Clarendon Press, 1989) and W. J. T. Mitchell (ed.), *Against Theory: literary theory and the new pragmatism* (Chicago, IL: University of Chicago Press, 1985). For a critique of Fish and other neo-pragmatists, see Norris, 'Right You Are (if you say so): Stanley Fish and the rhetoric of assent', in *What's Wrong with Postmodernism* (Hemel Hempstead: Harvester-Wheatsheaf, 1990), pp. 77–133.

63  Fish, *Doing What Comes Naturally* (op. cit.).

64  See Note 16, above.

65  de Man, *The Resistance to Theory* (op. cit.), p. 14.

66  For further discussion, see Norris, 'Against a New Pragmatism: law, deconstruction, and the interests of theory', in *What's Wrong with Postmodernism* (op. cit.), pp. 125–48.

67  See especially de Man, *The Rhetoric of Romanticism* (op. cit.).

68  de Man, *Aesthetic Ideology* (op. cit.); see also Philippe Lacoue-Labarthe and Jean-Luc Nancy, *The Literary Absolute: the theory of literature in German Romanticism*, trans. Philip Barnard and Cheryl Lester (Albany, NY: State University of New York Press, 1988).

69  de Man, *The Resistance to Theory* (op. cit.), p. 19.

70  de Man, *Aesthetic Ideology* (op. cit.), p. 73.

71  For a more detailed account of these problems from Kant and their 'continental'/'analytic' legacy, see Norris, *Minding the Gap: epistemology and philosophy of science in the two traditions* (op. cit.).

72  See for instance Derrida, 'The Principle of Reason', *Diacritics*, Vol. 13 (Fall 1983), pp. 3–20; 'Mochlos, ou le conflit des facultés', *Philosophie*, No. 2 (April 1984), pp. 21–53; *Du droit à la philosophie* (Paris: Minuit, 1990). I discuss these and related texts in Norris, *Reclaiming Truth: contribution to a critique of cultural relativism* (London: Lawrence & Wishart, 1996).

73  Immanuel Kant, *The Conflict of the Faculties*, trans. Mary J. Gregor (New York: Abaris Books, 1979); also *Kant's Political Writings*, Hans J. Reiss, ed. (Cambridge: Cambridge University Press, 1976).

74  See entries under Note 72, above.

75  Derrida, *Of Grammatology* (op. cit.), p. 158.

76  On this topic, see especially Cathy Caruth and Deborah Esch (eds), *Critical Encounters: reference and responsibility in deconstructive writing* (New Jersey: Rutgers University Press, 1995).

77  Derrida, *Of Grammatology* (op. cit.), p. 158.

78  Kurt Gödel, 'On Formally Undecidable Propositions of *Principia Mathematica* and Related Systems', trans. B. Meltzer (New York: Basic Books, 1962); also Ernest Nagel and James Newman, *Gödel's Theorem* (London: Routledge & Kegan Paul, 1971) and S. G. Shanker (ed.), *Gödel's Theorem in Focus* (London: Routledge, 1987).

79  For a range of views on these issues in philosophy of mathematics, see Paul Benacerraf and Hilary Putnam (eds), *The Philosophy of Mathematics: selected essays*, 2nd edn. (Cambridge: Cambridge University Press, 1983) and W. D. Hart (ed.), *The Philosophy of Mathematics* (Oxford: Oxford University Press, 1996).

80  See Norris, *Truth Matters: realism, anti-realism, and response-dependence* (Edinburgh: Edinburgh University Press, 2002).

81  Derrida, 'White Mythology' (op. cit.).

82  See entries under Note 2, above; also Derrida, 'The Time of a Thesis: punctuations', in Alan Montefiore (ed.), *Philosophy in France Today* (Cambridge: Cambridge University Press, 1983), pp. 34–50.

83  For a well-informed and witty account of these premature announcements, see Sean Burke, *The Death and Return of the Author: criticism and subjectivity in Barthes, Foucault and Derrida* (Edinburgh: Edinburgh University Press, 1992).

84  This issue is taken up from various angles in Jarrett Leplin (ed.), *Scientific Realism* (Berkeley & Los Angeles: University of California Press, 1984). See also Larry Laudan, *Progress and Its Problems* (U. California Press, 1977) and 'A Confutation of Convergent Realism', *Philosophy of Science*, Vol. 48 (1981), pp. 19–49.

85  See for instance Richard Boyd, 'The Current Status of Scientific Realism', in Leplin (ed.), *Scientific Realism* (op. cit.), pp. 41–82.

86  See Note 16, above.

87  See Note 16, above.

88  For a range of views on this topic, see William P. Alston, *A Realist Conception of Truth* (Ithaca, NY: Cornell University Press, 1996); Michael Devitt, *Realism and Truth*, 2nd edn. (Princeton, NJ: Princeton University Press, 1997); Michael Dummett, *Truth and Other Enigmas* (London: Duckworth, 1978) and *The Logical Basis of Metaphysics* (Duckworth, 1991); Michael Luntley, *Language, Logic and Experience: the case for anti-realism* (London: Duckworth, 1988); Norris, *Truth Matters: realism, anti-realism and response-dependence* (Edinburgh: Edinburgh University Press, 2002); Neil Tennant, *The Taming of the True* (Oxford: Clarendon Press, 2002); Crispin Wright, *Truth and Objectivity* (Cambridge, MA: Harvard University Press, 1992) and *Realism, Meaning, and Truth*, 2nd edn. (Oxford: Blackwell, 1993).

89  See especially James Robert Brown, *The Laboratory of the Mind: thought experiments in the natural sciences* (London: Routledge, 1991) and *Smoke and Mirrors: how science reflects reality* (Routledge, 1994); R. Sorensen, *Thought Experiments* (Oxford: Oxford University Press, 1992).

90  For an account of these quantum thought-experiments, see Norris, *Quantum Theory and the Flight from Realism: philosophical responses to quantum mechanics* (London: Routledge, 2000).

91  See Notes 16, 19, 56, 68 and 70 above.

92  Derrida, *Of Grammatology* (op. cit.), p. 158.

93  Ibid., p. 158.

94   See Note 83, above.
95   For a survey of these (mostly negative or hostile) assessments, see Norris, 'Raising the Tone: Derrida, Kierkegaard and the rhetoric of transcendence' and 'Of an Apoplectic Tone Recently Adopted in Philosophy', in *Reclaiming Truth* (op. cit.), pp. 73–126 and 222–53.
96   See entries under Note 88, above.
97   Derrida, 'Afterword: toward an ethic of conversation' (Note 4, above).
98   See especially Alain Badiou, *Being and Event*, trans. Oliver Feltham (London: Continuum, 2005); *Theoretical Writings*, ed. and trans. Ray Brassier and Alberto Toscano (Continuum, 2004); *Number and Numbers*, trans. Robin MacKay (Cambridge: Polity Press, 2008).
99   See Michael Dummett, *Elements of Intuitionism* (Oxford: Oxford University Press, 1977) and *Truth and Other Enigmas* (op. cit.).
100  See Note 89, above; also – for a first-rate survey and extended bibliography of the literature on thought-experiments – James Robert Brown's essay for the *Stanford Encyclopedia of Philosophy* at [http://www.seop.leeds.ac.uk/entries/thought-experiment/].
101  See for instance Derrida, *Monolingualism of the Other, or, the prosthesis of origin*, trans. Patrick Mensah (Stanford, CA: Stanford University Press, 1998); *Of Hospitality*, trans. Rachel Bowlby (Stanford U.P., 2000); *On Cosmopolitanism and Forgiveness*, trans. Mark Dooley and Michael Hughes (London: Routledge, 2001); *Ethics, Institutions, and the Right to Philosophy*, trans. and ed. Peter Pericles Trifonas (Lanham, Md.: Rowman & Littlefield, 2002); *Rogues: two essays on reason*, trans. Pascale-Anne Brault and Michael Naas (Stanford U.P., 2005); *Beast and the Sovereign*, Vol. 1, Michel Lisse, Marie-Louise Mallet and Ginette Michaud (eds), trans. G. Bennington (Chicago, IL: University of Chicago Press, 2009).
102  See Norris, *New Idols of the Cave* (op. cit.), for further argument against those (like Rorty) who seek to recruit Derrida – often through a highly selective or snippety reading – to the cause of their own wholesale anti-foundationalist, anti-realist or neo-pragmatist crusade.
103  See for instance Derrida, 'Afterword: toward an ethic of conversation' (Note 4, above).

# Chapter 4

1   Ludwig Wittgenstein, *Philosophical Investigations*, trans. G. E. M. Anscombe (Oxford: Blackwell, 1958), Sections 201–92 *passim*; Saul Kripke, *Wittgenstein on Rules and Private Language: An Elementary Exposition* (Oxford: Blackwell, 1982); Alexander Miller and Crispin Wright (eds), *Rule-Following and Meaning* (Chesham: Acumen, 2002).
2   See Paul Benacerraf and Hilary Putnam (eds), *The Philosophy of Mathematics: Selected Essays*, 2nd edn. (Cambridge: Cambridge University Press, 1983); W. D. Hart (ed.), *The Philosophy of Mathematics* (Oxford: Oxford University Press, 1996); Hilary Putnam, *Mathematics, Matter and Method* (Cambridge University Press, 1975).
3   See especially Alain Badiou, *Being and Event*, trans. Oliver Feltham (London: Continuum, 2005) and *Theoretical Writings*, ed. and trans. Ray Brassier and Alberto Toscano (Continuum, 2004).
4   Jacques Derrida, *Edmund Husserl's 'The Origin of Geometry': An Introduction*, trans. John P. Leavey (Pittsburgh, PA: Duquesne University Press, 1973) and *'Speech and*

*Phenomena' and Other Essays on Husserl's Theory of Signs*, trans. David B. Allison (Evanston, IL: Northwestern University Press, 1973).

5   See Note 3, above; also Michael Potter, *Set Theory and its Philosophy: A Critical Introduction* (Oxford: Oxford University Press, 2004) and – for an excellent entry-level text – John D. Barrow, *The Infinite Book* (London: Jonathan Cape, 2005).

6   Badiou, *Being and Event* (op. cit.).

7   See Note 3, above; also Badiou, *Number and Numbers*, trans. Robin MacKay (London: Polity Press, 2008).

8   See especially Badiou, *Metapolitics*, trans. Jason Barker (London: Verso, 2005); *Polemics*, trans. Steve Corcoran (London: Verso, 2006); *The Century*, trans. Alberto Toscano (Cambridge: Polity Press, 2007).

9   For further discussion, see Christopher Norris, *Truth Matters: Realism, Anti-Realism, and Response-Dependence* (Edinburgh: Edinburgh University Press, 2002) and *Badiou's* Being and Event: *A Reader's Guide* (London: Continuum, 2009).

10  See Notes 1 and 2, above.

11  See Note 2, above; also Michael Dummett, *Truth and Other Enigmas* (London: Duckworth, 1978) and *Elements of Intuitionism*, 2nd edn. (Oxford: Clarendon Press, 2000).

12  Badiou, *Theoretical Writings* (op. cit.); Plato, *Meno*, E. Seymer Thompson (ed.) (London: Macmillan, 1901); also Crispin Wright, *Truth and Objectivity* (Cambridge, MA: Harvard University Press, 1992) and Christopher Norris, *Truth Matters* (op. cit.).

13  See especially Michael Dummett, *Truth and Other Enigmas* (op. cit.) and *The Logical Basis of Metaphysics* (Cambridge, MA: Harvard University Press, 1994).

14  For a critical overview of these and related lines of argument, see Christopher Norris, *Truth Matters* (op. cit.) and *Philosophy of Language and the Challenge to Scientific Realism* (London: Routledge, 2004).

15  Badiou, 'Ontology is Mathematics', in *Theoretical Writings* (op. cit.), pp. 3–93.

16  Paul J. Cohen, *Set Theory and the Continuum Hypothesis* (New York: W. Benjamin, 1966).

17  Badiou, 'The Subtraction of Truth', in *Theoretical Writings* (op. cit.), pp. 97–160.

18  Badiou, 'The Paris Commune: a political declaration on politics', in *Polemics* (op. cit.), pp. 257–90.

19  See Michael Potter, *Set Theory and its Philosophy* (op. cit.).

20  See entries under Note 8, above.

21  Badiou, 'Theory of the Pure Multiple: paradoxes and critical decision', in *Being and Event* (op. cit.), pp. 38–48.

22  See Badiou, *Metapolitics* (op. cit.).

23  See especially Badiou, *Ethics: An Essay on the Understanding of Evil*, trans. Peter Hallward (London: Verso, 2001); also *Manifesto for Philosophy*, trans. Norman Madarasz (Albany, NY: State University of New York Press, 1999) and *Infinite Thought: Truth and the Return to Philosophy*, trans. Oliver Feltham and Justin Clemens (London: Continuum, 2003).

24  For a critique of these developments in (mainly) French cultural theory with particular emphasis on 'revisionist' readings of Kant, see Christopher Norris, *The Truth About Postmodernism* (Oxford: Blackwell, 1993).

25  For an early and widely influential sampling on the mainly 'analytic' side, see Richard Rorty (ed.), *The Linguistic Turn: Essays in Philosophical Method* (Chicago, IL: University of Chicago Press, 1967). I take a contrasting (highly critical) view of these

developments in Norris, *Resources of Realism: Prospects for 'Post-Analytic' Philosophy* (London: Macmillan, 1997) and *New Idols of the Cave: On the Limits of Anti-Realism* (Manchester: Manchester University Press, 1997).

26 See Badiou, *Manifesto for Philosophy* and *Infinite Thought*; also Christopher Norris, *The Truth About Postmodernism* (op. cit.) and *What's Wrong with Postmodernism?* (Hemel Hempstead: Harvester, 1991).

27 For further discussion, see Christopher Norris, *Minding the Gap: Epistemology and Philosophy of Science in the Two Traditions* (Amherst, MA: University of Massachusetts Press, 2000); also Frederick C. Beiser, *The Fate of Reason: German Philosophy from Kant to Fichte* (Cambridge, MA: Harvard University Press, 1987); Jürgen Habermas, *The Unfinished Project of Modernity: Twelve Lectures*, trans. Frederick Lawrence (Cambridge: Polity Press, 1987); Norris, *Deconstruction and the Unfinished Project of Modernity* (London: Athlone, 2000).

28 John McDowell, *Mind and World* (Cambridge, MA: Harvard University Press, 1994).

29 Christopher Norris, 'McDowell on Kant: redrawing the bounds of sense' and 'The Limits of Naturalism: further thoughts on McDowell's *Mind and World*', in *Minding the Gap* (op. cit.), pp. 172–96 and 197–230.

30 See Note 8, above.

31 See Notes 13 and 14, above.

32 See Notes 28 and 29, above.

33 Note 1, above.

34 Note 23, above.

35 All references to Badiou's *Being and Event* (op. cit.) henceforth given by page-number in the text.

36 See especially Badiou, *Theoretical Essays* (op. cit.).

37 Thomas S. Kuhn, *The Structure of Scientific Revolutions*, 2nd edn., revised (Chicago, IL: University of Chicago Press, 1970).

38 Michael Potter, *Set Theory and its Philosophy* (Note 3, above).

39 Thomas Nagel, *The View from Nowhere* (Oxford: Oxford University Press, 1986); also Norris, 'Not *Quite* the Last Word: Nagel, Wittgenstein, and the limits of scepticism', in *Minding the Gap* (op. cit.), pp. 231–59.

40 See the classic and much-discussed essay by Edmund Gettier, 'Is Justified True Belief Knowledge?', *Analysis*, 23 (1963), pp. 121–3.

41 See entries under Note 8, above.

42 Notes 13 and 14, above.

43 See Badiou, *Number and Numbers* (op. cit.).

44 Paul J. Cohen, *Set Theory and the Continuum Hypothesis* (op. cit.).

45 See especially Badiou, *Number and Numbers* (op. cit.).

46 See entries under Note 1, above.

47 Badiou, 'Theory of the Pure Multiple: paradoxes and critical decision', in *Being and Event* (op. cit.), pp. 38–48.

# Chapter 5

1 Jacques Derrida, *Of Grammatology*, trans. G. C. Spivak (Baltimore, MD: Johns Hopkins University Press, 1976), pp. 141–316.

2 Ibid., pp. 149–57. All further references to *Of Grammatology* given by *OG* and page-number in the text.

3   John R. Searle, 'Reiterating the Differences', *Glyph*, Vol. I (Baltimore, MD: Johns Hopkins University Press, 1977), pp. 198–208; also John M. Ellis, *Against Deconstruction* (Princeton, NJ: Princeton University Press, 1989).

4   For Jacques Derrida's essay on Austin – the one that sparked Searle's indignant and largely off-the-point response – see Derrida, 'Signature Event Context', *Glyph*, Vol. I (Baltimore, MD: Johns Hopkins University Press, 1977), pp. 172–97; also 'Afterword: toward an ethic of conversation', in Gerald Graff (ed.), *Limited Inc* (Evanston, IL: Northwestern University Press, 1989), pp. 111–54. For his classic early readings of other, mainly philosophical texts, see Derrida, *'Speech and Phenomena' and Other Essays on Husserl's Theory of Signs*, trans. David B. Allison (Northwestern U.P., 1973); *Writing and Difference*, trans. Alan Bass (London: Routledge & Kegan Paul, 1978); *Dissemination*, trans. Barbara Johnson (London: Athlone Press, 1981); *Margins of Philosophy*, trans. Alan Bass (Chicago, IL: University of Chicago Press, 1982); 'Parergon', in *The Truth in Painting*, trans. Geoff Bennington and Ian McLeod (U. Chicago P., 1987), pp. 15–147.

5   See for instance Donald Davidson, *Inquiries into Truth and Interpretation* (Oxford: Oxford University Press, 1984) and H. P. Grice, *Studies in the Ways of Words* (Cambridge, MA: Harvard University Press, 1989).

6   For an extreme version of this argument, see Donald Davidson, 'A Nice Derangement of Epitaphs', in Ernest LePore (ed.), *Truth and Interpretation: Perspectives on the Philosophy of Donald Davidson* (Oxford: Blackwell, 1986), pp. 433–46; also – for a dissenting commentary – Christopher Norris, *Resources of Realism: Prospects for 'Post-Analytic' Philosophy* (London: Macmillan, 1997).

7   Donald Davidson, *Inquiries into Truth and Interpretation* (op. cit.).

8   Ibid.

9   See especially Paul K. Feyerabend, *Against Method* (London: New Left Books, 1975); Thomas S. Kuhn, *The Structure of Scientific Revolutions*, 2nd edn. (Chicago, IL: University of Chicago Press, 1970); W. V. O. Quine, 'Two Dogmas of Empiricism', in *From a Logical Point of View*, 2nd edn. (Cambridge, MA: Harvard University Press, 1961), pp. 20–46; Benjamin Lee Whorf, *Language, Thought and Reality: Selected Writings*, J. B. Carroll (ed.) (Cambridge, MA: M.I.T. Press, 1956).

10  See for instance Cleanth Brooks, *The Well-Wrought Urn: Studies in the Structure of Poetry* (New York: Harcourt Brace, 1947) and William K. Wimsatt, *The Verbal Icon: Studies in the Meaning of Poetry* (Lexington, KY: University of Kentucky Press, 1954).

11  See especially Paul de Man, *Allegories of Reading: Figural Language in Rousseau, Nietzsche, Rilke, and Proust* (New Haven, CT: Yale University Press, 1979).

12  See Note 6, above.

13  Donald Davidson, 'A Nice Derangement of Epitaphs' (op. cit.), p. 173.

14  Ibid., p. 173.

15  Ibid., p. 171.

16  See especially Samuel C. Wheeler, 'Indeterminacy of French Translation: Derrida and Davidson', in LePore (ed.), *Truth and Interpretation* (op. cit.), pp. 477–94 and *Deconstruction as Analytic Philosophy* (Stanford, CA.: Stanford University Press, 2000); also Shekar Pradhan, 'Minimalist Semantics: Davidson and Derrida on meaning, use, and convention', *Diacritics*, 16(1) (1986), 66–77.

17  Shekhar Pradhan, 'Minimalist Semantics' (op. cit.), p. 75.

18  Jacques Derrida, 'Signature Event Context' (op. cit.).

19  Donald Davidson, 'On the Very Idea of a Conceptual Scheme', in *Inquiries into Truth and Interpretation* (op. cit.), pp. 183–98; p. 184.

20 Donald Davidson, 'Communication and Convention', in *Inquiries into Truth and Interpretation* (op. cit.), pp. 265–80; p. 280.

21 Donald Davidson, 'A Nice Derangement' (op. cit.), p. 171.

22 Ibid., p. 170.

23 See entries under Note 4, above.

24 See Jaakko Hintikka, *Models for Modalities* (Dordrecht: D. Reidel, 1969); G. E. Hughes and M. J. Cresswell, *A New Introduction to Modal Logic* (London: Routledge, 1996); W. and M. Kneale, *The Development of Logic* (Oxford: Clarendon Press, 1962); Michael J. Loux (ed.), *The Possible and the Actual: Readings in the Metaphysics of Modality* (Ithaca, NY: Cornell University Press, 1979); A. N. Prior, *Time and Modality* (Oxford: Clarendon Press, 1957).

25 Graham Priest, 'Derrida and Self-Reference', *Australasian Journal of Philosophy*, 72(1) (1994), pp. 103–11 and *The Limits of Thought* (Cambridge: Cambridge University Press, 1995).

26 W. V. O. Quine, 'Two Dogmas of Empiricism' (Note 9, above); Michael Dummett, *Elements of Intuitionism* (Oxford: Oxford University Press, 1977) and *Truth and Other Enigmas* (London: Duckworth, 1978). For a critical account of these developments, see also Norris, *Truth Matters: Realism, Anti-Realism and Response-Dependence* (Edinburgh: Edinburgh University Press, 2002) and *On Truth and Meaning: Language, Logic and the Grounds of Belief* (London: Continuum, 2006).

27 Donald Davidson, Inquiries into Truth and Interpretation (op. cit.).

28 See for instance Gilbert Harman, 'Inference to the Best Explanation', *Philosophical Review*, 74 (1965), pp. 88–95; Peter Lipton, *Inference to the Best Explanation* (London: Routledge, 1993); Charles S. Peirce, *Reasoning and the Logic of Things* (Cambridge, MA: Harvard University Press, 1992).

29 See especially J. L. Mackie, *Truth, Probability and Paradox* (Oxford: Clarendon Press, 1973), pp. 1–16; G. E. Moore, 'A Reply to My Critics', in P. A. Schilpp (ed.), *The Philosophy of G. E. Moore* (La Salle, IL: Open Court, 1968), pp. 535–687; Arthur Pap, *Semantics and Necessary Truth* (New Haven, CT: Yale University Press, 1958), pp. 276–9.

30 C. H. Langford, 'The Notion of Analysis in Moore's Philosophy', in P. A. Schilpp (ed.), *The Philosophy of G. E. Moore* (La Salle, IL: Open Court, 1968), pp. 321–41; p. 323.

31 Jacques Derrida, 'Afterword: toward an ethic of conversation' (Note 4, above), p. 117.

32 See Note 10, above.

33 See Note 4, above.

34 See especially Jacques Derrida, *'Speech and Phenomena' and Other Essays on Husserl's Theory of Signs*, trans. David B. Allison (Evanston, IL: Northwestern University Press, 1973) and *Edmund Husserl's 'Origin of Geometry': An Introduction*, trans. John P. Leavey (Pittsburgh, PA: Duquesne University Press, 1978).

35 Gottlob Frege, 'On Sense and Reference', in P. Geach and M. Black (eds), *Translations from the Philosophical Writings of Gottlob Frege* (Oxford: Blackwell, 1958), pp. 56–78; Bertrand Russell, 'On Denoting', *Mind*, 14 (1905), pp. 479–93.

36 J. L. Austin, *How to Do Things With Words* (Oxford: Oxford University Press, 1963); Ludwig Wittgenstein, *Philosophical Investigations*, trans. G. E. M. Anscombe (Oxford: Blackwell, 1953).

37 Gilbert Ryle, *The Concept of Mind* (London: Hutchinson, 1949) and *Dilemmas* (Cambridge: Cambridge University Press, 1954).

38 See Note 25, above.

39  See for instance Peter Gibbins, *Particles and Paradoxes: The Limits of Quantum Logic*
(Cambridge: Cambridge University Press, 1987) and Susan Haack, *Deviant Logic:
Some Philosophical Issues* (Cambridge U.P., 1974).

# Chapter 6

1  See for instance Alain Badiou, *Being and Event*, trans. Oliver Feltham (London:
Continuum, 2005); also *Manifesto for Philosophy*, trans. Norman Madarasz (Albany,
NY: State University of New York Press, 1999); *Ethics: An Essay on the Understanding
of Evil*, trans. Peter Hallward (London: Verso, 2001; *Infinite Thought: Truth and
the Return to Philosophy*, trans. Oliver Feltham and Justin Clemens (London:
Continuum, 2003); *Theoretical Writings*, ed. and trans. Ray Brassier and Alberto
Toscano (London: Continuum, 2004); *Metapolitics*, trans. Jason Barker (London:
Verso, 2005); *Polemics*, trans. Steve Corcoran (London: Verso, 2006); *The Century*,
trans. Alberto Toscano (Cambridge: Polity Press, 2007).
2  See especially Badiou, *Being and Event* and *Theoretical Writings* (Note 1).
3  See Badiou, *Being and Event*; also – for a useful survey of the field – Michael Potter,
*Set Theory and its Philosophy: A Critical Introduction* (Oxford: Oxford University
Press, 2004).
4  On this topic, see Ludwig Wittgenstein, *Philosophical Investigations*, trans. G. E. M.
Anscombe (Oxford: Blackwell, 1951), Sections 201–92 *passim*; Saul Kripke,
*Wittgenstein on Rules and Private Language: An Elementary Exposition* (Oxford:
Blackwell, 1982); Alexander Miller and Crispin Wright (eds), *Rule-Following and
Meaning* (Chesham: Acumen, 2002).
5  For a range of views on this issue, see Michael Dummett, *Frege: Philosophy of
Mathematics* (London: Duckworth, 1991); Paul Benacerraf and Hilary Putnam
(eds), *The Philosophy of Mathematics: Selected Essays*, 2nd edn. (Cambridge:
Cambridge University Press, 1983), pp. 272–94; W. D. Hart (ed.), *The Philosophy
of Mathematics* (Oxford: Oxford University Press, 1996); Jerrold J. Katz, *Realistic
Rationalism* (Cambridge, MA: M.I.T. Press, 1998); J. R. Lucas, *The Conceptual Roots
of Mathematics* (London: Routledge, 2000); Hilary Putnam, *Mathematics, Matter
and Method* (Cambridge University Press, 1975); Stuart G. Shanker (ed.), *Philosophy
of Science, Logic and Mathematics in the Twentieth Century* (New York: Routledge,
1996); Stewart Shapiro, *Thinking About Mathematics: The Philosophy of Mathematics*
(Oxford: Oxford University Press, 2000).
6  See especially Michael Dummett, *Truth and Other Enigmas* (London: Duckworth,
1978); also *The Logical Basis of Metaphysics* (London: Duckworth, 1991) and
*The Seas of Language* (Oxford: Clarendon Press, 1993). For further discussion
in a more-or-less critical or qualified anti-realist vein, see Neil Tennant, *The
Taming of the True* (Oxford: Clarendon Press, 2002) and Crispin Wright,
*Truth and Objectivity* (Cambridge, MA: Harvard University Press, 1992). For
an opposed (realist) line of argument, see Christopher Norris, *Truth Matters:
Realism, Anti-Realism and Response-Dependence* (Edinburgh: Edinburgh
University Press, 2002).
7  See Jerrold J. Katz, *Realistic Rationalism* (op. cit.); also (classically) Gottlob Frege,
'The Thought: a logical inquiry', in Robert M. Harnish (ed.), *Basic Topics in the
Philosophy of Language* (Hemel Hempstead: Harvester, 1994), pp. 517–35; Bob Hale,

*Abstract Objects* (Oxford: Blackwell, 1987); Scott Soames, *Understanding Truth* (Oxford: Oxford University Press, 1999).

8　See Note 6, above.

9　See Note 7, above; also – on the broader (physical-scientific) realist front – Michael Devitt, *Realism and Truth*, 2nd edn. (Oxford: Blackwell, 1986); Jarrett Leplin (ed.), *Scientific Realism* (Berkeley & Los Angeles: University of California Press, 1984); Norris, *Philosophy of Language and the Challenge to Scientific Realism* (London: Routledge, 2004); Stathis Psillos, *Scientific Realism: How Science Tracks Truth* (London: Routledge, 1999); Wesley C. Salmon, *Scientific Realism and the Causal Structure of the World* (Princeton, NJ: Princeton University Press, 1984).

10　See for instance Larry Laudan, *Progress and Its Problems* (Berkeley & Los Angeles: University of California Press, 1977).

11　See Badiou, *Being and Event* and *Theoretical Writings* (Note 1, above).

12　See Abraham A. Fraenkel, *Elements of Set Theory*, rev. edn. (Amsterdam: North-Holland, 1973), for a main source of Badiou's thinking and the basis of his formal approach to issues of set-theoretical ontology. For a helpful expository account of these developments, see Michael Potter, *Set Theory and its Philosophy: A Critical Introduction* (Oxford: Oxford University Press, 2004).

13　See especially the references to Cavaillès and Lautman in Badiou, *Metapolitics* (op. cit.).

14　See Badiou, *Metapolitics*, *Polemics*, and *The Century* (Note 1, above).

15　See especially Badiou, *Polemics*.

16　Paul J. Cohen, *Set Theory and the Continuum Hypothesis* (New York: W. Benjamin, 1966).

17　Sigmund Freud, 'Remembering, Repeating and Working-Through', in *Standard Edition of the Complete Psychological Works of Sigmund Freud*, James Strachey (ed.), Vol. XII (London: Hogarth Press, 1957), pp. 141–57.

18　See especially Badiou, *Manifesto for Philosophy* and *Infinite Thought* (Note 1, above); also Richard Rorty (ed.), *The Linguistic Turn: Recent Essays in Philosophical Method* (Chicago, IL: University of Chicago Press, 1967).

19　See especially Ludwig Wittgenstein, *Philosophical Investigations*, trans. G. E. M. Anscombe (Oxford: Blackwell, 1953) and *On Certainty*, ed. and trans. Anscombe and G. H. von Wright (Blackwell, 1969); also Crispin Wright, *Wittgenstein on the Foundations of Mathematics* (London: Duckworth, 1980); Cora Diamond (ed.), *Wittgenstein's Lectures on the Foundations of Mathematics* (Chicago, IL: University of Chicago Press, 1976); S. Shanker, *Wittgenstein and the Turning-Point in the Philosophy of Mathematics* (Albany, NY: State University of New York Press, 1987).

20　Benacerraf and Putnam (eds), *The Philosophy of Mathematics* (op. cit.), p. 15; cited by Badiou, 'Platonism and Mathematical Ontology', in *Theoretical Writings* (op. cit.), pp. 49–58; p. 49.

21　Badiou, ibid., p. 49.

22　Plato, *Meno*, E. Seymer Thompson (ed.) (London: Macmillan, 1901).

23　Badiou, 'Platonism and Mathematical Ontology'; p. 49.

24　Ibid., p. 49.

25　See Note 6, above; also – for a range of views on this topic – Paul Benacerraf, 'What Numbers Could Not Be', in Benacerraf and Hilary Putnam (eds), *The Philosophy of Mathematics* (op. cit.), pp. 272–94; Michael Detlefson (ed.), *Proof and Knowledge in Mathematics* (London: Routledge, 1992); W. D. Hart (ed.), *The Philosophy of Mathematics* (op. cit.); Philip Kitcher, *The Nature of Mathematical Knowledge*

(Oxford: Oxford University Press, 1983); Hilary Putnam, *Mathematics, Matter and Method* (op. cit.).

26  See for instance Crispin Wright, 'Moral Values, Projection, and Secondary Qualities', *Proceedings of the Aristotelian Society*, Supplementary Vol. 62 (1988), pp. 1–26; Mark Johnston, 'How to Speak of the Colours', *Philosophical Studies*, 68 (1992), pp. 221–63; Philip Pettit, 'Are Manifest Qualities Response-Dependent?', *The Monist*, 81 (1998), pp. 3–43 and 'Noumenalism and Response-Dependence', *The Monist*, 81 (1998), pp. 112–32; Neil Tennant, *The Taming of the True* (Oxford: Clarendon Press, 2002).

27  For further argument to this effect, see Christopher Norris, *Truth Matters* (op. cit.).

28  See Note 4, above.

29  Badiou, 'Spinoza', in *Being and Event* (op. cit.), pp. 112–20 and 'Spinoza's Closed Ontology', in *Theoretical Writings* (op. cit.), pp. 81–93. On this and other aspects of Spinoza's turbulent reception-history, see Frederick C. Beiser, *The Fate of Reason: German Philosophy from Kant to Fichte* (Cambridge, MA: Harvard University Press, 1987) and Norris, *Spinoza and the Origins of Modern Critical Theory* (Oxford: Blackwell, 1991).

30  Spinoza, *Ethics*, in *The Collected Writings of Spinoza*, trans. Edwin Curley (Princeton, NJ: Princeton University Press, 1985).

31  See Badiou, *Deleuze: The Clamor of Being*, trans. Louise Burchill (Minne apolis, MN: University of Minnesota Press, 2000); also Gilles Deleuze, *Spinoza: Practical Philosophy*, trans. Robert Hurley (San Francisco, CA: City Lights Books, 1988) and *Expressionism in Philosophy: Spinoza*, trans. Martin Joughin (New York: Zone Books, 1992), along with the various references to Spinoza in Deleuze and Félix Guattari, *A Thousand Plateaus* (*Capitalism and Schizophrenia*, Vol. 2), trans. Brian Massumi (Minneapolis, MN: University of Minnesota Press, 1987).

32  See also Etienne Balibar, *Spinoza and Politics* (London: Verso, 1998); Lewis Samuel Feuer, *Spinoza and the Rise of Liberalism* (Boston: Beacon Press, 1958); Jonathan Israel, *Radical Enlightenment: Philosophy and the Making of Modernity, 1650–1750* (Oxford: Oxford University Press, 2002); Paul Wienpahl, *The Radical Spinoza* (New York: New York University Press, 1979); Yirmiyahu Yovel, *Spinoza and Other Heretics*, Vol. 1: *The Marrano of Reason,* and Vol. 2, *The Adventures of Immanence* (Princeton, NY: Princeton University Press, 1989).

33  See for instance Louis Althusser, *For Marx*, trans. Ben Brewster (London: New Left Books, 1969) and 'Elements of Self-Criticism', in *Essays in Self-Criticism* (New Left Books, 1976), pp. 101–61; Althusser and Etienne Balibar, *Reading Capital*, trans. Brewster (New Left Books, 1970); Balibar, *Spinoza and Politics* (London: Verso, 1988); Pierre Macherey, *Hegel ou Spinoza?* (Paris: Maspero, 1979) and *In a Materialist Way: Selected Essays*, Warren Montag (ed.), trans. Ted Stolze (Verso, 1998).

34  See Note 31, above.

35  Christopher Norris, *Spinoza and the Origins of Modern Critical Theory* (op. cit.).

36  Spinoza, *Ethics* (op. cit.).

37  See for instance Ted Benton, *The Rise and Fall of Structural Marxism* (London: New Left Books, 1984) and Gregory Elliott, *Althusser: The Detour of Theory* (London: Verso, 1987).

38  See Note 4, above.

39  See especially Badiou, *Being and Event* and *Theoretical Writings* (Note 1, above); also entries under Note 5.

40  E. P. Wigner, 'The Unreasonable Effectiveness of Mathematics in the Physical Sciences', in *Symmetries and Reflections* (Bloomington, IN: Indiana University Press, 1967), pp. 228–38.

41  See Note 25, above.

42  See Note 26; also Crispin Wright, *Realism, Meaning and Truth* (Oxford: Blackwell, 1987) and *Truth and Objectivity* (Cambridge, MA: Harvard University Press, 1992).

43  See entries under Note 26, above; also Philip Kitcher, *The Nature of Mathematical Knowledge* (op. cit.).

44  For a classic statement of the realist case, see Gottlob Frege, 'The Thought: a logical inquiry', in Robert M. Harnish (ed.), *Basic Topics in the Philosophy of Language* (Hemel Hempstead: Harvester, 1994), pp. 517–35; also – for a range of opposed or dissenting views – entries under Notes 25 and 26, above.

45  See Note 19, above; also Martin Heidegger, *'The Question Concerning Technology' and Other Essays*, trans. William Lovitt (New York: Harper & Row, 1977).

46  Badiou, 'Mallarmé', in *Being and Event* (op. cit.), pp. 191–8.

47  See especially Martin Heidegger, *Poetry, Language, Thought*, trans. Albert Hofstadter (New York: Harper & Row, 1972) and *Early Greek Thinking*, trans. David F. Krell and Frank Capuzzi (Harper & Row, 1975).

48  Spinoza, *Ethics* (op. cit.).

49  See Note 31, above.

50  Spinoza, *Ethics* (op. cit.).

51  See especially Jacques Derrida, *'Speech and Phenomena' and Other Essays on Husserl's Theory of Signs*, trans. David B. Allison (Northwestern U.P., 1973); *Writing and Difference*, trans. Alan Bass (London: Routledge & Kegan Paul, 1978); *Dissemination*, trans. Barbara Johnson (London: Athlone Press, 1981); *Margins of Philosophy*, trans. Alan Bass (Chicago, IL: University of Chicago Press, 1982); also 'Signature Event Context', *Glyph*, Vol. I (Baltimore, MD: Johns Hopkins University Press, 1977), pp. 172–97 and 'Parergon', in *The Truth in Painting*, trans. Geoff Bennington and Ian McLeod (U. Chicago P., 1987), pp. 15–147.

52  See Note 31, above.

53  Daniel W. Smith, 'Badiou and Deleuze on the Ontology of Mathematics', in Peter Hallward (ed.), *Think Again: Alain Badiou and the Future of Philosophy* (London: Continuum, 2004), pp. 77–93.

54  See Badiou, 'Plato', in *Being and Event* (op. cit.), pp. 31–7.

55  Badiou, *Deleuze: the clamor of being* (op. cit.).

56  Badiou, 'Leibniz', in *Being and Event* (op. cit.), pp. 315–23.

57  See Note 4, above.

# Index of Names

CPSIA information can be obtained
at www.ICGtesting.com
Printed in the USA
LVOW04s1520161215
466814LV00004B/138/P